AF696281

MODERN AMERICAN HISTORY ★ A Garland Series

Edited by
FRANK FREIDEL
Harvard University

THE IMPACT OF THE GREAT DEPRESSION ON THE ARMY

John W. Killigrew

Garland Publishing, Inc.
New York & London ★ 1979

UA
25
.K47
1979

Helen-Jean Moore Library
Point Park College

© 1979 John William Killigrew

All rights reserved

Library of Congress Cataloging in Publication Data

Killigrew, John W
The impact of the Great Depression on the Army.

(Modern American history)
Reprint of the author's thesis, Indiana University.
Bibliography: p.
Includes index.
1. United States. Army—History—20th century.
2. United States—Military policy. 3. Depressions—1929—United States. 4. Depressions—1933—United States. I. Title. II. Series.
UA25.K47 1979 355'.00973 78-62385
ISBN 0–8240–3634–4

All volumes in this series are printed on acid-free, 250-year-life paper.
Printed in the United States of America

Preface

For many years military history has been of considerable interest to me, and in my graduate career in history at Indiana University I determined that for a dissertation subject I would select a topic in this area. But it was Dr. Stetson Conn, former Chief Historian, Office of the Chief of Military History (OCMH), Department of the Army, now called the Center for Military History, who urged me to study the problems and issues of military history from a broad point of view in contrast to the more popular but narrow focus of battles, campaigns, and leadership. Believing that the inter-war years were crucial in the development of military policy, Dr. Conn suggested that I undertake a study of the United States Army during this period, with particular attention being given to the years of the great depression. Furthermore, it was through the recommendation of Dr. Stetson Conn that I received an appointment as Associate in Military History at OCMH. This appointment, now called the Dissertation Fellowship, provided me with access to the facilities of OCMH, the privileges of a staff historian, and the critique, guidance, and review of the Chief Historian. Although shortcomings and errors of fact and interpretation contained in my study are my own responsibility, my intellectual indebtedness to Dr. Stetson Conn is obvious. I should also note the other distinguished historians on the staff of OCMH who gave me encouragement and inspiration: Dr. Stanley Falk, Dr. Vincent Jones, Mr. Martin Blumenson, and Lt. Col. William Bell.

Mention should also be made of my doctoral committee at Indiana University who cooperated by agreeing to the unique arrangement that I had as Associate in Military History with Dr. Stetson Conn and OCMH: the late Dr. R. Carlyle Buley, the late Dr. Joseph L. Sutton, Dr. S. Y. Teng, and Dr. Leonard Lundin. From the bibliographical note at the back of this book, the reader will note that the overwhelming bulk of my study is based on primary sources consisting of army records and documents deposited in the National Archives. Without the patient aid and knowledgeable guidance of the noted archivist, Mr. John Taylor, the sheer volume of this material would have inhibited effective research. Finally, I wish to acknowledge the encouragement given me by my wife, June Ann, whose abiding confidence in me had much to do in bringing this study to fruition.

The editors at Garland have suggested that it would be appropriate to review significant works that have been published on the army and military policy during the 1930's since I prepared my manuscript. Although there has been no specific work devoted to the identical topic, there are several works that are peripherally related. D. Clayton James, The Years of MacArthur, Volume I, 1880-1941 (Boston: Houghton-Mifflin, 1970), and the new biography of MacArthur by William Manchester should be noted. The James work relies heavily on my manuscript for MacArthur's career as Chief of Staff. Two developments that involved the Army during the depression, and which are discussed in my study, are the specific focus of some recent scholarship. In this regard I cite: The Civilian Conservation Corps by John Salmond (Durham: Duke University Press, 1967), and two definitive works pertaining to the Bonus March in the summer of 1932: Donald J. Lisio, The President and Protest (Columbia: The University of Missouri Press, 1974), and Roger Daniels, Bonus March (Westport, Connecticut: Greenwood Press, 1971). The Center for Military History, Department of the Army, has published two volumes in recent years pertaining to topics that are of long term historical development, and both briefly cover the problems of the depression years: James A. Huston, The Sinews of War: Army Logistics, 1775-1953 (Washington: USGPO, 1966), and James E. Hewes, From Root to McNamara: Army Organization and Administration, 1900-1963 (Washington: USGPO, 1975) I should also note that Chapter VII of this work pertaining to the Bonus Incident appeared in Military Affairs, Volume XXVI, Number 2, Summer 1962, pp. 59-65.

TABLE OF CONTENTS

Chapter

INTRODUCTION

The military policy of the United States in the period between the two world wars consisted of maintaining a small regular establishment complemented by a civilian component organized into the National Guard and the Organized Reserve Corps. The basic premise underlying this policy was the concept of organizing and maintaining a small professional force to serve as the nucleus for the mobilization of a large mass "citizen" army. This policy, outlined in the 1920 Defense Act, involved extraordinary expenses compared to the pre-World War I military organization and the unpreparedness that formerly was endemic with the republic.

The annual appropriation by Congress for the military establishment was the means through which American military policy was carried out, and as a consequence of this "power of the purse" any reductions in appropriations affected military activities, plans, and projects that the Army had formulated in carrying out the provisions of the 1920 legislation. With the advent of the Great Depression at the beginning of the third decade of the century, Congress, and more in particular the Executive, believed that it was of the utmost importance for the financial and economic stability of the country that government expenditures be reduced in order to balance spending with revenue. This belief was accepted as sound fiscal policy in a period of national economic recession. One facet of government spending that came under immediate close scrutiny in the battle to balance the budget was military expenditures.

The reaction by the Army to the policy of financial stringency and reduced expenditures was conditioned by the basic view of the military establishment toward the separation of the civil-military power in the United States as prescribed by the Constitution. The Army interpreted its role in the republic not as a formulator of policy but the executor of policy; policy formulation was the function of the civilian leaders of the government, with the President as the Commander in Chief and Congress as the ultimate power with its constitutional responsibility of raising and supporting the Army.

This role of subordination to civilian direction was reinforced during the depression by the general acceptance among military leaders of the orthodox economic theory that federal expenditures should balance federal revenue. The Army accepted the necessity of reduced expenditures in order to balance the federal budget, and supported and cooperated with the Commander in Chief in cutting spending and reducing its programs and projects. Thus the Army would not consider going over the head of the President and appeal to Congress and the public on the issue of obtaining "adequate funds," both because of its subordination to the civilian authority and its willingness to cooperate in keeping spending down in time of economic difficulty. Furthermore, the Army was extremely reluctant to appear to the public as a "special pleader" and lay itself open to the charges of its critics that it was seeking to foist on the American republic a "militaristic" mold.

As a result of the national policy of the Hoover and Roosevelt Administrations to stabilize and reduce military expenditures, the Army became acutely concerned about the manner and method of making the best use of the limited funds available to it. For the General Staff the problem was to determine how its multitudinous projects, plans, activities, and diversified organization could be maintained in a viable and efficient manner in the face of curtailed financial support. The issue was not how to obtain the maximum security with the available funds but how to minimize insecurity during a period of stringent financial crisis. The availability of funds determined policy; not all needs and requirements of the General Staff could be met and it became essential to military planners to determine where the greatest effort should be concentrated.

CHAPTER I

BACKGROUND OF ARMY ORGANIZATION AND PLANNING

American military policy and the development of the Army in the inter-war years was based on the National Defense Act of 1920. This legislation, which amended the 1916 Defense Act, remained the basic national military legislation with minor amendments until after World War II. Several significant aspects of the 1920 law are of importance as a background to military developments and military affairs during the years of the Great Depression the late twenties and the early thirties.

The law defined the Army of the United States as the Regular Army, the National Guard, and the Organized Reserves. The Regular Army, according to the law, was to be composed of branches and combatant arms and not to exceed 280,000 enlisted men, and as defined by law in 1923 not more than 12,000 officers. The act noted that the purpose of the peace establishment was to form the basis for "complete and immediate" mobilization in case of emergency. For the purpose of administration, the act granted the President discretionary power in organizing the Army, and specified only that the United States was to be divided into corps areas on the basis of military population.[1] Pursuant to this power the War Department

[1] *The National Defense Act* approved June 3, 1916, as amended to March 4, 1929 Inclusive (Washington: GPO, 1929), pp. 1-10.

organized the country into nine corps areas, replacing the old six territorial departments which formerly embraced the continental United States. In addition, the Philippines, Panama, and Hawaii were designated independent territorial departments giving the War Department twelve subordinate territorial commands.[2]

According to the National Defense Act of 1920 the General Staff was charged with preparing plans for national defense and the use of the military forces. The Chief of Staff was to preside over the General Staff and, under the direction of the President and the Secretary of War, to "cause the General Staff to plan for the recruiting, organizing, supplying, equipping, mobilizing, training and demobilizing of the Army of the United States."[3] The long standing controversy, between the supply branches of the Army, such as Ordnance, Quartermaster General, and Signal Corps, and the General Staff, was not solved by the 1920 legislation. In addition there was perpetuated through the establishment of the Office of Assistant Secretary of War dual control over the administration of supply between the General Staff and the various branches of the Army. Section 5a of the 1920

---

[2] Otto Nelson, National Security and the General Staff (Washington: Infantry Journal Press, 1946), p. 295.

[3] National Defense Act, p. 21. Note: The Main divisions of the General Staff were: G-1 Personnel, G-2 Intelligence, G-3 Plans and Training, G-4 Supply, and War Plans Division (WPD).

Defense Act gave the Assistant Secretary of War, in addition to other duties that might be assigned to him by the Secretary of War, the "supervision of the procurement of all military supplies and other business of the War Department...." Furthermore, the law specified that

> under the direction of the Secretary of War, chiefs of branches of the Army charged with the procurement of supplies for the Army shall report direct to the Assistant Secretary of War regarding all matters of procurement.[4]

Thus in an attempt by the framers of the 1920 law to draw a distinction between matter of supply and command, dual control over administration of supply between the General Staff and the Office of the Assistant Secretary of War was exercised. However, according to a student of the General Staff, during this period the General Staff and the Office of the Assistant Secretary of War worked together during the inter-war years and both modified their plans in the light of suggestions offered.[5] Besides being charged with procurement responsibilities, the Assistant Secretary was given supervision of planning for the "adequate provision for the mobilization of materiel and industrial organization essential to wartime needs."[6] As a student of the General Staff has pointed out, this was a planner's dream and at the same time a planner's

---

[4] *Ibid.*, p. 22.

[5] Nelson, *General Staff*, p. 304.

[6] *National Defense Act*, p. 22.

nightmare. Industrial mobilization planning for total war based on the nation's entire industrial might was a broad term and could mean mobilization under government direction until some form of totalitarian government was reached.[7] The Army was aware of this broad discretionary power, and as planning developed during the twenties, it realized that success of procurement planning for wartime mobilization depended upon such measures as price control, wage-price fixing, and labor-management arrangements to be adopted in wartime to insure that the entire economic resources of the country were brought into the war effort. However, this was regarded by the Army as a "sacred field" that should not be touched upon in planning because it involved the decisions of national policy beyond the scope of the military.[8] Although the Army sought to publicize its work in industrial mobilization planning in order to obtain the support and cooperation of industry, it failed to implement effectively these good intentions.[9] By the time plans were formulated in the late twenties and early thirties for economic mobilization, the depression had arrived and the Army, concerned over the charges that had been leveled against it by its critics and caught in the pinch of reduced expenditures, deemphasized

---

[7] Nelson, General Staff, p. 301.

[8] Ibid., p. 305.

[9] Marvin Kreidberg and Merton G. Henry, History of Military Mobilization in the United States Army, 1775-1945 (Washington: GPO, 1955), pp. 506-07.

mobilization planning. The depression dealt a death blow to realistic supply and procurement mobilization planning by the Army. Reports of industrial surveys and plant capacity became so unstable as to be useless, and visits to factories in an effort to bring statistics up to date turned into "mournful walks through empty shops and past halted belt lines."[10] Although industry offered little to the survey because of the depression, planning continued as before. It was aimed at the specific military requirements of the subsequent mobilization plans and it was divorced from the social and economic implications of the directive given the Army by the National Defense Act. In this area the Army was pre-empted by the New Deal planners and perforce was left to its mobilization requirements pertaining to armaments.

Central to any review of the military establishment of the Republic at the end of the third decade of the twentieth century was the all-pervasive problem of the airplane and air power. Basic to the entire issue was the question whether the airplane was just another weapon comparable to the tank and submarine, or a new and unique instrument of destruction with such power and potentiality as to demand a sweeping reorganization of defense doctrine and strategy. The Air Corps Act of 1926 had authorized the appointment of an Assistant Secretary of War for Air to foster military aeronautics, but this Assistant had little actual power. The General

[10] Dulany Terrett, "The Technical Services- The Signal Corps: The Emergency," UNITED STATES ARMY IN WORLD WAR II (Washington: GPO, 1956), p. 67.

Staff, by its authority over military planning, prevented the Assistant Secretary of War for Air from exercising any substantive control over air development. The 1926 legislation, in order to remedy existing deficiencies in personnel and equipment, authorized expansion of the Air Corps to 1,518 officers, 2,500 flying cadets, and 16,000 enlisted men, and provided for the procurement of 18,000 serviceable aircraft during a five year period.[11] This act did little to ameliorate the clamorous and strident struggle of the air enthusiasts for more autonomy and for a greater role in national defense strategy. Throughout the period under review the question of air power permeated any discussion of military affairs and was closely connected with the problem of providing an adequate defense with a modest expenditure of federal funds.

Any background summary of the organization and activities of the Army in the inter-war years must mention its non-military duties. Besides its specific military activities and procurement planning, the War Department was charged with a plethora of non-military activities. Improvement of rivers and harbors and flood control activities were under the direction of the Corps of Engineers. The Inland Waterways Corporation was created by Congress and given to the Army to run until such time as the transportation of freight on inland waterways could be "profitably undertaken by private

---

11 Wesley F. Craven and James L. Cate (eds.), "Plans and Early Operations: January 1939 to August 1942" Vol. I, The Army Air Forces in World War II (Chicago: The University of Chicago Press, 1948), p. 29.

enterprise."[12] Furthermore, the Army was in charge of the Panama Canal, and the Bureau of Insular Affairs in the War Department administered the Philippines and Puerto Rico.[13] The Army also operated all national cemeteries, national military parks, and the Washington State-Alaska Cable. These non-military activities were no small

---

[12] Report of the Secretary of War, 1930 (Washington: GPO, 1930), p. 18. For a discussion of these activities see the annual reports of the Secretary of War.

[13] Upon the acquisition of the territory ceded to the United States by Spain as a result of the Spanish-American War the necessity arose for the creation of an agency of the Federal Government especially equipped to administer the civil affairs of the new possessions. For this purpose there was established in the Office of the Secretary of War on December 13, 1898, a Division of Customs and Insular Affairs, which was charged with "all matters pertaining to the customs of the Islands of Puerto Rico, Cuba, and the Philippines, and all civil affairs relating to those islands as distinguished from matters of a military character connected with the government of the islands." The name of the agency was changed in 1900 to the Division of Insular Affairs, and in 1902 to the Bureau of Insular Affairs.

From time to time the designation of the Bureau as a Central Office to administer the affairs of all the noncontiguous territory of the United States was proposed, and the Bureau's organization was shaped in anticipation of this eventuality. In fact, it acted to some extent as a clearing house for information relative to all the territories and insular possessions, including the Philippines, Puerto Rico, Panama Canal, Hawaii, Alaska, Guam, Samoa, and the Virgin Islands. Hopes for the creation of an office of colonial affairs in the War Department were never realized, and on July 1, 1939, the functions of the Bureau were transferred to the Department of Interior and consolidated with those of the Division of Territories and Island Possessions.

Although the administrative powers of the Bureau of Insular Affairs in connection with the Philippines were never clearly defined, it may be said in general that its functions were primarily to gather information, to advise, and to formulate and recommend policies to the Secretary of War rather than execute them. The National Archives, Records of the Bureau of Insular Affairs Relating to the Philippine Islands, 1898-1935 (Washington: GPO, October 1942), p. vii.

sideline for the Army, and total appropriations for these activities for fiscal 1930 were $142,000,000.[14] Although they served to disperse Army concentration on purely military planning and activities as well as employ needed officers on non-essential activities, the non-military activities of the War Department were a convenient public relations vehicle which served to make the Army known to the public.

Perhaps one of the most important facets of this study is the relationship between budgeting for military appropriations and military policy. The mechanics of budget procedure pertaining to the annual military appropriations bill underwent a drastic change after World War I. Prior to 1921 the different War Department agencies and bureaus which were charged with procurement and other disbursing functions presented their estimates, not in a coordinated whole but as single and separate estimates. Any coordination by the War Department was negligible and each agency asked for all it could get. The total estimates were compiled by the Treasury Department and sent to Congress and assigned to the appropriate committees.[15]

---

[14] Report of the Secretary of War, 1930, p. 235.

[15] Lt Col Irving J. Phillipson, "War Department Participation in the President's Budget," Lectures Delivered at Army Industrial College, XI (1935), pp. 132-33. See also Cater Files, folder entitled "Budgetary Matters of the War Department," Office of the Chief of Military History, Washington.

Under the Budget and Accounting Act of 1921, the Secretary of War was required to submit to the Director of the Bureau of the Budget the estimate of funds necessary to sustain the Army for all its activities for the coming fiscal year. After review by the Budget Bureau, and after consideration in connection with other executive department estimates as part of the financial policy of the administration, the estimates were returned to the War Department with a figure limiting military expenditures for the coming fiscal year. Usually during this period the General Staff had to reconsider its original estimates and whittle them down to meet the Bureau of Budget's limitation. This process in general did not antagonize the War Department; in fact, it preferred an overall limiting figure set by the President or the Director of the Budget. What perturbed the Army was that the Director of the Budget in many instances took action himself in reducing or eliminating certain specific items of the military budget. After the War Department had completed its revised expenditure estimate, the Secretary of War submitted it to the Bureau of the Budget along with any supplementary estimates which the War Department felt were essential but which exceeded the Budget Bureau's original limit.[16]

---

[16] *Ibid.*, pp. 132-33.

This exercise of control over military expenditures by the Budget Bureau insured the predominance of civilian political authorities over military spending during the inter-war years. Military needs were studied as part of the total federal fiscal policy, which in turn reflected the political and economic policies and doctrine of the administration. In keeping with the American tradition, the control of the Budget Bureau over military expenditures meant the subordination of the military forces to civilian control.

One student of military history has noted that "routine, disciplined obedience of the Army to the President," that is, the subordination of military officers to the President as Commander in Chief and his chief fiscal agent, the Director of the Budget, was itself a handicap to the military program.[17] This, of course, is true, but it should be noted that besides the basic discipline, which made acceptance of orders from the Commander in Chief automatic, there were other factors underlining the Army's subordination to civilian direction in respect to military expenditures. Basically the Army accepted the concept that the military budget formulated by the President is the vehicle through which the civilian head of the executive branch of government carries out his military policy and that the military forces were subordinate to the elected political Commander in Chief. Congress, of course, in its role as the custodian

---

17 Mark S. Watson, "Chief of Staff: Prewar Plans and Preparations," UNITED STATES ARMY IN WORLD WAR II (Washington: GPO, 1950), p. 21.

of the purse, had the final prerogative in military appropriations and, although it would challenge the executive branch from time to time, it generally was willing to follow the Bureau of Budget's estimates.[18] The central tendency of this budgetary procedure was to give *de facto* authority to the executive branch of the government, specifically to the Bureau of the Budget, in matters relating to military expenditures.

The mechanics involved in preparing the War Department budget was another factor which tended to keep military expenditures to a minimum. In order to obtain efficiency, the routine and perfunctory mechanics of budget preparation became habitual; thus, the budget of one year tended to become the budget of the next. The mechanics of budget preparation may have served during the years of financial stringency to ingrain a conservative habit of mind into the officers responsible for budget estimates, and this tended to keep military activities to a minimum. In order to maintain efficiency and to avoid the painstaking and embarrassing defense of budget estimates for new activities, there may have developed within the Army a tendency to accept the same or similar budget from one year to the next. Generally, estimating agencies within the

---

[18] Elias Huzar, *The Purse and the Sword: Control of Army by Congress Through Military Appropriations, 1933-1950* (Ithaca: Cornell University Press, 1950), p. 138. Huzar also notes that Congress was quite willing to subscribe to a small military budget and, therefore, they usually went along with the figures presented by the Budget Bureau. Furthermore, Congress was technically ill-equipped to undertake an evaluation of the military budget.

War Department were called upon to submit their estimates based on a tentative directive of Army activities that had been issued by the Chief of Staff. After hearing and studying the various branch estimates, the Budget Advisory Committee of the War Department reported its recommendations to the General Council and the Chief of Staff.[19]

The Chief of Staff then generally reviewed the estimates and issued his final directive to all War Department organizations with instructions concerning submission of the final estimates. The Budget Advisory Committee would coordinate and check final estimates with the Chief of Staff and act informally on any necessary final change.[20] Of particular note in this sequence of preparation was the important role played by the Chief of Staff and the fact that he superseded the Secretary of War in the final preparation and check of the budget figure, although the Secretary of War legally had to approve the figure before its submission to the Bureau of the Budget.

The War Department started preparation of its budget in the spring of the calendar year for presentation to the Budget Bureau in September or early fall. This was followed by revision and

---

19

The General Council of the War Department consisted of all the branch and bureau chiefs and the General Staff Division chiefs. It met periodically at the summons of the Chief of Staff to discuss important policy matters. It was formed by MacArthur in 1931, and, unfortunately, minutes of the meetings were not kept.

20

Memo, Deputy Chief of Staff for the Budget Officer of the War Department, June 30, 1933. AG 111, Record Group (RG) 94, National Archives (NA).

final presentation to the Budget Bureau and submission to Congress the first of the succeeding calendar year. This meant that budget preparation was for activities several years in advance. During a period of economic stringency, the tendency was to continue or maintain a certain level of expenditures from year to year and to plan ahead not on what was needed for long range plans but what had been accepted by the Budget Bureau and Congress during the current fiscal year.

In discussions of the military policy during the inter-war years, it has been pointed out that because of the "spirit of the time" -- as reflected in the Kellogg-Briand Treaty, the renunciation of war by treaty, the repudiation of collective security, and the national policy of avoiding war by refusing to become involved -- it was easy to dismiss the military. In addition, it is claimed that the Army, in turn, gave no thought to the "ultimate causes" of war and tended to think of military doctrine in an isolated manner and to think that planning proceeded in a vacuum.[21] Nevertheless, military affairs played an important role during these years and, although the country had eschewed the Wilsonian version of collective security, it was hardly pacificistic and contemptuous of the military. The important political and social status of the National Guard and

---

21 Walter Millis, Arms and the State, Civil Military Elements in National Policy (New York: Twentieth Century Fund, 1958), pp. 15-25. Watson notes that the between wars idea that armed forces should be designed for defense only, reflected as it was in the Washington Treaty of 1922 and the Kellogg-Briand Pact, was so completely a national policy that it became a guide to Army planning. Watson, Prewar Plans, p. 35.

the Officers Reserve Corps, the popularity of the ROTC and CMTC program, the never-ending controversy over airpower, and the lingering impact of the Civil War on the nation reflected the fact that military affairs, if not military policy and the role of the military in national policy, were far from insignificant.

Army planning and theory during this period were based on the "insurance" concept of preparedness. According to Army thinking, the nation had to maintain a military strength imposing enough to discourage affront and aggression, to protect the liberties and property of its citizens, and to cope with any emergency that would challenge American safety and interests.[22] This was somewhat a pre-atomic version of the "deterrent" concept of national defense and served as the basis for Army planning and doctrine during the inter-war years.

A more detailed account of actual military thinking on the causes, probability, and possibility of war was presented to President Hoover by the General Staff in the fall of 1929. The President had asked for a complete survey of the military establishment and the role and position of the Army in carrying out national policy and the defense of the country. The reply to this broad directive indicates that the Army was not too strongly influenced by the Kellogg-Briand Pact.

---

22 Army Navy Journal, January 5, 1935, p. 381. Speech by Maj. Gen. James G. Harbord on January 4, 1935 to Civic Forum and League for Political Education in New York. Harbord had served as Pershing's Chief of Staff in the AEF and like his old chief kept his hand in military affairs during his retirement.

According to the General Staff, the pre-eminent economic position of the United States made it incumbent upon the nation to maintain a deterrent posture of defense; a policy of non-involvement would not suffice to prevent conflict with other less fortunate and jealous international powers. The General Staff emphasized the belief that war resulted from a conflict of the national policies of one country with those of another. These policies arose in connection with questions affecting their respective vital interests, which were the outgrowth of moral, economic, and political influences in the lives of nations and their people. The General Staff reported to Hoover that war was not the inevitable consequence of every clash or conflict, but the success in the application of diplomacy, conciliation, and arbitration was due "beyond question" to the weight which others gave to the American ability to sustain by force of arms its "rightful contention." Thus, according to Army planners, the state of preparedness would determine the respect and success in which the nation was held in the settlement of international disputes. National policies, according to the General Staff, were not arbitrary mandates directed aggressively against another country, but were "lines of conduct adopted and pursued as best for the interest of the country" and developed through experience, and to trespass these policies to such an extent as to do violence to them would create the "liability to war."

The General Staff went on to note seven national policies of the United States during the years of so-called "isolation" that might constitute a liability to war: maritime rights of neutrals, naval rivalry, Monroe Doctrine, Platt Amendment, Open Door Policy, Japanese immigration, and foreign debts and trade rivalry. In commenting on the last named national policy that presented a liability to war for the United States, the General Staff noted that there was a united front of world opinion against the United States, and "ordinary prudence" indicated a strong military position to meet the "contingencies of the final outcome." The General Staff emphasized to the President that the primary position of the nation in world trade made it extremely vulnerable for, as an "Historical fact," ascendancy in world trade coupled with a growth of sea power had always been a potential cause of war. The General Staff concluded its brief for the President by noting that the world situation in 1929 and in the foreseeable future appeared quiescent and there was no issue in foreign relations that could be considered as calling for "immediate military preparations" by the Republic. Nevertheless, Hoover was warned that the United States had clearly defined national policies which conflicted with those of other nations and that there were issues between the United States and other nations which "vitally affect our national interests" and therefore the possibility and probability of war existed.[23]

Perhaps one of the most perplexing problems faced by the military planners in the decade of the twenties was the fact that

---

23 Report of the Survey of the Military Establishment by the War Department General Staff, November 1, 1929, pp. 26-31. WPD/3345, RG 319, NA.

compared with the pre-World War I days military expenditures had risen sharply. Following World War I, appropriations were reduced until they reached a low of around $270,000,000 during fiscal 1924-1925. During the next few years appropriations began to increase gradually. A considerable portion of this increase was attributable to the Air Corps Act of 1926, as well as to the disappearance of surplus World War I equipment available for issue without replacement.[24] Since World War I, the Army had lived largely on these stocks, and by the late twenties these stocks were becoming exhausted. For this reason, articles, which were formerly available without cost, had now to be purchased. This fact alone increased the cost of the Army from year to year even though activities remained stabilized, and the cost of maintaining activities tended to increase annually in proportion to the decrease of surplus stocks.

Perhaps the main cause of the sharp increase in military expenditures in the postwar era was the increased strength of the Army and its new activities. The latter factor increased the budget for such items as the Chemical Warfare Service, Air Corps, tanks, Infantry School, Organized Reserve Corps, ROTC, and the CMTC. Furthermore, there was an increase in the annual National Guard expenditures of some $26,000,000, with minor increases in the budget for transportation and maintenance of buildings and other facilities. In addition, the strength of the Regular Army in the Medical Corps,

---

[24] Phillipson, <u>Lectures Delivered at Army Industrial College</u>, X (1933), p. 6.

Field Artillery, and the Air Corps had increased since 1916. Another main cause for an increase in military expenditures during the postwar years, as compared with the pre-World War I days of "normalcy," was the roster of new and expensive weapons of war: aircraft, tractor-drawn and railway artillery, antiaircraft artillery, sound-ranging equipment, anti-tank guns, tanks, automatic rifles and machine guns, gas and smoke projectors, gas masks, armored cars, radios, and motor transport. All these new developments, the General Staff reminded the Secretary of War, had caused the military budget to increase from a modest prewar figure of $144,000,000 for fiscal 1916 to the ever-increasing 1930 figure of approximately $332,000,000.[25]

---

[25] Memo, AC/S G-4 to the Chief of Staff, July 31, 1929. G-4/26986, RG 319, NA. Note: This memo was written at the direction of the Secretary of War in order for him to have available for the President the reasons why the cost of the Army had risen so sharply as compared with the last pre-World War I fiscal year. Memo, Chief of Staff to the AC/S G-4, June 26, 1929. OCS/26986, RG 319, NA.

CHAPTER II

REACTION TO HOOVER'S ATTEMPT TO REDUCE MILITARY EXPENDITURES

Although the Hoover Administration faced no financial deficit until after fiscal 1930 (June 30, 1930), the Army was alerted during the summer of 1929 to the fact that it faced a period of stabilized military expenditures, if not stringent reductions. The new administration was determined to curtail federal expenditures as a matter of principle, and Hoover sought the cooperation of the Army in his efforts to reduce the federal budget. Hoover accepted the "insurance" theory of preparedness and believed that one of the assurances of peace was "adequate preparedness," but the Chief Executive emphasized that preparedness was not to "exceed the barest necessity." Otherwise, he claimed, it became a cause of fear and animosity in the world as well as needless governmental expense.[1] The problem for Hoover was to define "adequate defense" and arrive at a modest figure of military expenditure that would provide this military posture.

---

1 William Starr Myers (ed.), The State Papers and Other Public Writings of Herbert Hoover (New York: Doubleday Doran & Company, 1934), Vol. I, p. 101. Radio Address on Preparedness and Peace, Dedication of Station WABC, New York, September 18, 1929.

Calling together his military advisors, both civilian and uniformed, at his Rapidan retreat during a weekend in late July, 1929, the Chief Executive ordered a thorough survey of all military activities in order to obtain a reduction of expenditures. Relying on the impartial judgment of the General Staff, Hoover assigned to it the task of surveying the Army. In accordance with the President's order, the Chief of Staff, General Charles Pelott Summerall, informed the entire Army that the General Staff would make a survey of the military establishment with a view toward making "extensive reductions in the cost of the Army in all or any of its components or activities, wherever the same can be made without manifest injury to adequate national defense."[2]

Continuing his instructions in a vein that indicated his desire for a thorough and critical reappraisal and re-examination of the military establishment, the Chief of Staff laid down a nine-point program to serve as a guide for the survey: (1) To review the status of Coast Artillery and determine whether coast and harbor defenses were obsolete and whether these activities could be deferred over a period of time without detriment to national defense; (2) to include in the survey a fair and unprejudiced statement of conditions

---

[2] Memo, Chief of Staff for all Corps Area Commanders and Chiefs of Branches and Bureaus, August 29, 1929. AG 333 EP, RG 94, NA. Note: the August 29 memorandum contained detailed instructions pertaining to the scope and mission of the economic survey. The General Staff had been assigned the responsibility for the survey earlier in the month, and branch, arm, service, and territorial chiefs had been informed of the survey in mid-August.

in all branches and arms, and what present programs could be omitted, reduced, or deferred; (3) to evaluate the Cavalry and the degree to which motorization or aviation could replace cavalry; (4) to consider the relation of aviation to other branches and analyze the five-year Air Corps program, to determine whether the program could be curtailed; (5) to make a comparison between the cost of a conscript Army and a small regular establishment with civilian components serving as a reserve; (6) to consider the value and relation to national defense of the civilian components and how one or more could be curtailed or abolished; (7) to estimate the result if the Army was reduced to pre-war posture of 1916; (8) to form a conclusion as to the manner in which the cost of the Army could be reduced, and its effect of this reduction on national defense; (9) to approach the survey with an "open mind" and with the realization that a complete readjustment and revision of the military establishment might result in a reduction in administrative costs, while still completely maintaining adequate defense.[3] An analysis of Summerall's nine-point program indicates that he sought a free and frank appraisal of the military policy, though he was aware that the Army was the executor, not the formulator, of this policy. The Army survey would serve as guide for the President in his reexamination of American military policy. WPD Division of the General Staff was given the task of preparing the study, but important subordinates of the Chief of Staff, such as branch, arm, and service chiefs, as well as Corps Area Commanders, were asked to submit their opinions and recommendations.

---

[3] Ibid.

While asking for sweeping recommendations from his chief subordinates in the Army, Summerall advised his Deputy Chief of Staff that the survey should be guided by certain "principles." Summerall advised that attention should be given to the accepted doctrine that a small highly trained force is "fundamental" to the preparedness of the nation, and that this force should be capable of emergency defense and at the same time provide the nucleus to train and mobilize a larger force which would take the offensive against the enemy. Another "principle" which Summerall laid down was that the strength of the military establishment must reflect the international situation, and its cost must be a "reasonable adjustment of income of the government to meet all needs." "If possible," the Chief of Staff continued, "the survey should arrive at a conclusion for stabilizing a balanced budget" and avoid expanding or maintaining certain military programs at the expense of equally essential items. A third "principle" that the Chief of Staff proposed was that the survey should consider the continuing high cost of aviation and the possibility that it would be better to maintain a small force in efficient condition than a large force in low efficiency.[4] Summerall appears to have been aware that the Army would have to adjust its plans to fit in with the administration's desire to reduce government expenditures, and that there should be a leveling off of military expenditures and a stabilization over the coming years. Summerall hoped that this could be obtained and still provide a balanced military program.

---

[4]Memo, Chief of Staff for the Deputy Chief of Staff, August 2, 1929. AG 333 EP, RG 94, NA.

Summerall was particularly desirous to remove the Army from any criticism of playing politics in maintaining and defending its annual appropriations, and he asked the Budget Officer for the War Department whether the military budget contained anything having political rather than military value. The view of this officer was that "no doubt" the military budget was capable of being divided into items for the Regular Army, having little or no political implication, with the exception of housing, Air Corps, and the retention of certain Army posts, and those items of the military budget which "unquestionably" had political tinge, such as the National Guard, and the other civilian components.[5] What this officer failed to realize was the fact that among certain liberal and pacificist groups, the entire military appropriation was wasteful and only reflected the political aims of the military establishment, and that a large military budget was an onerous political as well as economic burden.

The Chief of Staff let it be known that as head of the Army he supported Hoover in the aim of the survey. He wanted to dispel any idea that the War Department was reluctant, because of some fancied entrenched or privileged position, to put its own economic house in order, or that it was out to sabotage Hoover's desire to cut back on military spending. Informed that the American Legion in its 1929 convention at Louisville was preparing a resolution criticizing Hoover for mingling in military affairs and for his efforts

---

[5] Ltr, Budget Officer of the War Department for the Adjutant General, August 9, 1929. AG 333 EP, RG 94, NA.

to reduce military expenditures, the Chief of Staff wrote to the Commanding General of the 6th Corps Area asking the latter to use his influence to prevent the resolution from being passed. Summerall added that it was of the "first importance" that no such resolution be passed and that nothing which would tend to "criticize the action of the President, as far as the Army is concerned, should be presented." Summerall clearly indicated that the War Department was heartily in accord with the President's policies and that he believed Hoover's survey of the Army was an opportunity to take "beneficial measures that would be difficult to initiate without Executive action."[6]

If the Chief of Staff was seeking from his chief subordinates a vigorous intellectual analysis and criticism of American military policy and of Army thinking along the lines of possible reorganization, he undoubtedly was somewhat disappointed in the replies received to his August 29 memorandum. The replies were varied, perhaps reflecting the seniority and independence of the territorial commanders and their isolation from day-to-day thinking with the General Staff in Washington and the policies of the Hoover Administration. Although it is evident from the replies that the Army was hardly the homogeneous and monolithic structure that one would presume, there was a general reluctance to change the status quo and reduce military activities. Certain replies showed a dissatisfaction with the existing defense structure and a desire to make

---

[6] Ltr, Summerall for the Commanding General of the 6th Corps Area, August 20, 1929. AG 333 EP, RG 94, NA.

changes not only for economic reasons but for efficiency and a better establishment. On the other hand, some officers were adamant against any change and wanted the existing organization maintained and even expanded. These officers urged an increase in military appropriations.

Maj. Gen. Preston Brown, Commanding General of the 1st Corps Area, suggested a better organized and better trained Regular Army; he favored a small, mobile, and hard-hitting force ready for instant combat. Brown recommended transferring all non-military duties from the ARmy, merging of some supply branches, and the combining of the Field Artillery and the Coast Artillery. He intimated that he favored a reduction of Army activities in support of the civilian components and he urged that emphasis be placed on the quality rather than the quantity of the civilian components.[7]

Maj. Gen. Hanson Ely, Commanding General of the 2d Corps Area, made no recommendations and sent to the Chief of Staff the proceedings of a board of officers of his command which favored retention of present activities. Ely added, by way of endorsement, that he favored the abolition of the Marine Corps and the merger of the Coast Artillery and the Field Artillery.[8] The Chief of the 4th Corps Area, Maj. Gen. Richmond P. Davis, recommended vigorously that the existing military program be continued without any discussion of

---

[7] Ltr, Maj. Gen. Preston Brown for AG, August 30, 1929. AG 333 EP, RG 94, NA.

[8] Ltr, Maj. Gen. Hanson Ely for the AG, September 14, 1929. AG 333 EP. RG 94, NA.

the relationship of the program to expenditures or cost.[9] Dennis Nolan, Commanding General of the 5th Corps Area, presented a detailed account of economies, actual and planned, in his jurisdiction but offered "no other suggestions or other changes to be effected by administrative action of the War Department."[10] Maj. Gen. Frank Parker of the 6th Corps Area recommended possible relocation of the Regular Army, but no retrenchment whatever in activities in regard to the civilian components. He recommended that curtailment, if it came, should be through personnel rather than activities.[11]

In contrast to most of the replies, Maj. Gen. William Lassiter, Commanding General of the 8th Corps Area, presented a lengthy account of his ideas on national defense and military policy. Lassiter outlined the plan of a small force of 250,000, to include both Regular Army and National Guard. This force should be able to meet the first phase of an emergency and serve as a foundation upon which to mobilize. Lassiter was adamant that no violence be done to the theory of the citizen army in wartime and the principle of universal responsibility. Lassiter proposed some administrative changes, such as combining the

---

[9] Ltr, Maj. Gen. Richmond P. Davis for the AG, August 24, 1929. AG 333 EP, RG 94, NA.

[10] Ltr, Maj. Gen. Dennis Nolan for the AG, September 13, 1929. AG 333 EP, RG 94, NA.

[11] Ltr, Maj. Gen. Frank Parker for the AG, September 12, 1929. AG 333 EP, RG 94, NA.

Coast Artillery and the Field Artillery and urged the abolition of fixed coast defenses on the grounds that they were an anachronism.[12] The Commanding General of the 9th Corps Area, Maj. Gen. John L. Hines, urged that no reduction or change in the military program should take place, but if reduction did come about, it should be at the expense of the civilian components.[13] The Hawaiian Department commander, Maj. Gen. Edwin B. Winans, made no recommendations outside of his own area and situation in Hawaii.[14]

Maj. Gen. Douglas MacArthur, Commanding General of the Philippine Department wired to Washington that the only major economic move he would recommend would be to abolish the China garrison. He noted that this force had ceased to have adequate strength to perform its mission and that "changed conditions have rendered its presence in China a source of potential military danger rather than strength to the national defense."[15]

It was the bete noire of the Army, Maj. Gen. Johnson Hagood, Commanding General of the 7th Corps Area, who presented the most radical proposals for a "better national defense at less cost."

---

[12] Ltr, Maj. Gen. William B. Lassiter for the AG, September 14, 1929. AG 333 EP, RG 94, NA.

[13] Ltr, Maj. Gen. John L. Hines for the AG, September 13, 1929. AG 333 EP, RG 94, NA.

[14] Ltr, Maj. Gen. Edwin B. Winans for the AG, September 14, 1929. AG 333 EP, RG 94, NA.

[15] Telegram, MacArthur for AG, Manila 4409, August 23, 1929. AG 333, EP, RG 94, NA.

Hagood, long an opponent of the General Staff and its concept of a national army mobilized around the nucleus of the Regular Army, proposed radical changes in the military establishment. He proposed doing away with the General Staff and reorganizing the Army top command into three main bureaus to include administration, tactics, and supply. This he claimed would obviate the overlapping of the General Staff and the old line supply branches. Hagood proposed serious surgery on the National Defense Act of 1920 as the only way to make considerable budget savings, and he urged the curtailment of federal expenditures for the National Guard and the reorganization of the ROTC on a more economical basis.[16]

The branch, arm, and service chiefs, in their recommendations to the Chief of Staff, emphasized the importance and need of their particular branch, and reflected the tendency within the Army for inter-service rivalry and bureaucratic antagonisms to be sharpened during a period of economic stringency and reduced military spending. Undoubtedly the old line supply branches viewed Summerall's survey as a plot by the General Staff to increase its control over the entire Army. The Chief of the Air Corps used the opportunity to re-emphasize the importance and role of the strategic bomber and the need for the Air Corps to be independent from the rest of the Army. The Air Corps chief also added that the 1926 five-year program should be scrapped

---

[16] Ltr, Maj. Gen. Johnson Hagood for the AG, September 30, 1929. AG 121.62, RG 94, NA.

and a larger program inaugurated.[17] The Chief of the Air Corps disregarded Summerall's promptings for economy and cut back in activities and recommended greater expansion and expenditures for aviation instead.

The Chief of the Field Artillery rebutted the claims of the Air Corps, and charged that the Army was becoming increasingly unbalanced with the accentuation of the Air Corps and military aviation. He noted that the rate of the development of civilian aviation had removed the necessity of building up the Air Corps at the expense of the other combat arms. He claimed that the other combat arms were losing the fight for appropriations in an endeavor to carry the heavy responsibility of training in the Regular Army and at the same time to carry the responsibility for the civilian components. No reduction in appropriations for artillery was urged; instead, an increase in annual expenditures was recommended for a ten-year program of ordnance replacement, motorization of artillery, and a much-needed housing program. The Chief of Field Artillery urged expansion of the National Guard and Officers Reserve Corps, expansion of the Army school system, and maintenance of the Coast Artillery Corps as a separate arm because harbor defense was essential to national defense.[18] The Chief of Finance, responsible for the disbursement of all War

---

[17] Ltr, Chief of the Air Corps for AG, September 21, 1929. AG 333 EP, RG 94, NA.

[18] Ltr, Chief of Artillery for AG, September 21, 1929, AG 333 EP, RG 94, NA.

Department funds, urged the Chief of Staff to go slowly in any move toward transferring the non-military activities of the War Department to other federal agencies because such activities were a source of friendly and useful advertising for the Army both before Congress and the public. He noted that these activities were a "self-evident refutation of the charge that the Army is a useless, outworn appendage."[19]

The Chief of Infantry vigorously opposed any reduction in the CMTC regardless of the fact that it was not a fruitful source of officer material. To the Infantry the CMTC was of value because of its activities in increasing patriotism, and in improving the standards of health and citizenship of the youth of the nation. The only recommendation that the Chief of Infantry made was to urge the transfer of the non-military activities of the War Department to other federal departments.[20]

The Inspector General's Department gave a detailed and lengthy summary of military expenditures and noted that the Regular Army cost more than a force of its size should because of high overhead which resulted from the cost of recruitment and from the necessity of maintaining a large number of posts and depots. The Inspector General recommended that the CMTC be abolished, that the Regular Army be concentrated at a fewer number of posts, that there be a

---

[19] Ltr, Chief of Finance for the AG, September 20, 1929. AG 333 EP, RG 94, NA.

[20] Ltr, Chief of Infantry for the AG, September 23, 1929. AG 333 EP, RG 94, NA.

transfer of non-military activities to other agencies, and that the War Department staff in Washington be reduced.[21]

An example of the bureaucratic jealousy and the tenacious defense of the existing organization and methods that Summerall engendered with his economic survey was presented by the Chief of the Insular Affairs Bureau and by the Chief of Cavalry. The former proposed that his bureau remain with the War Department because the relationship between civil government and national defense in the "dependent colonies" was such that the "desirability of continued control" by the Army should continue. Unified control of civil and military affairs militated against any transfer of the Insular Affairs Bureau to any other civilian agency.[22] The Chief of Cavalry deprecated the denigration of Cavalry in post-World War I military developments and warned that the geographical situation in Mexico, "our most probable antagonist" in a future war, made the need for Cavalry all the more greater.[23]

---

[21] Ltr, The Inspector General for the AG, September 19, 1929. AG 333 EP, RG 94, NA. According to The Inspector General there were 114 officers of the General Staff on duty in Washington, while the French Army General Staff in Paris consisted of 175 officers for their Army of 650,000 on duty with the colors and 5 million in the reserves. The Inspector General urged the merging of the following War Department bureaus: Signal Corps-Engineers, Chemical Warfare-Ordnance, Cavalry-Field Artillery-Coast Artillery-Infantry.

[22] Ltr, Chief of the Insular Affairs Bureau for the AG, September 21, 1929. AG 333 EP, RG 94, NA.

[23] Ltr, Chief of Cavalry for the AG, September 21, 1929. AG 333 EP, RG 94, NA.

The Chief of the Engineers urged continuance of Army work in rivers and harbors activities, and defended this activity on the basis of not only being economically administered but also of value in preparing officers for war service through the experience of utilizing the resources of the country during peacetime.[24]

The Chief of the Militia Bureau urged the Chief of Staff to expand the National Guard and noted that savings could be made by curtailing ROTC and CMTC programs.[25] The Quartermaster General stoutly defended existing supply procedures and urged an increase in the military budget for the maintenance activities of the Quartermaster Corps.[26]

The Commandant of the Command and General Staff School at Fort Leavenworth, Brig. Gen. Stuart Heintzelman, though making no recommendations, admitted that the "time has come to restate the Army's mission in new legislation or in executive policies" which will bring appropriations and the mission of the Army into harmony. According to General Heintzelman the Army had too many "Irons in the fire" and something must be cut away to place the service on a practicable working basis. According to the Commandant, ever since 1920 appropriations for carrying out the Army's role under

---

[24] Ltr, Chief of Engineers for the AG, September 20, 1929. AG 333 EP, RG 94, NA.

[25] Ltr, Chief of the Militia Bureau for the AG, September 20, 1929. AG 333 EP, RG 94, NA.

[26] Ltr, The Quartermaster General for the AG, September 19, 1929. AG 333 EP, RG 94, NA.

the National Defense Act had been curtailed and the War Department was forced to draw on war reserves to keep many of its projects in being. He warned the Chief of Staff that obligations imposed by the National Defense Act and the limiting budget figure of past years and the future years did not permit continuing the policies of the past.[27] General Heintzelman seems to have come to the essence of the problem that faced Summerall and the General Staff: too many activities and programs and too limited appropriations. Very few of the other senior officers of the Army in 1929 were able to grasp this point. Instead, they showed an amazing unconcern for the needs of the Army as a whole by vigorously defending their own activities and programs.

Another perspicacious study on the issue of military expenditures and the requirements of national defense came from the Office of the Assistant Secretary of War (ASW). This study, prepared for the Assistant Secretary and not forwarded to the General Staff, was entitled "Studies of Trends of Appropriations and Army Strengths," and included several important insights into the problem of defense appropriations that were in general overlooked in most of the correspondence dealing with this problem. The ASW's study began by emphasizing the fact that it was difficult to prove that any one program was essential to national defense, and that the favorable geographical position of the country and its defensive military policy

[27] Ltr, Commandant of the Command and General Staff School for AG, September 19, 1929. AG 333 EP, RG 94, NA.

were of vital importance in estimating the fiscal requirements of the military policy. This apparently was an implication that perhaps the Army's desire to hold on to all its various activities in the face of budgetary pressure was unsound and invalid.

According to the study, the history of the past decade had proved that no military program could be successfully set up and maintained at 100 percent capacity, and that it was futile to assume that the Army could convince Congress that all the various projects the Army had were essential and should be included in full in the military budget. Nevertheless, the Assistant Secretary was advised, the Army was attempting to keep all its activities going and even to expand some, even in the face of probable budget decreases. "This cannot be done," the study exhorted, "Something is bound to suffer." The Army could continue its widespread activities for the present because it was living on its war reserves, but this would soon end, for the reserves were not being replaced.

In order to build a military posture intelligently for the future, the Assistant Secretary was advised, the Army must know or estimate what expenditure for military purposes the country would approve, for the level of military expenditures was the controlling factor in developing military policy, and should determine the military program. Although no one could definitely decide how much money would be appropriated for military purposes over a period of years, the study estimated that the military expenditures would soon be stabilized at around $200,000,000 and the Regular Army strength would be set at around 100,000 to 150,000.

According to the study, this estimate was based on the "present and prospective political situation" in the country and on the fact that there was no "war scare" that could be used to emphasize the need of military expenditures. The study pointed out that one of the main planks of the Democratic and Republican platforms in 1928 had been the reduction of taxes, and regardless of which party came to power in future years the trend definitely pointed to a period of reduced military expenditures.[28]

The Adjutant General, in presenting the case for the ROTC and CMTC, pointed out that the mission of the ROTC was to replace some 7,000 reservists annually and that this figure was at no time since 1920 actually achieved. Noting that the total cost of the ROTC for fiscal 1928 was almost $8,000,000, The Adjutant General admitted that administrative savings and the curtailment of junior ROTC units in high schools could save approximately one million dollars a year. In discussing the CMTC program, The Adjutant General noted that its main mission was to bring together

---

[28] Memo, Lt. Col. E. D. Pek, OASW, for Maj. Schimelfenig, OASW, August 26, 1929. ASW/26986. Note: G-4 likewise warned of the ominous probability of reduction in military spending. "Should this continue and should it be made manifest through reduction in the War Department limiting figure or in annual appropriations, the War Department will shortly find itself faced with the necessity of reducing its activities to meet the budget." Memo, AC/S G-4 for the Chief of Staff, August 28, 1929. G-4/26771, RG 319, NA.

youths from 17-21 with a view to "stimulate interest in military training" and to provide a body of young men partially trained, who could furnish along with the Regular Army the nucleus of an emergency force. The Adjutant General pleaded against any abolition of the CMTC and noted that if a decrease in its activities was absolutely necessary, such a decrease could be achieved through reducing the number of individuals trained or in the number of camps conducting CMTC training.[29]

The War Plans Division of the General Staff (WPD) was given the task of preparing the War Department study on the possibilities of effecting economies in the military establishment for submission to the President. Its objective, as directed by the Chief of Staff, was to survey the military establishment with the aim of "making extensive reductions" in the military budget without "manifest injury to the national defense." This reflected the understanding by the Chief of Staff that all military needs were not going to be met, and all that adequate preparedness could do would be to mitigate insecurity, not eliminate it. The problem in 1929, as it is today, was to provide an adequate military force within a politically feasible and financially sound budget figure.

The WPD outlined three ways in which the problem could be attacked and possibly solved. The first method would be to estimate the cost of the present military establishment and its planned

---

[29] Ltr, AG for the Chief of Staff, September 23, 1929. AG 333 EP, RG 94, NA.

projects; admittedly this would mean a constantly increasing military budget and was unacceptable to the Hoover Administration. The second method would be to assign a stable military budget figure from year to year fixed at approximately $350,000,000; this would mean having the Army "tailor its suit to fit the cloth." The final solution, as the WPD saw the problem, would be to plan for a reduced budget figure based on legislative changes in military policy and the National Defense Act of 1920 and aimed at organizing a small, highly trained regular force with no skeletonized units. This would mean an annual budget of around $200,000,000 and would mean the curtailment and discontinuance of the training and support of the civilian components by the Regular Army.[30]

It is significant to note the cost as well as the importance given to the training and maintenance of the civilian components by the General Staff. Throughout the period under review, whenever the problem of curtailment of expenditures was raised, the program that the War Department defended most strenuously was that of the civilian components. Their continuance and efficiency was a matter of the utmost concern to the General Staff because it was on these components of the Army of the United States that the nation would depend in time of emergency and total mobilization.

The final 165-page report submitted by the WPD with the concurrence of the other General Staff division chiefs reflected the

[30] Memo, AC/S WPD for the AC/S G-4, September 25, 1929. WPD/3345, RG 319, NA.

staff's views on the problem of balancing military requirements with budget appropriations. The first part of the report covered the authority and purpose of the survey and the mission and organization of the Army. The report then outlined the international situation and concluded that, although foreign relations presented no immediate danger of a conflagration, the existing military establishment must be adequately maintained in order to provide for the possibility and probability of war.[31] The General Staff, however, recognized the necessity of the "minimum expenditures on the peacetime establishment at the same time providing a proper basis for the mobilization of a wartime army."[32]

In analyzing the various arms and services in the light of modern science and weapons technology, the General Staff reaffirmed the doctrine that Infantry was the basic arm, with Cavalry as an "essential component" and the Field Artillery as "indispensable."[33] This was the basic doctrine of the American Army and the General Staff vigorously charged that nothing had occurred since 1918 to change the doctrine that the military establishment was a team built around the Infantry arm, and that there was no short cut nor any economical weapons to replace this fact.

The need for coastal harbor defense was reaffirmed and defended by the General Staff on the grounds that the Air Corps and Navy were

---

[31] Report of the Survey of the Military Establishment by the War Department General Staff, November 1, 1929, p. 23. WPD/3345, RG 319, NA.

[32] Ibid., p. 36

[33] Ibid., pp. 38-41.

too expensive to preclude fixed coastal defense.[34] Granted unlimited funds, the Navy could be increased so that it would be possible to disperse it for harbor defense in detachments superior to any force the enemy could bring to bear. Perhaps reflecting the need for economy, as well as its antipathy toward the claims of the Army aviators, the General Staff threw cold water on the idea of air autonomy by stressing the fact that the air arm was auxiliary to the other combat arms, though capable of performing separate missions. Nevertheless, the General Staff urged completion of the expensive five-year Air Corps expansion program and recommended further study of the air program after the completion date.[35]

In discussing the participation of the Regular Army in the training of the civilian components the General Staff stressed the fact that the National Guard must be kept reasonably efficient and, to this end, the detail of a "considerable number of officers" from the Regular Army was essential. In the case of the Organized Reserves, the General Staff emphasized that supervision by the Regular Army was necessary to insure efficiency; in addition, it was pointed out that the assignment of Regular Army officers to ROTC units was necessary in view of the fact that a lowering of standards of instruction would result in lower efficiency and would be resented by the institutions maintaining ROTC units.[36]

---

[34] *Ibid.*, pp. 42-44.

[35] *Ibid.*, p. 47.

[36] *Ibid.*, pp. 55-57.

The General Staff then delineated its idea of how an adequate defense establishment should be organized. In the continental United States it was recommended that the strength must be sufficient to carry on the overhead duties of peacetime training of the civilian components and to provide adequate protection during time of emergency before the large citizen army could be brought into being. The General Staff believed that the size of this force must be determined by an estimate of the possible hostile forces which could be brought to bear against the nation. Under existing world conditions the General Staff considered that this force should be a Regular Army of approximately 14,000 officers and 165,000 men, a National Guard of 250,000, and an Officer Reserve Corps of 116,000. This force was believed to be adequate to provide for the minimum effective force for the immediate defense of the nation's continental limits and insular possessions. This force was called "Plan I" in the General Staff's survey and was considered the mean between the organization set up by the National Defense Act of 1920, and the actual annual force provided for by the yearly appropriations.[37]

Realizing that Plan I was extremely expensive, the General Staff urged that this cost be looked upon as insurance; the value of the property of the country and the value of principles for which the nation would fight meant that insurance would be necessary. Plan I, according to the General Staff report, would cost under 1929 dollar value $438,000,000 for the first year, and rise gradually to about

---

[37] Ibid., p. 102.

$500,000,000 in the tenth year. In the eleventh year it was estimated that the cost would be lowered to around $450,000,000 and then gradually stabilize at this figure. The General Staff noted that the plan was to be put into effect gradually and spread over a period of a year.[38]

Plan I was the General Staff's recommendation for "adequate defense," although the Staff certainly knew that such a cost figure would be viewed with disfavor by the Hoover Administration. In fact, it is surprising that the General Staff presented such an outline of military requirements when the Commander in Chief had specifically asked for reduction in expenditures and activities. Realizing that to attain Plan I was impossible with the present attitude of Hoover and Congress, the General Staff submitted what it called "Plan II." This plan was based on the assumption that Congress and the Executive would consider Plan I too expensive and perhaps not "necessary for adequate defense."[39]

The General Staff admitted that Plan I was somewhat greater in magnitude and cost than the existing establishment, and in case "responsible authority" considered the present establishment adequate the General Staff believed that more efficient results could be obtained for the money spent by the adoption of certain reforms. These reforms concerned minor administrative policies, such as the transfer of items listed as military activities in the

---

[38] *Ibid.*, pp. 102-04.

[39] *Ibid.*, p. 124.

budget to the non-military category. In addition, it was urged that all real estate and surplus property of the War Department not used for military purposes be sold, and that personnel transfers be limited.[40] The General Staff recommended that if "responsible authority" considered the present establishment adequate for national defense that the budget estimated for fiscal 1931, $359,000,000, be taken as the amount necessary for the maintenance of defense and should be used as a guide and budgetary limit to military planning.[41]

In outlining Plan II, the General Staff stressed that the most essential requirement for the Army was that it be properly maintained regardless of size, and for that reason, the General Staff considered that pay be raised and that the least important military activities be curtailed in order to meet the necessary pay raise. Plan II would not involve any changes in the "basic character" of the mission of the Army, as set forth in the National Defense Act, but would materially reduce the scope of the mission and thus increase the time necessary to mobilize the citizen army and put it in the field ready for combat. The General Staff admitted that this was no great threat to the nation provided the country had allies when war broke out, or if the Navy could control the seas while the powerful forces could be mobilized and organized, as they were in the First World War.[42]

---

[40] Ibid., p. 105.

[41] Ibid., p. 125

[42] Ibid., pp. 132-33.

Plan II was to meet the existing budget for fiscal 1931 and still maintain "adequate defense" by curtailment of minor activities and adoption of certain administrative reforms. According to the General Staff, if material reductions below existing expenditures were desired, it could only be at the expense of major items in the appropriations bill. The General Staff advised against such a move as it would "depreciate the influence and standing of the United States" and so weaken the military preparedness of the country as "to jeopardize the continued existence of the nation as a sovereign state."[43] According to the General Staff, if there were to be any reductions in military expenditures below those outlined in Plan II, it would necessitate the withdrawal of overseas garrisons, discontinuance and abolition of the CMTC, ROTC, Organized Reserves, harbor defense fortifications, war reserves, industrial mobilization planning, and research and development projects.[44]

---

[43] Ibid., p. 162.

[44] Ibid., pp. 135-38. Note: The General Staff discussed at length the role of overseas garrisons, noting that they are "our strategic outposts." While affirming the strategic vulnerability and expense of maintaining these outposts, the General Staff recommended no change. In respect to the Philippine garrison, the General Staff noted that its mission was to hold the Manila Bay area until the fleet could gain supremacy in the Western Pacific. To do this would involve considerable mobile forces and aircraft, because the United States was precluded by treaty from adding to the fortifications of Manila Bay. Moreover, this would be such an additional expense as to make it prohibitive. The solution recommended by the General Staff, both from a cost and efficiency standpoint, was the development of Filipino citizen forces, which together with the American garrison would be sufficient to hold Manila Bay until the fleet could gain supremacy of the Western Pacific. "By judiet cious handling, it is quite possible that the expense" of this development could be transferred to the Philippine Government. Ibid., pp. 70-71.

The strong and vehement opposition of the General Staff to any substantial reduction in military spending below $350,000,000, indicated to the administration that the best it could hope for, with the cooperation of the Army, would be to aim at a stabilization of the military budget. This became in early 1930 the goal of the President and his Secretary of War.

The entire economic survey of the General Staff reflected its satisfaction with the provisions of the National Defense Act of 1920 and the belief of the Army that this legislation should remain inviolate. To the Army, no substantial reduction of military spending was possible without violating this act and thereby seriously betraying the requirements of national defense. The survey reflected the basic conservatism of the General Staff in that it eschewed the possibility of reorganization and economy, and the unwillingness of a peacetime Army under constant budgetary pressure to adopt new and untried procedures and programs:

> It is patent that military expenditures should for economic reasons be kept to the lowest level consistent with adequate national defense. It is desirable also that the annual budget be brought to a state of reasonable stabilization. This can be accomplished to some extent through adoption of all possible measures of economy and the pre-determination of military programs.[45]

An interesting aspect of the General Staff's survey is the emphasis that it placed on the role of the civilian components, particularly the National Guard. The General Staff, in warning against any reductions in military appropriations, defended the

[45] Ibid., p. 163

role of the National Guard as the foundation for the mobilization of a mass citizen army. No longer was it the despised "militia" of former years.[46] The General Staff clearly stressed the fact that higher military costs were the necessary result of the Regular Army supporting and training the National Guard. An efficient National Guard could not be guaranteed without this expense. By stressing the National Guard as the keystone of the citizen army, and the complementing role of the Regular Army played in training and equipping the civilian components, the General Staff assured itself of political support to meet the challenges of those groups in the country who were adamantly opposed to the Army and its various activities.

Perhaps the most significant aspect of the General Staff's report was the emphasis by the Army planners on the bedrock of American military doctrine: In battle it is man and not machines that is the decisive element. Therefore, the General Staff stressed numbers and personnel and, in particular, the vital role of the Regular Army in training and equipping the civilian components who would play the main role in a mass army. The report reflected the

---

[46] The military policy of the Root-Upton-Garrison-March school of thought deprecated the role of the militia or the National Guard in national defense, preferring instead a national volunteer or continental force based on an expansible Regular Army. The militia of the states would serve as state forces and as replacements in time of war to the federally raised national army. See Politics of National Defense (GPO: Washington, 1940). For Root's views of the National Guard, see Elbridge Colby, "Elihu Root and the National Guard," Military Affairs XXIII (1959), pp. 20, 28-34.

concept that victory in any future war would not come through rapid technological advancement, but in a mass citizen army, and that there was no economical short cut for adequate preparedness.

CHAPTER III

STABILIZATION OF THE MILITARY BUDGET, 1930

At the end of the first decade after the Armistice of 1918, the Army, except for the Five-Year Program of Air Corps expansion and augmentation, was still basically equipped with World War I equipment. During late 1929 the new Secretary of War, Patrick J. Hurley, sought to remedy this situation through a modest but systematic and well-coordinated research and development and re-equipment program. Hurley, succeeding to the Office of Secretary of War upon the death of James W. Good on November 14, 1929, brought to the office wide experience and contact with military affairs. Forty-six years old in 1929, Hurley was married to the daughter of Admiral Henry B. Wilson (Ret.). He had been affiliated with the militia and National Guard in the old Indian Territory and the State of Oklahoma since 1902, and had served with the AEF in France during the first World War. Before succeeding to the secretaryship Hurley had been Assistant Secretary of War.

On November 30, 1929, Hurley directed that in making its estimates for the next fiscal year (1932) each arm and service having supply and procurement functions should list in detail its research and development projects. It is significant to note that although the Assistant Secretary of War was generally responsible for procurement there was no overall guidance given to research and development, and each arm, service, or branch having supply functions maintained its own research program without general control or coordination. Hurley sought to give some sort of direction and control to this effort. He directed each supply bureau to submit separate reports listing projects of research and development in connection with new equipment, projects for the substitution of critical materials and the improvement of manufacturing processes, and new equipment that was scheduled to undergo extended service tests before being accepted. The list was to include cost estimates for all the projects. Hurley emphasized that a clear distinction should be drawn between research and development and re-equipment. In general, the Secretary of War advised, until equipment had passed the experimental stage and tests warranted adoption as standard equipment, funds for testing this equipment should come from research and development appropriations.[1] Under this definition funds for research and development would therefore for some years run greater than procurement for rearmament and re-equipment. Perhaps Hurley's aim was to emphasize research and development and the perfecting of pilot models of equipment that could be procured more readily upon mobilization, with less concern being placed on the actual rearmament of the Army with costly new weapons. Hurley definitely hoped to bring closer coordination and control over the

[1] Memo, Acting AC/S G-4 for the AG, November 29, 1929. AG 111, RG 94, NA.

entire research and development program and in his memorandum seems not to have been overly concerned with the problem of immediate budget reductions and the curtailment of military spending. However, by instituting a strict priority listing of projects, the Secretary of War was in a position to continue research and development on at least high priority items if reduction and curtailment was directed by the President.

It is doubtful that Hurley visualized a large scale program because a little more than a month after his memorandum on the research and development program he directed that the Army should prepare for fiscal 1932 the "minimum of additional and continuing major projects."[2] Thus he inaugurated the policy of stabilization of military spending, generally along the lines of the General Staff's Plan II that was submitted in the economic survey in November 1929.

Although research and development was an important aspect of military affairs during the twenties, the advancement of military technology, except perhaps aircraft, did not warrant the General Staff preparing any re-equipment and modernization program. The General Staff was hesitant about investing appropriated funds in untried equipment and generally was of the opinion that the military establishment could be considered adequately prepared with its vast

---

[2] Report of the War Department Budget Advisory Committee Estimates for Fiscal Year 1932, May 26, 1930, p. 2. RG 129, AG 198. Note: Hurley's letter advising the War Department of this policy was reproduced and appeared in the Report of the BAC.

reserve stocks left over from World War I. By the beginning of the 1930's, however, this equipment was obsolete or obsolescent and it was essential that some modest program be initiated. Unfortunately, the advent of the depression occurred precisely as the World War I stocks were becoming out of date and the policy of retrenchment and stabilization of military spending, inaugurated in early 1930, made it difficult to plan on the realization of any worthwhile modernization and re-equipment program.

Nevertheless, the General Staff was of the opinion that it was possible to make some progress, at least in the development of pilot models of certain pieces of equipment, if not an expensive program of re-equipment. An example of this policy of strict apportionment of priorities in the development of certain items was the preparation of the Ordnance Department estimates for fiscal 1932. Ordnance had submitted an estimate of $2,400,000 for limited service tests and the purchase of semi-automatic rifles, 3-inch antiaircraft guns, and as many tanks as possible with the remaining money. The final directive of the War Department reduced this amount to less than $1,000,000 and proposed a corresponding reduction in each of the items to be purchased. The General Staff then decided that the entire amount should be concentrated for use on the highest priority item, the semi-automatic rifle, and perhaps a few tanks.[3]

---

[3] Memo, AC/S G-4 for the AG, January 27, 1930. AG 111, RG 94, NA.

The General Staff was of the opinion that progress in tank development did not warrant more than a few token purchases to test tactics and keep up with the latest in tank technology, and that the 3-inch antiaircraft gun would not be an economic investment in view of the rapid advance of aircraft technology and the probability of its swift obsolescence. The perspicacity of the General Staff decision in this case was amply demonstrated in later developments; while tank, anti-tank, and aircraft development through the thirties continued in a constant flux and made the testing and adoption of any one weapon in this category difficult, the development of the Garand semi-automatic rifle gave the American Infantry a weapon that became standard before World War II and proved itself the outstanding shoulder weapon of the Second World War.

Hurley's annual report for 1930, submitted at the end of fiscal 1930, was a generally bland and complacent report which concluded with the statement that Army efficiency had perhaps increased, and mentioned nothing about reductions, stabilization, or curtailment due to the economic policy of the administration.[4] However, the Chief of Staff, General Summerall, in his accompanying report emphasized that it was the policy of the War Department to follow the "expressed desire" of the Commander in Chief and "stabilize" military expenditures. Fixing this limitation, according to the Chief of Staff, was admittedly "a governmental necessity" but

---

[4] Annual Report of the Secretary of War, 1930 (Washington: GPO, 1930), pp. 1-33.

he noted that the War Department was concerned over the possibility that the Bureau of the Budget, acting for the President, would usurp the responsibility of the military in determining which items of the military budget should be reduced or stabilized in order to bring the total estimates within a limiting figure.[5] If stabilization was the policy, Summerall wanted Hoover to give the War Department a financial ceiling and make it the responsibility of the Army to stay within this limit.

In his report as Chief of Staff Summerall had considerable to say in respect to budget and appropriations. In general his remarks reflected his concern that the gap between what was desired for the Army and actual appropriations was indeed significant and suggested that military planning should be more attuned to the meager funds that could be expected. Summerall admitted that the means of making military policy effective was through the budget and that the sufficiency of appropriations for military purposes had to be considered in connection with the general financial condition of the country.[6]

Notwithstanding Summerall's acceptance of the necessity to curtail military spending he charged that funds were insufficient for approximating the military system of national defense set up by the National Defense Act of 1920. The essential feature of

---

[5] *Ibid.*, p. 140.

[6] *Ibid.*, p. 137.

Summerall's final peroration as Chief of Staff was that limited funds must be spread around all projects and all activities in order to have a balanced military establishment: "No element in our military forces is independent of the other, but each is affected by the state of development of the other." He rebuked the air enthusiasts by charging that too much emphasis had been given to the strength of bombardment aircraft. Reflecting the belief that modest and unspectacular equipment development was consonant with a "stabilized" budget, if closely controlled and coordinated, the Chief of Staff urged that all elements of the Army be considered simultaneously and that development should be expressed in "general projects extending over a period of years."[7]

It was Summerall's announced policy to maintain the cost of the Army at "not less than the existing budget." Aware of the fact that President Hoover was adamantly opposed to "mounting" military expenditures, particularly after the end of fiscal 1930 and the beginning of federal fiscal deficiency, the Chief of Staff was of the opinion that Hoover would accept a military budget stabilized at the 1931 figure of about $350,000,000. According to Summerall the Army could maintain itself in a "reasonable state of efficiency within the existing budget."[8]

---

[7] *Ibid.*, p. 140.

[8] Ltr, Summerall for Maj. Gen. Frank Parker, Commanding General 6th Corps Area, August 18, 1930. Summerall Papers, Library of Congress, Container No. 4.

Pressure from the White House after the beginning of fiscal 1931, which was the summer and fall of calendar year 1930, indicated that Summerall's hope of stabilizing the military budget at the 1931 figure would be difficult of attainment, particularly if government revenues continued to drop and the administration continued its demand for a balanced budget. In late July 1930 the President notified Hurley that he wanted the expenditure of appropriated money reduced for the fiscal year 1931. According to Hoover it was of the "utmost importance in this time of depression" that government outlays for procurement be reduced in every possible manner, and the War Department was admonished that besides minor administrative savings it was desirable to defer expenditure on major programs until "such time as government revenues have recovered."[9] The Commander in Chief requested cooperation of the War Department in his efforts to reduce government spending and directed the Army to return to the White House a statement as to the amount of appropriated funds for the current fiscal year of 1931 that could be deferred from expenditure.[10]

Hurley directed G-4 and the Budget Officer of the War Department to come up with the desired figure of deferred expenditure for Hoover, and at a conference on August 7, 1930, the Army proposals were prepared and forwarded to the Secretary.[11] The Assistant Secretary of

---

[9] Ltr, Hoover to Hurley, July 29, 1930. AG 111, RG 94, NA.

[10] Ibid.

[11] Memo, Deputy Chief of Staff for the Budget Officer of the War Department, August 4, 1930. AG 111, RG 94, NA.

War Frederick H. Payne, answered the President on September 15, noting that the Army had estimated that it was possible to withhold $20,000,000 from total military and non-military appropriations for fiscal 1931. At the same time the Assistant Secretary admonished Hoover that the non-withdrawal of appropriated funds from the Treasury for Army spending would keep money out of circulation and in almost every instance would "further aggravate and increase the unemployment situation."[12] Hoover replied with a strident and almost panicky warning that the budget for fiscal 1931 could not be balanced without "drastic reduction of current expenditure" and notified the Army that it should limit its total expenditures for fiscal 1931 to $444,200,000 and specified explicitly that Army proposals to defer $6,300,000 for rivers and harbors should be spent and not deferred.[13] Hoover's limiting figure of $444,000,000 for both military and non-military funds meant that War Department spending for fiscal 1931 would be less than the appropriated figure of $509,000,000 by some $65,000,000. Apparently Hoover viewed rivers and harbors projects as a modest form of public works

---

[12] Ltr, Payne for Hoover, September 15, 1930. AG 111, RG 94, NA. Frederick H. Payne brought unusual qualifications to his position as Assistant Secretary of War. Born November 10, 1876 in Greenfield, Mass., he had been a banker and industrialist in New England. He was appointed Assistant Secretary of War on March 6, 1930 and served in that position until March 4, 1933. Payne had wide experience as an Ordnance procurement officer in New England during the First World War and from 1919 until his appointment as Assistant Secretary of War served as assistant district Ordnance chief affiliated with the Office of the Assistant Secretary of War in Bridgeport, Conn.

[13] Ltr, Hoover for Hurley, September 23, 1930. AG 111, RG 94, NA.

which could be spread around the country and he was reluctant for this reason to have them stopped or deferred.

According to the G-4 an analysis of the deferments proposed by the War Department in following out the orders of the President "indicates that no essential military activity of the War Department is curtailed or seriously affected." However the various estimating agencies of the Army would have to "revise or modify" their schedule of procurement or expenditure in order to conform with the directives of the President.[14] Undoubtedly the smugness of the G-4 reflected the attitude that by the winter and the spring of 1931 and the next fiscal year <u>at the latest</u>, the economy would right itself and the need for further deferments or curtailments of military projects would be obviated.

If G-4 was not alarmed by the policy of the President the Air Corps certainly was concerned and vigorously charged that it had contracted for the procurement of a certain number of aircraft based on the appropriated money and had assigned procurement and operating requirements for fiscal 1931 based on the idea that what was appropriated could be expended. The Air Corps warned that if its appropriated money was not made available, it would be unable to execute its mission and prevent what would shortly be an "economic catastrophe" to the aviation industry in the United States.[15] The

---

[14] Memo, AC/S G-4 for the Chief of Staff, September 24, 1930. AG 111, RG 94, NA.

[15] Ltr, Assistant Secretary of War for Air, F. Trubee Davison, for the Director of the Bureau of the Budget, Clawson Ropp, November 3, 1930. AG 111, RG 94, NA.

Air Corps readily grasped the significant link between military procurement and the aviation industry of the United States. Without government orders and the procurement of military aircraft the aviation industry of the United States would have been in dire financial straits.

The issue developed into quite a controversy with the General Staff taking the Air Corps to task for its failure to heed the warning of the President in the summer of 1930 to defer spending. The Air Corps stressed that it needed to withdraw $40,000,000 to meet its contracts instead of the $33,700,000 that had been set by the Bureau of the Budget. The final solution of the problem was that the Air Corps was permitted to spend around $36,000,000 but only after the funds were obtained from the money appropriated to the other arms and services.[16] Although the amount that was taken from the other arms and services was small in present day standards of military appropriations, around $2,000,000, it is easy to visualize the reaction of the arms and services which were forced to come to the relief of the Air Corps. Action such as this during times of financial stringency and reduced spending was hardly likely to make for mutual respect and understanding within the military service, and exacerbated the already tenuous relationship between the older branches and combat arms and the self-assertive Air Corps.

Besides transferring funds from the ground combat arms to the Air Corps, the policy of building up the enlisted strength of the

---

[16] Memo, AC/S G-4 for the Chief of Staff, October 21, 1930. AG 111, RG 94, NA.

Air Corps at the expense of the other arms was also a sore point in intra-service relations. In order to provide for the annual increment of personnel for the Air Corps, in 1929 approximately 1,900 men were transferred from the other arms to the Air Corps. This resulted in the deactivation of five battalions of infantry and one regiment, less one battalion of field artillery.[17]

Although the Assistant Chief of Staff G-4 had more or less supported the decision of the President and the Budget Bureau in curtailing military expenditures in the fall of 1930 in order to balance the federal budget, his views were not generally accepted throughout the service. As mentioned, the Air Corps was strongly against any curtailment of appropriated funds. Pique was also expressed by other military spokesmen over Hoover's tactics of limiting treasury withdrawals regardless of the fact that the money had been duly appropriated by Congress. The Budget Advisory Committee of the War Department, made up of representatives of the General Staff and the various branches, informed the Chief of Staff that the President's call for savings and deferments involved good old fashioned politics brought about by "alarming" treasury estimates of sharply reduced federal receipts and revenues. According to the Budget Advisory Committee the Army would have to suffer while Hoover made political capital out of his efforts to balance the federal budget. Furthermore, the Budget Advisory

---

[17] Annual Report of the Secretary of War, 1930, p. 3.

Committee reported to the Chief of Staff that Hoover was not really worried over the deficit, but his action in deferring military expenditures may have been "slightly due to pending elections and a forthcoming lame duck session of Congress."[18] Rarely is there to be found in Army files such a candid appreciation of the fact that military policy and military affairs in the United States are closely involved in the political arena.

Army petulance over Hoover's alleged tactics of playing politics with military appropriations was reflected in the tenor of comment in the unofficial but influential Army Navy Journal. The "house organ" of the military and naval services attacked the President for curtailing money that had lawfully been appropriated by Congress and charged that Hoover's action would "eventually raise the question of the constitutional right of Congress to provide for national defense."[19] According to the Journal there was some resentment because of the blatantly "political conditions" under which Hoover linked the economy move.[20]

Throughout the congressional election campaign of 1930 the unofficial spokesman for the services kept up its mild rebuke toward President Hoover. It chided him for being inconsistent in his views toward the Army; by encouraging on the one hand national defense

---

[18] Memo, Budget Advisory Committee of the War Department for the Chief of Staff, November 4, 1930. AG 111, RG 94, NA.

[19] Army Navy Journal, October 18, 1930, p. 145.

[20] Ibid., September 27, 1930, p. 73.

through various public pronouncements the Chief Executive had reversed himself through his day-to-day "seeming inattention" to Army activities and Army problems. The President was urged to "learn from personal knowledge" what the Army was doing so he would be more considerate of the "needs of national defense."[21] During the congressional campaign the <u>Army Navy Journal</u> stressed the fact that the administration's policy of cutting down on military spending was in contradiction to its efforts to urge businessmen to embark on replacement and expansion of industry.[22] If Hoover was hesitant about spending how could he expect private enterprise to invest and spend in plant equipment and expansion?

The election of the Democrats to control of the House of Representatives of the 72nd Congress in November 1930, and the repudiation of Hoover and the GOP, led the <u>Army Navy Journal</u> to gloat that the results were in the nature of a "general disapproval" of the policies of the administration, and that it was fair to assume that the results demonstrated that there was no "popular approval" to the diminution of national defense.[23] Accordingly the <u>Journal</u> championed the cause of increased military expenditures, and urged Congress to prime the pump through military spending. To relieve unemployment, the <u>Journal</u> pointed out that it

---

[21] <u>Ibid</u>., October 11, 1930, p. 130.

[22] <u>Ibid</u>., September 27, 1930, p. 82.

[23] <u>Ibid</u>., November 8, 1930, p. 226.

was necessary to increase Army pay, continue the housing program, increase the size of the Regular Army, and expand the Air Corps' Five-Year Program. By spending "adequate appropriations" the Army could be used as a means of lifting the country out of its economic doldrums.[24]

The idea of using military expenditures, manifestly for the development and modernization of the Army, as a means of pulling the economy up by its boot straps fell on the unsympathetic ears of the lame duck session of the 71st Congress which convened in December 1930. It was difficult for Congress to comprehend the logic and consistency of cutting the military budget, ostensibly to balance the budget, and at the same time increase expenditures for military activities in order to afford relief from unemployment. Nevertheless, the idea of pump priming through military expenditures was not at all alien to White House thinking at this time. The second session of the 71st Congress convened in December, 1930, and the Hoover Administration considered presenting to Congress some sort of public works program that would include spending for military activities. The War Department was asked orally on November 10, 1930, by the Bureau of the Budget to ascertain how much money could "properly and profitably" be expended in order to combat the "unemployment situation which apparently has developed and grown so acute in recent months.

---

[24] Ibid., November 29, 1930, p. 298.

throughout the United States."[25] Interestingly enough this request implied that the Army would be given some vague role as the coordinator and planner of a modest and mild public works program that could be undertaken efficiently and economically within a reasonable period of time.

War Department studies on pump priming in late 1930 included activities within the Department's jurisdiction and did not include activities pertaining to other government agencies. The Army sent to the Budget Bureau a figure of $47,600,000 for spending on military projects and a proposal for the expenditure of $27,000,000 for non-military activities, a total of some $74,000,000. The Bureau of the Budget held hearings on these proposals with representatives from the War Department, and the President transmitted to the Speaker of the House a request for $57,000,000 on December 4, 1930. Of the total requested by Hoover $30,500,000 was for military projects and $27,000,000 for non-military activities. The entire reduction by the President had been in the military items and was based on Hoover's idea of requesting money for projects which had been at one time authorized by Congress but never completed because of the lack of funds. Furthermore, Hoover wanted the money spent on projects for which it was planned to provide funds if and when federal finances would

---

[25] Ltr, Frederick H. Payne, Acting Secretary of War to Senator Wesley L. Jones, Chairman Senate Appropriations Committee, January 9, 1931. AG 111, RG 94, NA.

permit. Although some of the military projects, for which Hoover requested money, would not be completed within six months, and would entail future continuing expenditures to complete, it was hoped that Congress would disregard this problem and grant the money in order to provide employment relief.[26]

Under Public Law 550, 71st Congress, approved on December 20, 1930, some $116,000,000 for unemployment relief work were authorized for the entire government. The War Department received a total of some $25,500,000 for rivers and harbors projects and $3,000,000 for flood control; the request for money for military programs was refused by Congress.[27]

The issue of pump priming through military expenditures was raised again in the early part of 1931, when the War Department estimates for fiscal 1932 were before the Senate Appropriations Committee. The War Department, at the initiative of Senator Wesley Jones of the Senate Appropriations Committee, was asked to give a "succinct account" of how the 1932 budget figure could be considered

---

[26] _Ibid._ The list of military activities that Hoover forwarded to Congress contained the following breakdown:

Quartermaster Corps	$9.69 million	Chemical Warfare	$1.45 million
Seacoast Defense	3.16 "	USMA	1.46 "
Signal Corps	.39 "	National Guard	2.04 "
Air Corps	4.75 "	ROTC	.67 "
Ordnance	6.90 "		
		Total	$30.5 million

[27] _Ibid._

as an "aid to unemployment." The Army, hoping that this was an "opportune time" to present its request for additional funds for military projects outside of its regular appropriations,[28] presented to the Senate Appropriations Committee the original figure that Hoover had sent to the Speaker of the House in early December.[29] Nothing came of this effort and the use of funds for strictly military activities in pump priming endeavors was not brought up again until the advent of the New Deal.

During the late fall of 1930 Hurley had forwarded to President Hoover's Budget Bureau the War Department estimates for fiscal 1932 which totalled some $346,400,000 for military expenditures. This was a revised figure which had $20,000,000 deducted by the Secretary of War from an original figure of some $360,000,000, which had been forwarded to the Secretary of War by the Budget Advisory Committee of the War Department and the Chief of Staff. Some of Hurley's deductions were taken from the ROTC, CMTC, Ordnance, and Quartermaster, but the main cut was in the Air Corps estimates which were pruned from $56,900,000 to around $45,500,000. In transmitting this figure to the White House, Hurley noted that his policy was to "stabilize" the War Department estimates for the next several years at a third of a billion dollars, and in order to carry out this policy every "project had been reduced to the utmost" and except for the Fifth

---

[28] Memo, Budget Officer for the War Department for the Secretary of War, January 3, 1932. AG 111, RG 94, NA.

[29] Ltr, Payne to Jones, January 9, 1931. AG 111, RG 94, NA.

increment of the Air Corps' Five-Year program the budget carried no provision whatever for the augmentation of the military establishment.[30]

The Bureau of the Budget flatly rejected Hurley's reduced figure and instructed the War Department to revise the figure downward through the elimination of such activities as the Air Corps depot reserve of aircraft, one-half of the aircraft augmentation program, as provided in the annual increment of the Air Corps Act of 1926, and other activities pertaining to the Air Corps. No limiting figure was set by the Bureau of the Budget, much to the chagrin of the War Department.[31]

In his appearance before the House Sub-committee on Military Appropriations, Hurley outlined to the Committee the revised figure for fiscal 1932, $343,200,000. According to the Secretary of War this amount would suffice to carry out his policy of stabilization while continuing the "operation and maintenance of existing routine activities" in the most economical manner.[32] According to Hurley the original War Department estimates aggregated almost a half billion dollars, but through review they had been lowered to a

---

[30] Memo, Hurley for the Budget Officer of the War Department, June 28, 1930. AG 111, RG 94, NA.

[31] Memo, AC/S G-4 for the Chief of Staff, September 9, 1930. Memo, Budget Officer for the War Department for the Secretary of War, undated. AG 111, RG 94, NA.

[32] _Hearings_: War Department Appropriations Bill, 1932 (December 11, 1930), p. 992.

figure totalling around a third of a billion plus a supplemental Air Corps estimate of $7,500,000. Hurley, reflecting the War Department's concern over the attempt of the Budget Bureau to reduce certain specific items, rather than in setting a limiting figure, added that he had requested the cooperation of the Budget Bureau to set up a total for "military requirements" and thus assure a "degree of freedom" essential to the responsibilities of his office. According to Hurley the figure before Congress was unchanged from the final War Department estimate that had been forwarded to the Budget Bureau.[33] The Secretary emphasized that the War Department, under pressure to reduce its annual budget, should be given a limiting figure rather than have the Budget Bureau determine arbitrarily where reductions were to be made and by how much.

Appearing before the Sub-committee on Military Appropriations in early December 1930 was the new Chief of Staff, General Douglas MacArthur. In speaking to the Sub-committee, MacArthur noted that he had just returned from a long tour of foreign service and had been Chief of Staff for only a few days. He affirmed his general support for the military budget for fiscal 1932 and added that in his opinion it was free from the "eccentricities af any individual or group." This was a subtle thrust at the Air Corps, and an indication to the Sub-committee that he favored a balanced military program. In addition, MacArthur remarked that he thought that the

---

[33] Ibid., pp. 992-93.

budget represented the "best thought of the executive branch of the government" in respect to a military program. The new Chief of Staff noted that the actual figures for fiscal 1932 approximated those of fiscal 1931, and that this lack of provision for augmentation and expansion of the military establishment indicated a certain "crystallization of routine administration and training for the fiscal year 1932."[34] When asked whether he thought the estimates were sufficient for the military program for 1932, the Chief of Staff equivocated somewhat by answering:

> The estimate will carry out the routine training, supply and operation of the Military Establishment in a satisfactory way. I think that they represent the necessary balance that must always be maintained, in time of peace, between the financial structure of the Government and its provision for National Defense.[35]

Thus the Chief of Staff affirmed the fact that the policy of the Army would be to accept the necessity for reduced spending and cooperate with the administration in "stabilizing" expenditures. Army estimates would, therefore, be based not on what was needed or sufficient, but on what was to be expected and practical of being appropriated in time of economic and budgetary stringency.

If the Chief of Staff was more or less satisfied with the Army estimates and the "crystallization of routine administration and training" in the Army, such cooperation was not forthcoming from the Air Corps. Air Corps spokesmen before the House Subcommittee voiced concern and apprehension over the impact of reduced

---

[34] *Ibid.*, p. 980.

[35] *Ibid.*, p. 982.

appropriations on aviation development. F. Trubee Davison, Assistant Secretary of War for Air, pointed out the dilemma of the modern military budget by stressing the fact that with restricted funds all that was possible was to keep day-to-day activities going and make some modest improvement each year on equipment that was on hand. In other words, what Davison was bringing out was that technological advancement was difficult if not impossible without increasing expenditures. According to Davison, the Air Corps was on a treadmill: it was making moderate development each year but unable to go ahead with "big, important projects because of a lack of funds."[36] When Congressman Taber asked Davison why more money should not be put into the budget for experimental work and research and development and less in procurement, Davison replied that this would not be a good idea, except to a very limited extent, because it was the Air Corps policy to take available funds and buy the best available aircraft for an expanding Air Corps.[37] His reply reflected the basic antagonism in time of financial stringency: whether the limited funds available should be used for research and development and the maintenance of a small nucleus for training and testing in pilot models, or whether the limited money should be used for procurement and the equipping the forces with the latest available equipment. In general, the General Staff favored the former solution to the problem and Davison's testimony indicated that Air Corps thinking favored the

---

[36] _Ibid._, p. 779.

[37] _Ibid._, p. 781.

latter solution.

The testimony of General James E. Fechet, Chief of the Air Corps before the House Sub-committee on Military Appropriations is revealing in helping to understand the problem faced by the Army in the early 1930's of attempting to "stabilize" spending and at the same time provide a strong viable defense for the nation. Fechet told the Sub-committee that although the prices of aircraft and aircraft equipment were down in 1930 and 1931 because of the deflation and the depression, this fact had little effect on aircraft procurement. Fechet stressed the fact that by the time series production of an aircraft was begun and the price was brought down the "thing is obsolescent, and we do not buy it any more."[38] The Chief of the Air Corps noted that modern military equipment, in this case aircraft, cannot be stabilized or standardized because improvement is constant and so great that one model cannot become standard and produced year after year.

The "crystallization" of military training and administration, given the world situation and problems of national defense faced by the General Staff in 1930, perhaps was a valid goal consistent with the fiscal policy of a "stabilized" budget. But military technology cannot remain crystallized and stagnant and because of its very nature is in a constant state of flux demanding increasing funds. This problem led to an exacerbation of the struggle between the "tradionalists" in the General Staff and the old line combat arms

---

[38] <u>Ibid</u>., p. 739.

on the one hand and the air enthusiasts and their civilian supporters on the other. In general, the former proposed that in time of economic stringency it was possible to stabilize but cutting back on everything except the essential training activities. Behind this view was the belief that man and not weapons was the ultimate and deciding factor in warfare. The Air Corps supporters viewed aircraft as a new weapon possessing radical and revolutionary influence over the future of warfare that must be developed and expanded at the expense, if necessary, of the older combat arms and the civilian components.

CHAPTER IV

PROBLEMS OF STABILIZATION

While Congress was dealing with the War Department appropriations bill for 1932 and reducing the figure sent to it by the President from $343,200,000 to around $339,700,000, the Army began its annual task of preparing the 1933 fiscal year estimates. This task was initiated in early 1931, one year before final action was scheduled by Congress on the estimates. The Deputy Chief of Staff advised his colleagues on the General Staff that in making estimates for fiscal 1933 they should be guided by the instructions from the Secretary of War that he would not submit any estimate aggregating over one-third of a billion dollars.

While Congress went to work on the appropriations bill for fiscal 1932, the Army planners were advised that there were certain increases over the pending bill that must be included in 1933 estimates because of their statutory or legal status, and must be given priority over all other items to be considered for increase. Included in the items that would have to be marked for increase because of their statutory basis were retirement benefits, longevity pay, acquisition of land, and the Five-Year Air Corps program. The General Staff was advised that if there were to be any recommendations for the augmentation of any activity the increased cost must not only be justified, but financing of this cost must come from a reduction or elimination of less necessary activities.[1]

This peremptory admonition meant that Army planners would have to shelve any expensive plans and ideas and how to routine programs and projects that had been based on what to expect: one-third of a billion dollars. If rapid and large scale augmentation and modernization was dealt a severe blow through the policy of the Hoover Administration to stabilize military spending it was difficult to arouse much opposition to this policy in the Army outside of the clamorous Air Corps aviators. The Deputy Chief of Staff viewed the directive of 1933 as falling short of "all the activities and requirements" of the Army but recognized that it was based on the "present economic and military policy" of the President and would be adequate to provide for the "minimum activities essential to the continuing mission of the Army," and would provide to a limited extent for new requirements, increased activities, and possibly some augmentation.[2] The effect of this attitude was that the Army became habituated to accepting limited funds and conservative in its outlook toward new and expensive

---

[1]Memo, Deputy Chief of Staff for all Assistant Chiefs of Staff, December 24, 1930. AG 111, RG 94, NA. Augmentation is defined as the increase of personnel and equipment of the tables of organization or equipment, occasioned by variation from normal function. Dictionary of United States Army Terms, Department of the Army, 1950.

[2]Memo, Deputy Chief of Staff for the Chief of Staff, January 2, 1931. AG 111, RG 94, NA.

ideas. Financial stringency meant reluctance to adopt change because new programs meant increasing annual costs and expense. While the emphasis throughout the country was on economizing in government expenses, the Army was extremely reluctant because of the adverse effect on public opinion to appear as demanding more money for national defense regardless of how important the needed appropriations were.

It was suggested to the Chief of Staff that the Army could "reasonably anticipate" an eventual appropriation for fiscal 1933 of around one-third of a billion dollars. In this case why should it not simplify the entire budget procedure for the Army and instead of having the estimating agencies of the War Department forward their individual estimates to the Chief of Staff and the Secretary of War, let the latter specify to each estimating agency the total figure it would receive? Because of the responsibility and the authority of the Secretary of War this could be done and would be helpful for the estimating agencies in planning their detailed estimates, for they would know the exact figure they were scheduled to receive. According to the suggestion this would not preclude each estimating agency having the right to "protect its activities" and to appeal to the Secretary of War against what it considered was an "unreasonable limitation."[3]

---

[3]Memo, Acting Deputy Chief of Staff for the Chief of Staff, undated, AG 111, RG 94, NA.

Apparently nothing came of this suggestion and no record is available of the Chief of Staff's reaction. Undoubtedly in the interest of maintaining harmony between the General Staff and the old-time supply branches, the Chief of Staff was reluctant to approve such a plan, although in fact he did issue a limiting figure to each branch but only after its original estimate had been forwarded to the Chief of Staff's office.[4] Already the General Staff and the Secretary of War, through the Budget and Legislative Planning Branch of the General Staff, was exerting control over the branches in respect to budget estimates and the omitting of the procedure of allowing each branch to originate its own estimates would have exacerbated the old fissure between the General Staff and the supply branches. The budget stabilization policy and limited funds made available to the Army during the depression tended to increase the control of the General Staff over the one-time autonomous War Department bureaus.[5]

---

[4] Memo, Deputy Chief of Staff for the Chief of Staff, August 10, 1931. AG 111, RG 94, NA.

[5] One of the principal obstacles to the General Staff in its struggle for control of the War Department bureaus was the fact that the latter were financially independent up to 1921. Each bureau before that time compiled its own budget which was presented to the Treasury Department through the Office of the Secretary of War. Each chief of bureau allotted his own fund, which made him financially independent. After the passage of the Budget and Accounting Act in 1921, the War Department established a Budget Office which considerably moderated the financial independence of the War Department bureaus. This Budget Office had the task of assuring that funds requested and appropriated for the Army could and would be used to the interest of the Department as a whole. While the Department's funds after 1921 were still, in many cases, appropriated

The Deputy Chief of Staff viewed the tentative budget figure for 1933, around a third of a billion dollars, with cheery complacency, and believed it to be the best budget that could be expected, given the existing economic situation. He thought that the budget would insure a "coordinated and reasonable program which is adequate for minimum requirements of national defense."[6] He noted that the program for fiscal 1933 would provide for personnel, training, and supply on the same basis as in the preceding years, and also provide for some essential equipment on a limited basis. In summarizing the estimates for the Chief of Staff he noted that the Regular Army would be at the same strength, but that longevity requirements and the augmented numbers on the retired lists would be the principal factors in causing the pay of the Army to increase. The Chief of Staff was advised that because of the fall in commodity prices the "routine operations and maintenance activities" of the Army would be on more generous terms. Construction of buildings and the Air Corps estimates were down for 1933 but Ordnance and Quartermaster figures were up because of a planned limited expansion of training ammunition, and the purchase of tanks

---

under titles indicating the service primarily responsible for performing the functions for which the appropriations were made, the funds were allocated by the Budget Officer for use in accordance with Staff direction. Cater Files, "Budgetary Matters of the War Department," Office of the Chief of Military History, Department of the Army, (OCMH).

[6]Memo, Deputy Chief of Staff for the Chief of Staff, March 9, 1931. AG 111, RG 94, NA.

and a few armored cars, as well as motor trucks under the replacement program. The civilian components would be on the same basis and strength as previous years although at corresponding lower costs.[7]

The Chief of Staff, in writing to the Budget Officer of the War Department in order to brief the latter prior to his appearance before the Budget Bureau in defense of the Army's estimates, emphasized that the 1933 estimates made provision for a "limited program" of modernization of organizational equipment (motor truck replacement) and for the partial maintenance of war reserve ammunition. These, according to the Chief of Staff, were of "vital and immediate importance."[8] The final figure that was recommended by the Budget Advisory Committee to the Chief of Staff for presentation to the Bureau of the Budget for fiscal 1933 totalled $329,000,000.[9]

---

[7] Memo, Deputy Chief of Staff for the Chief of Staff, March 9, 1931. AG 111, RG 94, NA.

[8] Memo, Chief of Staff for the Budget Officer of the War Department, August 10, 1931. AG 111, RG 94, NA.

[9] Rpt, Budget Advisory Committee, sub: "Estimates for fiscal year 1933," July 27, 1931, p. 3. AG 125, RG 94, NA; Memo, Deputy Chief of Staff for the Chief of Staff, August 10, 1931. AG 111, RG 94, NA. The budget for fiscal 1933 for the War Department would have a stormy time in the upcoming first session of the 72nd Congress, and would be considerably reduced by the Bureau of the Budget and Congress before final allocation and appropriation. The alteration of the Army appropriation bill for fiscal 1933 by Congress during the spring and summer of 1932 will be covered in a succeeding chapter.

During the spring of 1931, while the onerous task of budget preparation was being conducted in the War Department, the controversial General Johnson Hagood presented to the Chief of Staff his radical proposals for reorganizing the ROTC program in order to achieve substantial reduction of cost, as well as for a general improvement of the entire program. Hagood charged that the existing ROTC program while being needlessly expensive was not turning out an adequate product. He claimed that only 20 percent of the students in the basic ROTC courses went on to complete the advanced course and qualify for reserve commissions. According to Hagood, 80 percent of the ROTC effort was wasted and 30,000 college graduates left campuses each year with no obligation to the nation. Thus, two hundred hours of basic military instruction were wasted. In general, Hagood's sketchy proposals consisted of abolishing training in the various arms, such as field artillery and infantry, and giving one basic ROTC course to be standard throughout all colleges. Graduates of the basic course would be commissioned as second lieutenants at the age of twenty-one, and students who desired could continue on to the advanced course and qualify for commissions as first lieutenant or captain. Each commission would be good for five years with no further obligation. Hagood advocated this length of service because existing appropriations did not permit reserve officers to be trained more than once in every five years. Hagood visualized an annual turnover of 40,000 reserve officers and a constant force of around 200,000. He warned MacArthur

MacArthur that the existing system was inadequate to supply officers for mobilization and that his proposal for a pool of 200,000 reservists would meet mobilization needs and still cost no more than the present ROTC setup.[10]

MacArthur forwarded Hagood's proposal to the G-3 for comment and recommendation. G-3 vigorously tore into the Hagood plan, and reflecting the adamant stand of the General Staff against any change in Army projects in time of economic stringency, pointed out that Hagood had proposed major changes in the National Defense Act and the annual appropriations bill "at a time when any attempt to change these instruments of policy is inappropriate."[11] G-3 further denied that the ROTC program was inefficient, noting that a recent survey of 110 colleges showed that 108 institutions reported favorably and recommended against any radical change in the program.

The main charge of G-3 against Hagood's plan was that proposed changes would be harmful because they would disturb "organized and functioning activities" and such disturbances would develop "bitter controversies" before Congress and offer the kind of "opportunity that is most desired by pacificist elements for exploitation."[12]

---

[10] Ltr, General Johnson Hagood for the Chief of Staff, March 1, 1931. AG 320.2, RG 94, NA. Hagood was Commanding General of the 7th Corps Area.

[11] Memo, AC/S G-3 for the Chief of Staff, March 31, 1931. AG 320.2, RG 94, NA.

[12] Ibid.

G-3 obviously was alarmed that a change in the ROTC program on War Department initiative as an economy measure would certainly bring congressional critics and economizers to seek an additional review of the Army program in order to obtain increased savings. A controversy over the ROTC program might lead to a review of the entire National Defense Act of 1920 in order to substantially reduce military spending. In a political tightrope act nothing pertaining to the essential activities must be disturbed.

During an early weekend in May 1931, President Hoover, chagrined and perturbed over the impending budget deficit for fiscal 1931, called together his military chiefs and congressional leaders at his Rapidan retreat in order to review the possibility of further substantial reductions in military spending. It appears that Hoover sought to obtain a reduction in personnel as well as the closing of about 30 Army camps and the concentration of the Regular Army at fewer posts. Secretary Hurley and the military chiefs strongly opposed the former proposal but were willing to consider the possibility of the latter.[13] The President also found that Senator Dan Reed, Chairman of the Senate Appropriations Committee, who attended the conference was lined up with the military leaders in opposing any reduction in personnel. Upon his return to the Capitol, Reed announced to the press that the "greatest cut" in military expenses could be made by closing superfluous camps, but that the present combat force of the

[13] Army Navy Journal, May 16, 1931, p. 873.

Army could not be reduced. Reed noted that expenditures for arms and equipment were next to nothing and that the training activities of the civilian components and the Regular Army were already cut to the bone to the detriment of the efficiency of the entire military establishment.[14]

In proposing a reduction of personnel in the military establishment, Hoover was touching a most sensitive spot in the Army program and one sure to bring about a sharp reaction. Hoover, pressing for reduction in military spending, was told by the Army that the bottom had been reached and further reduction would seriously cripple the Army in carrying out its mission. In order to have something in "readiness should the War Department be called upon to make recommendations" on military expenditures below the stabilized figure of a third of a billion dollars, General George Simonds, Assistant Chief of Staff, War Plans Division, prepared an ominous report for the Chief of Staff on the entire problem of further budget reductions. Simonds emphasized to his chief that his remarks were based on the extensive survey of the Army made in

---

[14] Ibid., May 16, 1931, p. 892. The Army Navy Journal's editorial tenor toward President Hoover began to shift from the critical position that it held during the fall and winter of 1930 to a more sympathetic attitude in the summer of 1931. The Journal commented that Hoover's acceptance of the Army's position on personnel reduction reflected his "intimate knowledge of the reductions" that had been made in the Army, and that he "understands and appreciates" the missions of the Army, especially the peacetime mission of training the civilian components, and that there would be no reduction in personnel. Ibid., May 23, 1931, p. 897.

the fall of 1929, which furnished all the information necessary, and he added, in a subtle thrust at Hoover, that the survey had not been made public perhaps because of the fact that the "consequences" of any reduction below present appropriations were vividly described.[15]

Simonds, in his lengthy memorandum for MacArthur, agreed that it was necessary because of the financial condition of the country to reduce military spending to the "lowest level" consistent with national defense, and that the budget should be stabilized through "measures of economy and predetermination of the military program." Simonds charged that this was being done and if any further reductions were planned it would mean major modifications on defense policies and the National Defense Act of 1920. However, in case "higher authority" considered that a reduction in military expenditures was mandatory, four steps for possible reductions were outlined. The first step proposed would save $11,000,000 and included the reduction of the ROTC and ORC program, elimination of warrant officers in the Regular Army, and the abolition of the CMTC program. The second step involved a further savings of some $27,000,000 by the additional curtailment of the ROTC and reserve activities as well as a cutback in research and development and the reduction in

[15] Memo, AC/S WPD for the Chief of Staff, July 25, 1931. WPD/3543, RG 319, NA.

Regular Army personnel.

According to General Simonds the result of these two steps would be to increase the length of time necessary for mobilization in time of emergency and would leave the United States without sufficient protection during a critical period. Simonds added that if the United States had powerful allies this would not be too serious a risk, as they would provide defense while the homeland mobilized. Simonds then proposed that if any significant reductions were desired beyond this point that it would necessitate radical changes in the military policy of the country and a return to the pre-1916 military posture. The result of such a development, the Chief of the WPD warned, would be a small professional force whose training mission with the civilian components would be practically eliminated and which would constitute a force in being for minor engagements. Simonds ventured to estimate that in case this situation came about the National Guard would be reduced to its pre-Dick Bill status, and the reserve corps would be of negligible value. Simonds concluded by stressing that the Army was practicing economy in every way possible consistent with its mission, and emphasized that if any "material reductions" were to be made a new military policy would have to be introduced and initiated by the "responsible authorities" who were responsible for the conduct of the government.[16]

---

[16] Memo, AC/S WPD for the Chief of Staff, July 25, 1931. WPD/3543, RG 319, NA. Note: The salient feature of the Dick Bill, passed in

General Simonds' memorandum for the Chief of Staff was a vigorous defense of the 1920 Defense Act and the role and the necessity of the Regular Army in complementing the civilian components. It was a strong brief for the maintenance of a "stabilized budget" at around a third of a billion dollars during the depression years, and its emphasis that further reduction of military expenditures would be a serious risk to national defense was of little comfort to the harassed President who was vainly trying to balance the budget.

The War Department announced that it was planning to abandon some fifty-three posts, ten of which were occupied with troops and the remainder on a "caretaking" status.[17] The issue would not be raised again until the summer of 1933 when President Roosevelt's Director of the Budget, Lewis Douglas, would come up with a vast program of concentrating the Army in a small number of posts.

Consonant with and related to the pressure to economize by concentrating activities, eliminating duplication, and curtailing

---

1903, was that for the first time the federal government was mentioned in reference to the organized militia. The bill provided that within five years the "organization, armament and discipline" of the organized militia was to be the same as regular army. Furthermore, the organized militia was to be paid during its activities and regular army officers were to be detailed to camps of instruction or for temporary duty with the militia. William A. Ganoe, The History of the United States Army (New York: D. Appleton and Company, 1924), pp. 417-18.

[17] Army Navy Journal, May 16, 1931, pp. 897-909.

any proposed expansion, the Chief of Staff in May 1931 made a decision which significantly influenced the early doctrine and organization of tanks and tank warfare in the United States Army. At that time, MacArthur ordered the disbanding of the embryo independent mechanized force and directed that it be organized and developed as part of the existing infantry and cavalry units.[18] The first test of an independent mechanized force for the United States Army was held at Fort Meade, Maryland, during the spring of 1928 using in the main materiel that was of World War I vintage, and as a consequence the results of the test were of little value. Nevertheless, on May 10, 1928, a board of officers recommended to the Secretary of War that a mechanized force, self-contained and capable of acting independently, be organized. Its role was conceived as being essentially offensive with the mission of acting as flank guard to a main body of troops, turning the enemy flanks, disrupting lines of communication, or exploiting a breakthrough of a defensive position. The board's recommendations, which were approved by the Secretary, proposed the organization of an "experimental Mechanized Force having its own means of administration, reconnaissance, operation, and supply."[19] Equipment for this force would be provided by three appropriation increments for fiscal 1931,

---

[18] Memo, Deputy Chief of Staff for the AC/S G-3, May 4, 1931. AG 537.3 IR (12-8-34) Section 1-B, RG 94, NA.

[19] Memo, AC/S G-3 for the AC/S WPD, May 28, 1929. Part VII, "Survey of the State of Preparedness." G-3/22614, RG 319, NA.

1932, and 1933, totalling respectively $1,200,000, $1,000,000, and $1,360,000.[20]

According to MacArthur, because of "budget intricacies" the original procurement program never reached Congress.[21] The procurement proposals came right at the time when "stabilization" was initiated and the organization of an independent armored force to experiment in tactics and in the development of suitable equipment was deterred.

In October, 1930, the Mechanized Force was finally assembled at Fort Eustis, Virginia. It was deemed advisable to assemble the unit with the equipment then available and to plan for the future development of equipment on the basis of experience gained from maneuvering a permanent mechanized force.[22] In May of the following year, General MacArthur reversed this policy and ordered the Mechanized Force to be split up and disbanded and organized under the control of the infantry and cavalry chiefs. The realization that adequate funds to equip and organize an independent armored force would never be forthcoming because of the extreme expense involved undoubtedly had an important influence in the Chief of Staff's decision. The Army Navy Journal pointed out that the

---

[20] Ibid.

[21] Hearings before Committee of Military Affairs, House of Representatives, 73rd Congress, 1st Session. April 26, 1933 (Washington: GPO, 1933), p. 32.

[22] Burton O. Lewis, "The Mechanized Force, U.S. Army," Army Ordnance, XI, No. 66 (May-June 1931), pp. 429-34.

decision was for the best because of the fact that it was basically not an independent unit, and because of the fact that its "extreme cost" would hold in abeyance any large scale procurement and adequate development until an actual emergency was upon the United States.[23]

MacArthur's concept was that those units of the former Mechanized Force which performed basic cavalry missions would be developed under the cavalry arm, and those parts of the mechanized unit which had infantry missions would come under control of the infantry arm. According to MacArthur's doctrine of 1931, the "tank" was a term to be used only when the track laying vehicle was used with infantry, and "combat car" when it was used with cavalry in such missions as reconnaissance and flank protection.[24] The Chief of Staff's decision had profound significance on the future development of tank organization and doctrine in the United States Army. After MacArthur's disbanding order of May 1931, the development of armored equipment and tactics would be decentralized under the various arms until July 1940, when the spectacular

---

[23] Army Navy Journal, May 23, 1931, p. 898. As would be expected, the advocates of mechanization claimed that it was less expensive than the maintenance of infantry units. According to one writer the total annual cost of a light tank battalion was only $.605 million compared to $3.2 million a year for an infantry regiment. According to this writer the initial cost of equipment could be carried into annual maintenance costs and spread over a period of years. John K. Christmas, "Is Mechanization Expensive," Army Ordnance, XI, No. 61 (July-August 1930), pp. 22-24.

[24] Memo, Deputy Chief of Staff for the AC/S G-3, May 4, 1931. AG 537.3 IR (12-18-34) Section 1-B, RG 94, NA.

German successes in France moved the General Staff to form an independent armored force.[25]

Although the Chief of Staff based his decision on doctrinal principles, he was well aware of the fact that adequate funds for the experimentation of armored equipment would be difficult to come by during a prolonged economy period. In this respect, budget appropriations influenced the development of doctrine and tactics. The cost of mechanization in 1931 was "terrific" and even to equip a light tank battalion, not including the cost of overhead that would be involved in a separate administration, it was estimated that it would cost over $2,000,000, an unrealistic figure in the early thirties. While Congress might feel "kindly toward the mechanization of the Army" it was realized that the extreme cost of any extensive mechanization would run up against the "wall of budgetary limitations."[26]

---

[25] This policy of decentralization held throughout the early thirties and MacArthur's term as Chief of Staff until July 1940. In 1935 the organization and operation of one battalion of the 68th Field Artillery as part of the Mechanized Cavalry Regiment at Fort Knox once again raised the question as to the responsibilities for the coordination of combined training. At that time G-3 re-emphasized the policy that each arm was authorized to continue its own development of mechanization which would continue decentralized. Memo, AC/S G-3 for the Chief of Staff, January 21, 1935. AG 537.3 IR (12-18-34) Section 1-B, RG 94, NA.

[26] Army Navy Journal, May 23, 1931, p. 898. Note: Major General J. F. C. Fuller, noted British military writer, stressed in 1931 the heavy burden involved in the cost and expense of developing armored warfare tactics, organization, and doctrine. According to Fuller, mechanization would prove extremely costly, possibly as costly as the mechanization of naval power had proved. While in 1931 it was possible to produce an efficient tank for around $20,000, when international

MacArthur's doctrine toward mechanization and the influence of budgetary pressure and economy on his ideas was vividly outlined two years later during an appearance before the House Committee on Military Affairs. Asked to discuss the use and organization of armored units, the Chief of Staff affirmed that he was going slowly toward mechanization, and was seeking to develop first a "completely suitable combat machine." According to MacArthur, to attempt to do more, given the present state of technology, would entail "useless expense without compensating advantage."[27] The Chief of Staff hoped that eventually a "degree of stabilization would apply to tank technology" and the "effective life" of each model would be enough to warrant increased investment in mechanization. Under present conditions, MacArthur pointed out, to maintain large independent units equipped with the latest models would entail replacement every few years, and "manifestly the expense of such a procedure would be enormous."[28] This had an effect on training and tactical doctrine,

---

competition in tanks began improvement would follow improvement, and the price of machines would consequently rise. According to Fuller, no nation was likely to be in a position to build and maintain more than a comparatively small mechanized army, for improvements and construction would be so rapid that each new batch of machines produced would be obsolete the moment they were "launched." Thus Fuller believed that the tendency toward increased mobility would find reaction in attempts to obviate the high cost of mobility by means of permanent field fortifications which would promise a cheaper defense over a longer period of time. J.F.C. Fuller, "The Mechanization of War," Army Ordnance, XI, No. 65 (March-April 1931), pp. 360-63.

[27] Hearings before Military Affairs Committee, 1st Session, 73d Cong. April 26, 1933, p. 28.

[28] Ibid., p. 29.

for, as MacArthur pointed out, the cost of mechanization was so great that for "some years to come" there would not be available in the initial stages of any emergency large units equipped with mechanized vehicles and the Army would be unable to participate in peacetime maneuvers and master the tactics and doctrine of large-scale armored warfare.

MacArthur reminded Congress that the Army would like to move ahead with modernization and mechanization as rapidly as possible but all modern developments were expensive. He cited the example of the machine gun, which, though it had the fire power of fifty riflemen, did not reduce military expenditures. As the Chief of Staff emphasized, the more complicated the weapon the more costly trained manpower was to operate it, as well as the organization of large and expensive supply, maintenance, and repair organizations, which were required for the support of modern armies.[29]

In order to alleviate some of the pressure from the White House, in regard to economy moves within the Army, the General Staff directed sweeping cutbacks in the personnel assigned to various Corps Area and Department headquarters during the spring of 1931. These Corps Area headquarters had sprouted a plethora of staff officers and had developed into nine miniature War Departments. To the General Staff in Washington this development was viewed with noticeable concern both as a movement toward

---

[29] *Ibid.*, pp. 30-32.

semi-autonomy on the part of the Corps Areas and as a further increase in the administrative overhead that militated against the Army's basic mission of providing a fighting force for the nation's defense.

In August 1931, the Assistant Chief of Staff G-1, alarmed over the growing increase of Corps Area Staff personnel, urged the Chief of Staff that the "time for study and correspondence had passed and positive action was needed." In addition, it was stressed that this was an important sector of the military establishment in which to make noticeable economies, for the trend over the past several years had been to increase the number of officers at Corps Area headquarters with a corresponding increase in expenditures for per diem and housing allowances.[30] G-1 noted that it would be impracticable for the War Department in Washington to regulate the exact organization of the Corps Area headquarters because of the geographical isolation and the methods and policies of each Corps Area commander "rendered long distance detached direction" difficult. However, by centralized control over expenditures for allowances from Washington it would be possible to force a curtailment in Corps Area staffs. The general goal was a fifteen percent reduction of personnel at Corps Area headquarters that would curtail the "progressive increase of staffs" and at the

---

[30] Memo, AC/S G-1 for the Chief of Staff, August 7, 1931. AG 320.2, RG 94, NA. Per diem allowances is money allowance given to personnel on detached duty away from their home station to defray the necessary added living expenses.

same time achieve the "immediate necessity" of controlling expenditures and forcing the Army to "live within the means available."[31]

Curtailment and reduction of the Corps Areas staffs and administrative overhead was not the sole administrative reduction that was proposed in the summer of 1931. As previously noted, many officers, in replying to Hoover's economic survey in the summer of 1929, had suggested that savings could be obtained through the consolidation or reduction of War Department bureaus and branches in Washington. General Hagood had proposed the elimination of the General Staff as the first move in such a plan. The issue of combining and consolidating the Coast Artillery Corps and the Field Artillery was brought up again and proposed as an economy move. To the proponents of such a move, the Coast Artillery and fixed defenses were obsolete and could easily be sacrificed for economy. The General Staff was skeptical over this proposal and was adamant that such a consolidation was unnecessary and "not desirable" under present conditions.[32]

During the spring of 1931, Congressman Ross Collins of Mississippi, a member of the House Sub-committee on War Department Appropriations, asked the Secretary of War to make a study looking toward recommendations on the issue of consolidation of the Coast

---

[31] Ibid.

[32] Memo, AC/S G-1 for the Chief of Staff, August 7, 1931. AG 320.2, RG 94, NA.

Artillery and the Field Artillery. Although Hurley was sympathetic toward consolidation, he deferred to the judgment of the General Staff that such a move would be disadvantageous to the Army and of doubtful economy. The main point that the General Staff presented in its defense against consolidation was that whereas the mission of the Coast Artillery was purely defensive, the Field Artillery was an offensive arm and therefore the thinking and general attitude of the two arms were so different that consolidation would have a deleterious effect on the efficient performance of the proposed combined arms.[33]

Congressman Collins, when he became Chairman of the House Sub-committee on Military Appropriations when the Democratic-controlled House of Representatives of the 72nd Congress convened in December 1931, brought up the issue of consolidation again. Not easily rebuffed by the report of the General Staff, he questioned the Chief of Coast Artillery, during the latter's appearance before the Military Appropriations Sub-committee, on the role of Coast Artillery in modern war with emphasis on its enormous cost and lack of mobility. Collins deprecated the War Department's view toward consolidation and charged that the General Staff wanted to "cling to an old toy" in its reluctance to move toward consolidation.[34]

The entire episode on the consolidation of Field Artillery and

---

[33] Army Navy Journal, March 28, 1931, p. 705.

[34] Hearings: War Department Appropriations Bill, 1933 (December 30, 1931), p. 531.

Coast Artillery reflected the unwillingness of the Army to effect radical changes in its organization and procedure under budgetary pressure. If one consolidation was effected for the sake of economy, what would prevent further and more dangerous consolidations and reorganizations from being brought to fruition under pressure from the White House and Capitol Hill? The War Department had held out against any reorganization by Hoover during the fall of 1929, and girded itself during the winter of 1931-32 for an expected onslaught by the economy-minded Democrats in the House of Representatives. Hostile critics of the Army, such as John Nance Garner and Ross Collins, were now in charge of the House and the Army could expect that its activities would be brought under close scrutiny and criticism.[35] It is difficult to distinguish a purely bureaucratic attitude in the Army's opposition toward consolidation of some of its branches and bureaus, and a genuine concern that such consolidation would be a detriment to national defense. Given the need of harbor defense and the General Staff's belief that coastal defense had an important role to play because of the ineffectiveness, as well as the high cost of aircraft and naval protection, Army planners felt that its position was justified and sound.

---

[35] Army Navy Journal, June 30, 1931, p. 1000. The Journal apprehensively noted that the Democrats would organize the new House and that National Defense would be in the hands of Ross Collins of Mississippi, who had "definite ideas" on Army consolidation as a means of reducing military appropriations. Furthermore, his "hostility to the ROTC and CMTC has been repeatedly expressed."

The issue of consolidation of the Field Artillery and the Coast Artillery was being fought out at the same time as the problem of the National Guard and the "stabilized" budget erupted. The National Guard under the terms of the National Defense Act of 1920 was authorized a strength of 250,000 officers and men.[36] However, due to financial limitations imposed on the Guard during the 1920's, the total strength approximated 190,000 officers and men at the end of fiscal 1931.[37] The Militia Bureau, the agency in the War Department which was responsible for National Guard affairs, began plans as early as January 1931 to increase the strength of the Guard by about 5,000 men. The Chief of the Militia Bureau, in his testimony before the House Committee on Appropriations in early 1931, indicated that an increase in appropriations would be needed to cover this planned increase at a future date. This brought the Secretary of War up sharp. Sensing that perhaps the Militia Bureau was going over his head and playing politics with the strong National Guard supporters in Congress, by seeking to obtain additional funds over and above the estimates that the War Department had assigned, he sternly called General William G.

---

[36] The actual wording of the section of the National Defense Act of 1920 dealing with the strength of the Guard specified that the number of men of the National Guard for each state should be in the proportion of two hundred men for each Senator and Representative in Congress and to be increased each year thereafter in proportion of not less than fifty percent a year until a total peace strength of not less than eight hundred enlisted men for each Congressman and Senator was reached. National Defense Act 1920, p. 55.

[37] Annual Report of the Secretary of War, 1931, p. 84.

Iverson, the Chief of the Militia Bureau, to account for his remarks before the congressional committee. Hurley directed that General Iverson be informed that an increase in National Guard appropriations for fiscal 1933 was not consistent with the administration's policy of stabilization and that any augmentation of National Guard activities would have to be financed by reductions of other items in the Militia Bureau's estimate so that total appropriations would not be increased over the figures for fiscal 1931.[38]

General Iverson defended his remarks by informing Hurley that an increase in the strength of the National Guard had been approved by the War Department, and that he felt this increase could not be accomplished without corresponding increases in appropriations. Iverson denied that he was aware of a "definite" policy that fiscal 1933 estimates could not be increased over 1931 figures; furthermore, he felt that it was necessary to "lay the cards on the table with Congress" and tell them that an increase in strength would of necessity entail additional expenditures for fiscal 1933 and for the future years. According to Iverson, "I felt that it was due the Committee that they should know that."[39] In reviewing the National Guard program for Hurley, Iverson pointed out that

---

[38] Memo, AC/S G-4 for the AG, January 10, 1931. AG 111, RG 94, NA.

[39] Ltr, Chief of the Militia Bureau for the AG, January 17, 1931. AG 111, RG 94, NA.

there had been a "most insistent" demand for an increase in the Guard's strength to 210,500, to be accomplished over a period of years. This pressure, he noted, came from the National Adjutant General Association, the National Guard Association, and the American Legion, all of whom were "chafing under the slowness" of the National Guard's progress.[40] Iverson concluded his remarks to Hurley by stressing the fact that he would cooperate with the Secretary's fiscal policies and only such number of the 5,000 man increase would be allowed as could be provided for under the financial limitations imposed upon the Militia Bureau.[41]

This mild misunderstanding apparently grew out of the fact that the War Department planners, including the General Staff and the Secretary of War, had authorized an expansion of the National Guard and at the same time tried to hold the line in budget estimates. Thus it was hoped to satisfy the National Guard and at the same time meet the political exigencies of the Hoover Administration. The War Department thought apparently that the two goals were not contradictory and that a modest increase in personnel could be absorbed through administrative savings imposed by the Militia Bureau on itself. Iverson, eager for an increase in strength, was extremely reluctant to achieve this goal at the expense of other activities of the National Guard and perhaps thought that the National Guard lobby in Congress would rescue him from his dilemma.

---

[40] Ibid.

[41] Ibid.

During the summer of 1931, with the attendance of the National Guard at its annual summer encampment, the issue of funds for the Guard and an increase in appropriations came again to the fore. Appropriations for the National Guard for fiscal 1932, beginning July 1, 1931, were based on the estimated attendance at the summer camp during 1931 of 86 percent of the authorized strength of 190,580 officers and men at a per capita cost of $55.50. Instead of this estimated figure whole regiments of the Guard were turning out at 100 percent of the authorized strength for the summer encampment.

This "greatly increased attendance" of the National Guard at summer camp meant that funds would not be sufficient to last out the entire year if other activities of the National Guard were to be met. It was clear that funds would be depleted well before the end of the fiscal year. According to the Militia Bureau, the increased attendance was due chiefly to the "unemployment crisis" throughout the country and also because of the fact that the men were interested in the Guard and willing to devote their time to it.[42]

Iverson realized that the Secretary of War was most adamant about "stabilizing" military spending and for political reasons would be extremely hesitant about asking Congress for a deficiency appropriation to cover the expected Guard deficit. Hurley urged that all agencies of the War Department do their utmost to hold down

---

[42] Ltr, Chief of the Militia Bureau for the AG, September 29, 1931. AG 111, RG 94, NA.

military spending and added that it would cause "political embarrassment" for the administration if it were to ask the Democratic-controlled House of Representatives of the 72nd Congress for a deficiency appropriation.[43]

However, General Iverson could see no other solution to the problem -- to curtail armory drills and other training activities scheduled for the remainder of the fiscal year would present a problem "fraught with difficulties." Such a solution, he claimed, would be a severe blow to the morale of the National Guard; in addition, curtailing armory drills would mean operating expensive armories at less than capacity, thus creating an economic loss. But Iverson's most telling rebuttal to Hurley was his implication that the abandonment of armory drills and summer camps would have serious political reaction. Iverson pointed out that a curtailment of National Guard activities before the end of the current fiscal year (FY 1932) would bring a "storm of protest" on the War Department that could not be resisted, and that the National Guard was spread over a wide geographical area and the units were located in states from which a large amount of "political pressure" could be brought to bear. In the face of the current economic situation, and the fact that in certain instances the armory drill pay constituted the bulk of the real earnings of a National Guard enlistee, General Iverson

---

[43] Ltr, Secretary of War for the Chief of the Militia Bureau, August 11, 1931. AG 111, RG 94, NA.

advised that it would not be "good policy" to curtail armory drills. In conclusion, Iverson urged the submission of a deficiency bill, and if the Secretary of War was unwilling to do this then it would be necessary for the latter to order drill curtailment and limit the attendance at drills of field officers and company grade officers.[44]

In advising the Chief of Staff concerning the problem of expected deficiency in National Guard appropriations, support for the Militia Bureau's position came from the Legislative and Budget Planning Branch of the General Staff. According to the chief of this branch, Lt. Col. Irving Phillipson, any of the expedients, such as curtailing camps and drill attendance, would be of "doubtful legality," as well as being highly detrimental to the morale of the Guard. Reduction of training, the Chief of Staff was advised, would militate against the value of the National Guard as a component of the Army and would subject the War Department and the General Staff to "severe criticism" in Congress.[45]

Although the Hoover Administration's political face would be slightly tarnished by asking for a deficiency appropriation during a presidential election year, the General Staff felt that there was no other way out. If it recommended a curtailment of National

---

[44] Ltr, Chief of the Militia Bureau for the AG, September 29, 1931. AG 111, RG 94, NA.

[45] Memo, Chief L&PB Branch for the Chief of Staff, October 8, 1931. AG 111, RG 94, NA.

Guard activities it would come under attack by National Guard supporters in Congress and in the several states for its willingness to see the National Guard sacrificed, and the General Staff's sincerity toward a viable and efficient National Guard would be questioned. This in turn would serve to inflame suspicions and jealousy between the National Guard and the War Department General Staff.

The administration remained adament against the submission of any deficiency appropriation bill to Congress. The Director of the Bureau of the Budget notified the War Department in early November 1931 that it was "mandatory" that the Militia Bureau finance its activities within its limiting figure, and the Secretary of War directed that the National Guard armory drills be reduced from 48 to 43, a decrease of five between November 1931 and June 1932. Informing the Corps Area Commanders of this action, the Chief of the Militia Bureau expressed his regret and emphasized that regardless of the vigorous opposition of the War Department and the General Staff, the order came from the President through the Director of the Budget, and that there was to be no expenditure of additional funds for the National Guard for fiscal 1932.[46]

Less than ten days later, President Hoover inexplicably changed his mind and authorized the submission of a deficiency bill provided that it could be financed from Regular Army savings. This

---

[46] Ltr, Chief of the Militia Bureau for all Corps Area Commanders, November 12, 1931. AG 111, RG 94, NA.

would mean the use of money appropriated for Regular Army activities, which through administrative savings or deferments had not been used, but would require congressional authorization before it could be transferred to the National Guard. The General Staff readily agreed with the President's compromise. "This will be done," MacArthur wrote gleefully to the Chief of the Militia Bureau in advising him of the full resumption of National Guard armory drills and other activities.[47]

The exigencies of budget pressure brought the National Guard and the General Staff into close harmony, and at no time was there a willingness on the part of the Staff to cut the activities of the National Guard for the sake of economy. The National Guard was given high priority in the national defense structure by the General Staff because of the role it played in mobilization and the acceptance by the latter of the National Guard as an integral part of the skeletonized "mass" citizen army. Any curtailment of training on the part of the National Guard, in order to reduce military expenditures, was vigorously opposed by the General Staff, who were willing to see Regular Army funds transferred for use by the National Guard, rather than accept a reduction in the latter's activities and program.

---

[47] Ltr, Chief of Staff for the Chief of the Militia Bureau, November 20, 1931. AG 111, RG 94, NA.

CHAPTER V

THE CRITICAL YEAR - 1932: THE ARMY UNDER ATTACK

Reviewing military developments at the end of 1931, the Army Navy Journal reflected that although the past twelve months had been a depression year with stringent economy measures, "only in its dying days and in the outlook for 1932" was the picture alarmingly dark for the military establishment. According to the Journal, the Army under its new Chief of Staff had taken several steps which to all appearances were forward, and in particular, it voiced optimism over the adoption of a "definite policy" toward mechanization and motorization. The Journal added ominously that the outlook for 1932 carried with it threats against the efficiency of the Army, and with members of Congress calling for further budget reductions over the drastic ones already made by the President and the Budget Bureau, the military could "hardly expect much improvement" in the coming year.[1]

In the opinion of the Chief of Staff, the most notable feature of fiscal year 1932 (July 1931 - June 1932) having an impact on the Army, over and above the Manchurian incident and the Geneva disarmament conference, was the "increased severity of the prolonged economic depression." The necessity of retrenchment in spending continued to be an onerous burden for the Army, and this fact had become the dominant factor in shaping national military policy. MacArthur pessimistically

---

[1] Army Navy Journal, January 2, 1932, p. 422.

added that the War Department had "rigidly" excluded from the 1933 budget estimates every item that was not essential for the "bare maintenance of existing strength" and the figures before Congress were "only the amounts on which the military establishment can be temporarily maintained, rather than meeting the continuing annual requirements of national defense."[2]

The comments of the Chief of Staff and the Army Navy Journal reflected rather succinctly the general tenor of the times, and the latter in particular realized the impatience and restlessness of Congress toward the Hoover Administration. The 1933 military appropriations bill came before the new 72nd Congress in December 1931, and Democratic critics of the President in the House of Representatives were determined to perform major surgery on the estimates in order to reduce government expenditures. Hearings before the House Subcommittee on Military Appropriations began in late 1931 with General MacArthur leading the way. MacArthur's testimony generally affirmed the intention of the General Staff to reduce costs and noted that savings had been made possible by limiting all maintenance and repair projects and by postponing essential augmentation and improvement of equipment. The Chief of Staff added that the increase in pay and allowances appearing in the 1933 estimates were specified by law, and that length of service was the controlling factor in fixing this part of the military estimate. MacArthur concluded his testimony by noting that the estimates for 1933 also indicated another increase over the 1932 figure in the initiation of a replacement program for worn-out and obsolete motor equipment and

---

[2] Report of the Secretary of War, 1932, p. 54.

an increase in funds for mechanization. Training activities for the Regular Army, he noted, remained essentially at the same level, as did the civilian components.[3] MacArthur's remarks were quite general and mild in support of the figures that had been forwarded by President Hoover to Congress.

The one issue which aggravated the House Subcommittee in reviewing the budget estimates for fiscal 1933 was the predominance of the fact that the estimates were in essence a pay bill. This led to the conclusion that if reductions were to be made, they would have to come through cutting down on personnel, both officer and enlisted, and perhaps restricting pay and allowances awarded to the expensive reserve and other civilian components. Secretary Hurley affirmed that, of the $329,000,000 asked for by the War Department for fiscal 1933, $134,600,000 were for pay and allowances. Hurley noted that because of the critical unemployment situation throughout the country, the attrition rates for all personnel in the military establishment had decreased, and, thereby, had increased expenditures for pay and allowances in all components through additional longevity rates. Hurley claimed that lower commodity prices, coupled with the exercise of rigid economy, had reduced expenditures, but widespread unemployment in industry had increased the re-enlistment rate to unprecedented proportions, and correspondingly had reduced separations from the service. The unemployment situation in the country had caused an increase in the total pay of the Army, much to the consternation and chagrin of congressional economizers. Hurley also pointed out

---

[3] Hearings: War Department Appropriations Bill, 1933 (December 21, 1931), p. 3.

that the War Department was curtailing enlisted activities as far as possible and re-enlistment in the Army was being restricted to "desirable soldiers" within ninety days of their discharge.[4]

The Secretary of War warned Congress against tampering with personnel in efforts to reduce the military estimates, noting that this would impair the combat forces at home and overseas "at a time of unrest both here and abroad." Concluding his entreaty to Congress, Hurley emphasized that the enlisted strength of the Army was well below the authorized figure, and that it was decreasing each month in an orderly fashion as rapidly as conditions would permit. Non-commissioned officers, the Secretary reminded Congress, had a legal right to re-enlist and were availing themselves of this right so that reductions were being made in non-rated enlisted grades, thus, decreasing the total manpower of the Army.[5]

Hurley's remarks fell on unsympathetic ears in Congress. Chairman Joseph W. Byrns of the House Appropriations Committee admonished the Secretary of War that the best way to save money was to stop all new enlistments and reduce the Army to 110,000 from the existing strength figure of 118,750. Byrns added that "prompt and vigorous" measures should immediately be adopted to reduce the enlisted strength of the Army, and added in a scathing rebuke to Hurley that the latter need not

---

[4]Ltr, Hurley to Hon. Joseph W. Byrns, Chairman of House Committee on Appropriations, December 28, 1931. AG 111, RG 94, NA.

[5]Ibid.

be burdened with making a reply to the Congressman's remarks.[6]

Testifying before the Subcommittee on Military Appropriations, Hurley again struck out at proposed reductions in personnel. The Secretary vehemently claimed that the Army proposed to "make every possible savings without permanently crippling the Military Establishment as would a decrease in the number of men and officers in the Army."[7] Such a decrease, in the opinion of the Secretary of War, would strike at the very foundation of the citizen army and tend to "destroy the integrity of National Defense."[8] A stronger position by the civilian chief of the War Department in support of the doctrine of the General Staff could not have been desired.

The General Staff doctrine of stressing men, rather than material, was the basis of the dispute between House leaders and the Army during the first part of 1932, and underlay the action of the House in passing an appropriations bill which called for a reduction of officer personnel. Congressman Collins received support for his contention -- in a future war the decisive element would be weapons and machines, and less emphasis should be placed on personnel -- from the Chief of the Air Corps,

---

[6]Ltr, Hon J. W. Byrns for Secretary of War, January 13, 1932. AG 111, RG 94, NA. At the conclusion of his testimony before the House Subcommittee on War Department Appropriations, Hurley was caustically rebuked by Ross Collins. Collins, a long time critic of the Army, and now chairman of this subcommittee, said he was very disappointed in Hurley's testimony, because of the wonderful statement made three years ago by Hurley that he would show the committee a "real saving." Collins added that although he had a high regard for the Secretary, he knew that he must be very busy with rivers and harbors and flood control, and the Filipinos, and so on and that he did not have much time to spend on "strictly military duties." <u>Hearings</u>: War Department Appropriations Bill, 1933 (January 15, 1932), p. 1102.

[7]<u>Hearings</u>: War Department Appropriations Bill, 1933, p. 1102.

[8]<u>Ibid</u>., p. 1103.

Maj. Gen. Benjamin F. Foulois. The latter, in his testimony before the Subcommittee, presented a strong case for the air advocates' claim for strategic bombing and the need for an independent air force. Foulois claimed that the mobilization plans as of 1932 based on personnel were detrimental to the development of the Air Corps, and that this should be changed and plans based "entirely on the materiel needs" in time of war should be prepared. General Foulois charged that materiel should dominate over personnel, and "it would be a splendid thing if additional expense would be put in materiel, meaning heavy bombers, rather than into personnel."[9]

Foulois was making a bid for the long-range strategic bomber, which in Air Corps doctrine would be the ultimate weapon in a future war. He interjected the issue of a separate air force by the comment that as far as the Air Corps was concerned the problem was not so much getting adequate money, but allocation of funds and a viable air policy.[10] This was a wedge to present the Air Corps brief for the strategic bomber and the need for a separate air force where the doctrine of strategic bombing would be given adequate support through budget allocation. Foulois reflected the wide gulf in military thinking between the General Staff and other traditionalists on the one side, and the Air Corps on the other, by concurring in Collins' thesis that the civilian components as well as Regular Army officer strength could be cut without damaging the efficiency of national defense. When asked about a proposed reduction of officer personnel from 12,000 to 10,000, General Foulois

---

[9] _Ibid._, pp. 1040, 1051

[10] _Ibid._, p. 1041-42.

replied that many Regular Army activities now considered essential, such as training with civilian components, must ultimately be curtailed bec because of their high cost.[11]

Foulois' heretical pronouncements, while giving Collins ammunition for his attack against the General Staff and the doctrine of the War Department, brought the other chiefs of the War Department more strongly to the defense of the orthodox view that the civilian components were essential and that, to all extremes, personnel should not be sacrificed for economy's sake. The passionate defense by the Army of its personnel-first policy engendered among congressional circles the suspicion that the Army was a selfish pleader, and was using national defense as a shield to continue its various activities and maintain its officer strength at an unduly high level. Congress was not very enthusiastic toward the "insurance" theory of national defense -- that it was necessary to maintain a certain trained and ready strength as insurance against any possible aggressor -- and was willing and eager to see military appropriations curtailed in order to reduce governmental expense.

More important, the Democrats in control of the House of Representatives were cognizant of the fact that 1932 was an election year, and that the issue of reduced military expenditures presented them with political ammunition to use against the harassed Hoover Administration. Representative Collins vigorously affirmed the fact that there would be an expected deficit in the budget of two billion dollars for fiscal 1933, and that to preserve "national integrity" and keep the budget balanced it was necessary to reduce spending, and there was no other

---

[11] Ibid., p. 1051.

place to make considerable reductions except in the Army and Navy appropriations bill.[12]

Faced by this pressure, Army leaders remained determined and prepared their own campaign of rebuttal to meet congressional threats. They emphasized to the subcommittee that everything except personnel, training, and the civilian components could be sacrificed. Maj. Gen. Charles L. Bridges, The Adjutant General, in his testimony before the Collins Subcommittee defended the military estimates:

> I know we are hard pressed for money, or the government seems to be, but they are still appropriating millions of dollars for other things, and I think national defense is important -- more important than a great many other items Congress is appropriating for and we should carry on.[13]

Bridges emphasized that the discontinuing of reserve officer training during the summer would be a psychological blow to the entire reserve program:

> If you discontinue it this year you can discontinue it next year and then you could discontinue it forever... If you stop training the whole movement might break up entirely and then we would lose all we have done in the last 11 years.[14]

This was a concise and adequate summary of the Army's position concerning reducing the activities of the civilian components as an economy measure. These activities must be maintained intact because once the activities pertaining to the civilian components were temporarily discontinued, it would be difficult to reactivate them again as essential to national defense.

---

[12] _Ibid._, p. 793.

[13] _Ibid._, p. 793.

[14] _Ibid._,

The Army felt that the suspension of these activities would signal the end of the reserve program which had been built up tenaciously by the Army over the last decade, as well as youth training in the CMTC, and eventually destroy the system of national defense established by the National Defense Act.[15]

The National Guard came in for its share of criticism from Representative Collins, but a vigorous and able defense of the Guard and its activities was presented by Maj. Gen. George E. Leach, the Chief of the Militia Bureau. Leach emphasized the fact that because the Guard was a part of the first line of defense, mobilization plans contemplated its immediate employment in an emergency, a reduction of any of its units as an economy measure would be inappropriate. Leach noted that because the administration's budget for fiscal 1933 allowed less than for fiscal 1932, his only alternative was to reduce the strength of active National Guard units by 20% of private enlistees. "In any readjustment effected," Leach advised the subcommittee, "I would insist that the officer and noncommissioned officer personnel of the National Guard remain intact."[16] Although Representative Collins was not enamored with the National Guard, it need fear little in the annual battle of the budget because of its powerful political support in Congress.

Support for the National Guard in its travail in the subcommittee hearings came from a not unexpected source when in late January 1932, the Governor of New York, Franklin D. Roosevelt, sent a strong letter of protest to Congress against any contemplated cuts in National Guard

---

[15] Army Navy Journal, January 23, 1932, p. 488.

[16] Hearings: War Department Appropriations Bill, 1933, p. 708.

funds. The Governor reminded Congress that if it wanted to reduce military spending it should look at the supply and construction items of the bill rather than in the essential training sections.[17] The year 1932 was an election year and the principal actors were preparing for the summer conventions and the fall campaign.

Alarm over the intention of the appropriations subcommittee to reduce expenditures by curtailing the activities of the civilian components brought Secretary Hurley into action. The Secretary of War called on Speaker Garner twice in late January at the time when the subcommittee was preparing to send its bill to the House and urged Garner to prevent any reductions in the essential features pertaining to the civilian components or in Regular Army personnel. It was believed at the time that veiled threats from the Military Affairs Committee to investigate any personnel cuts, along with pressure from patriotic societies, brought a halt to the proponents of personnel reductions and cuts in the civilian components.[18] Representative Collins was incensed over Hurley's action in pressing Garner to withhold budget cuts and charged that "if we are going to delegate our authority to a cabinet member we might as well go home."[19] Furthermore, to congressional critics of the Army, Hoover's pontificating about economy in government did not square with Hurley's attempt to maintain the military budget at the administration's estimate and rankled the Democrats on the Military Appropriations Subcommittee.

Reacting to pressure by the Army and the administration to maintain

---

[17] Army Navy Journal, January 30, 1932, p. 524.

[18] Ibid., February 6, 1932, p. 529.

[19] Ibid., February 6, 1932, p. 551.

the budget and provide for the proposed personnel activities of the Army, the Democratic leaders of the House adopted a political maneuver which they apparently hoped would cause the maximum embarrassment to the Hoover Administration. They simply postponed reporting their bill out of the committee. This may have been done with the idea of pushing the bill through Congress late in the session on the eve of adjournment, with the possible political advantage of having reduced government spending and economizing in the face of the "big-spending" Hoover Administration. House Democrats were eager to cut the "Hoover-economized" budget, and in particular still contemplated a reduction in personnel and in the activities of the civilian components as the best way of cutting expenses. Representative Byrns, Chairman of the House Appropriations Committee, affirmed the fact that while he favored a "big Navy," he believed it was a small matter for the Army to call to arms and train manpower, and that national defense would not suffer if the officer corps was cut to 10,000.[20] Thus, the Army, standing in the path of congressional leaders eager to make political capital by reducing Hoover's military estimates, was threatened by personnel cuts which the General Staff viewed as detrimental to national defense and the role of the Regular Army as the nucleus of a mobilized citizen army.

Throughout February, March, and April of 1932, the failure of the appropriations subcommittee of the House to report its bill out of committee wrought consternation and alarm to military leaders, and gave them grave fears that Representative Collins would bring a bill out of committee at the end of the current session and push it through a Congress

---

[20] _Ibid._, January 23, 1932, pp. 481-83.

eager to adjourn and get on with the conventions and political campaign of 1932. The Army Navy Journal, as expected, rallied to the defense of the Army and the budget that the administration had sent to Congress. Vitriolically, it charged that the Democrats in Congress were playing politics with national defense, and accused Speaker Garner of holding back the military appropriations bill in order to push it through Congress at the last minute without adequate discussion and consideration. Such selfish tactics, the Journal charged, were designed to cripple national defense.[21]

The Army was cognizant of the fact that the government was spending more than it was taking in, and that the result would be further retrenchment in federal fiscal policies and that the Army would be among the first to be sacrificed. There was a touch of bitterness over this fact in the Army, and it was felt that while the federal government continued to become increasingly paternalistic, the basic purposes of the Constitution and the essential needs of defense were gradually being considered as a needless expense. A sense of helplessness and resignation prevailed in some military circles, and it was felt that the remedy for the continuing budget deficiencies probably would be a further skeletonization of the Army in order to meet the demands of the "newcomers to the federal payroll and the scope of the federal government."[22]

During the late winter and early spring of 1932, while the appropriations bill remained in committee, military leaders were deeply

---

[21] Army Navy Journal, February 27, 1932, p. 608; March 12, 1932, p. 656.

[22] Army Ordnance, (XII, March-April 1932), p. 351.

concerned that Representative Collins would succeed in "kicking the props out" from under the National Defense Act. The Army Navy Journal pessimistically noted that among military leaders in Washington there was an "air of apprehension" and worriedly told its readers that all "indications point" to a probable reduction in officer personnel and the curtailment or abandonment of the CMTC, and summer camps for reserve officers. According to the Journal, the National Guard, because of its powerful friends in Congress, was faring well and would not only get restored to it the training funds cut by the Budget Bureau, but also enough money to insure that there would be no reduction in the total number of armory drills.[23] In strident and bitter tones, unusual for the unofficial voice of the Army keeping in mind the separation of military men from the political arena in American tradition, the Army Navy Journal caustically warned that Representative Collins and his coterie on the appropriations subcommittee were a "little group of willful men" out to scuttle national defense, who if they had their way would determine by appropriations

> what shall be the military policy of the United States, and then past and future legislation would be valueless. These men, forming the majority of the subcommittee will become the real military dictators of the Republic.[24]

The War Department appropriations bill was reported out of committee during the first week of May 1932, and not surprisingly it indicated the intent of Representative Collins to reduce the military expenditures on personnel. Introduced in the House on May 5, total

---

[23] Army Navy Journal, January 30, 1932, pp. 505-07.

[24] Ibid., January 30, 1932, p. 505.

military appropriations came to $281,000,000, a figure $24,000,000 less than Hoover had requested. The Army Navy Journal quickly took up the cudgels for the military establishment, calling the bill an "assault" upon national defense, and urged Congress to repudiate the appropriations committee bill.[25] The chief irritant of the bill which rankled and embittered the Army was the provision calling for a reduction of the officer corps of the Regular Army from 12,000 to 10,000. The House approved the bill and sent it to the Senate; although amendments were offered and passed by the House providing for pay of the organized reserves, ROTC summer camp, and funds for the CMTC, the House failed to eliminate the onerous proposal for the reduction of officer personnel.[26] The passage of the House bill and the reduction of officer personnel brought the Army into the political arena and heavy pressure was now brought to bear to prevent Senate passage of this legislation which was considered a mortal blow by the Army and its supporters.

Collins had first intimated his intention to reduce officer personnel in a "confidential" letter to Hurley on December 28, 1931. The Mississippi Congressman informed the Secretary of War at that time that he was undecided concerning a possible reduction in personnel but in any event needed information, should it be decided to reduce officer personnel, as to the result in appropriations and projects. He further advised Hurley to treat the matter as confidential, should "uneasiness unnecessarily"

---

[25] Ibid., May 7, 1932, p. 841.

[26] Congressional Record, 72nd Cong., 1st Sess., Vol. 75, Part 10, May 19, 1932, pp. 10718-10719.

be experienced among officers potentially concerned.[27] This explains why MacArthur did not comment on reduction during his testimony. Hurley replied at length on January 14, 1932, noting the "seriousness of even the suggestion" to reduce officer personnel of the Army. The Secretary of War reviewed and emphasized the National Defense Act of 1920 and the role of the Regular Army officer as the nucleus of the mass trained citizenry, and warned that a reduction in the officer corps would strike at the most important pillar of national defense. Hurley added that a reduction of 2,000 officers would result in a $5,500,000 savings, but an increase in retired pay would leave a net savings of little more than $2,000,000. Concluding his personal letter to Representative Collins, Hurley defended the Regular Army officer from the charge of militarism by emphasizing that the American officer was called to perform a wide variety of duties and was in intimate touch with the problems of civil life.[28]

When the appropriations bill incorporating the reduction of officer personnel was reported out of committee to the whole House for debate, the Chief of Staff, never one to turn from a political fight when military affairs and policy were involved, wrote to Congressman Bertrand D. Snell and reviewed the entire question of officer reduction and urged the Missouri Republican to defeat the insidious proposals of Representative Collins. MacArthur noted that he had been tricked by Collins because during the hearings in January the latter had given no indications that

---

[27]Ltr, Representative Ross Collins, Chm War Dept Subcom on Appropriations, for Hurley, December 28, 1931. AG 111, RG 94, NA.

[28]Ltr. Hurley to Collins, January 14, 1932. AG 111, RG 94, NA.

he was contemplating a reduction of officer personnel, and that as Chief of Staff he had had no opportunity to express an opinion on such a revolutionary step. Speaking as military advisor to the government, including Congress, MacArthur noted that he was taking the liberty of presenting to Representative Snell the views of the General Staff on the pending legislation.

MacArthur patiently pointed out that skilled officers were the product of continuous and laborious study and constituted the most vital element in modern warfare; the Army could be poorly housed and equipped but it must have adequate leadership. MacArthur pleaded that the Regular Army was the bulwark and basis of the entire defense structure and served as the instructor, model, and leader of the whole establishment, including, of course, the civilian components, and that the latter would be ineffective without the guidance of the Regular Army officer corps.

MacArthur defended the military budget for fiscal 1933 and affirmed the fact that everything in excess of the bare necessities had been sacrificed for the need of economy and that the sum presented to Congress by the Hoover Administration represented the minimum that the Army must have in order to exist for a single year rather than the true requirements of national defense. The Chief of Staff urged that no reductions be made as this would have the effect of bringing the country close to a condition "not conducive to security at home nor respect abroad."[29]

The War Department continued its vigorous opposition to the appropriations bill in the Senate and sought to stiffen its supporters in the

---

[29]Ltr, General Douglas MacArthur to Hon. Bertrand D. Snell, May 9, 1932. AG 111, RG 94, NA.

upper house in opposition to the machinations of Representative Collins and his cohorts. Hurley wrote Senator Wesley L. Jones, Chairman of the Senate Committee on Appropriations, and warned of the serious consequences that would ensue if a reduction in officer personnel was permitted to become law. Hurley emphasized that Collins and the House was "bamboozling" the Senate and that the House bill was a fraud because of the fact that the retirement of 2,000 officers would not reduce savings as much as Collins claimed.[30]

Although the Army was confident that Senate support in upsetting the House legislation would be forthcoming, particularly in view of the Republican majority, the Army nevertheless took no chances and re-emphasized its familiar arguments against any reduction in officer personnel. Hoover's public statement in early April that no further reductions in military appropriations should be made, although addressed to the House of Representatives, served to strengthen Republican members of the Senate to support the Army in voting against the Democratic acceptance of the proposal to reduce officer personnel.[31] Hoover reportedly was prepared to veto any bill Congress would pass that would reduce the strength of the officer corps of or the Army.[32]

The Army based its opposition to any reduction in officer personnel on the claim that officers were not superfluous and were needed for the training of civilian components and that officers on duty with troops,

---

[30]Ltr, Secretary of War to Senator Wesley L. Jones, June 3, 1932. AG 111, RG 94, NA.

[31]Army Navy Journal, April 2, 1932, p. 721.

[32]Ibid., p. 728.

or the ratio of officers to enlisted men, was no criterion with which to judge the needed strength of the officer's corps. The Army emphasized the fact that the officer corps could not be cut beyond the existing 12,000 figure and still maintain efficient training of the civilian components and carry out the mission of being the nucleus of a mass citizen army in the event of mobilization. Assistant Secretary of War Frederick H. Payne, in writing to his fellow citizen of the Bay State, Senator David J. Walsh, stressed the fact that there were 12,133 officers on the active duty list, and 5,031 of these were with tactical units while another 1,200 were carrying out duties directly connected with the sanitation, administration, and supply of other units. Payne added that a total of 1,653 officers were serving with the civilian components and a total of 2,400 were on school duty including the faculties and student bodies of all military educational institutions. Payne defended the military school system, as initiated by Elihu Root, and emphasized that it had proved its value during World War I, that through the school system the Army was kept abreast of the latest in military thought, and that it was the best method of providing for the development of skillful and capable leaders.[33]

On June 9, 1932, the Senate defeated the House bill calling for a reduction in the officers corps by 2,000, and on July 12, when representative Collins sought to override the Senate vote and have the House

---

[33]Ltr, Assistant Secretary of War Frederick H. Payne to Hon. David J. Walsh, May 27, 1932. AG 111, RG 94, NA. (Note: Payne's letter was drafted by the Secretary to the General Staff, Major Dwight D. Eisenhower.)

vote against accepting the Senate amendment, he was defeated.[34]

The vehement opposition by the Army and its vocal supporters, coupled with the fact that the Senate had voted against a reduction of officer personnel, and the threat of a veto by Hoover which would cause the Army to be without current operating funds well into fiscal 1933, all tended to give an impetus to a reversal by the House of its previous vote. The Army rightly considered it had won an important political victory and that the doctrines it viewed as essential to national defense had been preserved. The Chief of Staff, jubilant over the victory, wired joyously to Assistant Secretary Payne, vacationing at his Massachusetts home before attending the Republican convention: "Just hogtied a Mississippi cracker. House voted our way one seventy-five to fifty-four. Happy times are here again. /s/ MacArthur."[35]

The entire episode of the original action by the House to reduce officer personnel and its subsequent <u>volte-face</u>, along with Senate opposition to such a reduction, brought the Army and its concept of national defense into the political arena. On the grounds of economy and the necessity of further reducing military spending in time of financial stringency, the House had originally voted to reduce the officer corps. The Army led by its politically astute Chief of Staff was ready for the challenge and accepted the political battle, basing its position on the claim that officer reduction was false economy as well as being a most serious threat to the national security. The basic premise

---

[34]<u>Congressional Record</u>, 72nd Cong., 1st Sess., Vol. 75, Part 11, June 9, 1932, p. 12429; Vol. 75, Part 14, July 12, 1932, p. 15145.

[35]Tel, MacArthur to Payne, July 12, 1932. AG 111, RG 94, NA.

to the Army's argument was that maintenance of the Regular Army officer corps was essential to the American defense strategy of a mass "citizen" army. While certain financial cutbacks were necessary and acceptable, the Army would not countenance a cut in the officer personnel and would fight to preserve what it considered was an adequate officer personnel strength.

Significantly, the incident served to link the Army up with the already politically disgraced Hoover Administration. President Hoover was against further action by the House in cutting military spending and the proposed officer reduction. Secretary Hurley and Assistant Secretary Payne stressed the position of the Army when they held that a reduction of the officer corps by the Democrats in the House would weaken the national defense and efficiency of the Army. The incident, originally planned as a political blow to the Hoover Administration, should have redounded to the latter's credit, coming as it did immediately before the summer convention and the campaign of 1932. Nevertheless, posing as the defender of the integrity of the Army and national defense proved of little value to Herbert Hoover in his efforts to present his story to the electorate in the fall of 1932. The squire from Hyde Park dexterously dodged military policy during his campaign and rode to victory on his personal magnetism and by hammering away on the "Hoover-conspired depression."

The Chief of Staff viewed the congressional attempt to reduce the officer corps as a vital threat aimed at the essential efficiency of the of the military establishment: "No other attack aimed exclusively at the Army was so surely calculated to accomplish the disastrous emasculation of our defensive system as this one."[36] According to the Chief of Staff, a reduction in officer personnel would have crippled the troop contingent and tactical units of the Army and not the so-called administrative overhead. MacArthur held that the latter, consisting of officers assigned to mobilization planning, general administrative duties, and the design and development of needed equipment, as well as to schools and faculties, were already at a minimum.[37] The Army Navy Journal commenting on the House vote of July 12, 1932, noted that the reversal in the lower house was caused by various factors such as the failure of progress at the Geneva disarmament conference, the portentous presence of the bonus army in Washington, and the "untoward possibilities" which continued unemployment throughout the country could engender during the coming winter. Although these factors figured in influencing the House vote in upsetting Representative Collins, according to the Army Navy Journal, it was the "masterful way" in which General MacArthur presented the case for the Army and his leadership and genius in "creating and directing the organization which disrupted the pacifist machine."[38]

Basically, however, Collins' proposal for reducing the Army was the result not of any commitment to pacifism or an emotional anti-militaristic ideology, but of a passionate concern that the Army, under the leadership of the General Staff, was not moving ahead fast enough in policy and plans toward a modernization of doctrine and organization.

---

[36] Report of the Secretary of War, 1932, p. 60.

[37] Ibid., p. 62.

[38] Army Navy Journal, July 16, 1932, p. 1072.

During the long and bitter debates on his officer reduction plan in the House of Representatives, he stressed the fact that the "theory behind the reductions" was based on the need to emphasize materiel in the Army organization rather than manpower. On May 10, 1932, in a three hour speech in the House, Collins proclaimed that while other nations, particularly Great Britain, were moving toward modernization, the American Army and General Staff were "utterly unable to lift ourselves ou of the rut and apply new principles to military science in the United States." The Mississippi legislator charged that military planning must not be based on the last war, that reorganization was urgently needed, and that the "vested interests of various branches must not be permitted to stand in the way of progress." Quoting extensively from the famous British military writer, Basil H. Liddell-Hart, Collins claimed that widespread mechanization of the Army was needed and that money should be spent on materiel such as tanks, modern guns, and planes and not on the wasteful civilian components and the "transient training of schoolboys." Collins indicted the General Staff for shortsightedness and went on to charge that either their good judgment was lacking or that the power of the vested traditional combat branches was so great that something outside of the War Department was needed to break the shackles of military conservatism. Denying the pertinency and value of the prevailing concept of the mass "citizen" army, and doubting that warfare in the future would use a large mass army mobilized around the nucleus provided by the regular establishment, Collins championed the concept that the "defense of this country lies in the utilization of science and warfare by a comparatively small army of trained experts." He urged that Congress forget the expensive training of the masses and provide for scientific advancement and mechanical means for defense. Appropriations were sufficient, according to Collins, and all that was needed was a redirection of effort and planning by the General Staff. In summation, he voiced his concern over the fact that the General Staff put the bulk of appropriations into pay and allowances for personnel to the neglect of material, and that a pre-World War I Army was being maintained rather than a force modeled along modern lines.[39]

In his lecture to the House on military doctrine, Collins did not relate how the reduction of officer personnel would give the impetus to reorganization and modernization. Apparently he was of the opinion that by abolishing funds for the reserve components, exclusive of the National Guard, and by curtailing the pay and allowances through an officer reduction, he could coerce the General Staff into compromising its doctrine and organization and stress weapons rather than manpower. Frustrated over the fact that the Army leaders gave his doctrine little serious consideration, Collins hoped to strike back at them by forcing a reduction in officer personnel. As indicated earlier, Representative Collins continually scored the Army during the hearings on the appropriations bill in January 1932. He was aghast at the reluctance of the military leaders to espouse enthuiastically his doctrine of a small modernized and mechanized Army as the key to modern warfare, and was appalled at the "go slow" policy of the General Staff and its conservative

---

[39] Congressional Record, 72nd Cong., 1st Sess., Vol. 75, Part 9, pO, 9932-35.

approach in experimenting in order to obtain a "proper balance between mechanization and the horse."[40]

The Army policy toward mechanization and modernization was laid down by MacArthur in the fall of 1931. This policy rankled Collins, particularly MacArthur's willingness to put preservation before progress and his plan to seek a balance in organization and tactics between the old horse cavalry and the modern tanks. The Army felt that cost prevented it from moving ahead in any large scale modernization and adoption of new weapons. The Chief of Field Artillery, Major General Harry G. Bishop, in testimony before the appropriations subcommittee in January 1932, replied, when asked about adoption of new weapons, that the artillery was reluctant to adopt a larger caliber field gun as standard equipment because of the cost of experimentation and re-equipment. The project of first priority, according to the Chief of Field Artillery, and the "most important" effort that should be made toward modernization, was the improvement of material in the war reserve left over from World War I. This was the venerable "soixante quinze" — the famous French seventy-five of World War I fame. The Army view was that in any future war it would enter hostilities with this equipment on hand and if any money was to be spent on modernization it should be spent on improving existing equipment.[41]

Representative Collins scored General MacArthur over his hesitancy in adopting more tanks during the hearings on the 1934 budget in late November 1932. MacArthur fired back that mechanization was going on

---

[40]*Hearings*: War Department Appropriations Bill, 1933 (January 9, 1932), p. 680.

[41]*Hearings*: War Department Appropriations Bill, 1933 (January 8, 1932), p. 670.

and that the only thing handicapping the embryo force was the fact that "Congress will not give them enough money to equip them properly with modern tanks; but even at that we are making the best of what we have ...."[42] Collins quickly rebuked the Chief of Staff by noting that military spokesmen always asked for more money and although Congress appropriated "about 40% more money for the War Department than any other nation.....it all goes for pay and more pay and more men."[43] Collins' point was that if Congress appropriated more money for the Army, MacArthur would spend it not on tanks but on more men and on the civilian reserve components. MacArthur in reply defended the General Staff policy and emphasized that training of men was more important because without training there could be no effective army. He added that Great Britain was spending $5,000,000 a year on its mechanized forces and commented that although this might be a "wise plan" no one could tell what would happen. Implying that the British plan was not too wise in the long run, MacArthur affirmed the fact that the American General Staff was not preparing for any specific type of war or specific situation, but was planning the general defense of the Republic.[44] MacArthur clearly was reluctant to put the limited funds into anything except training leaders for a large, expansible Army that could be mobilized to face whatever danger threatened the nation; therefore, mechanization was fine but of secondary importance to personnel. The Army viewpoint was that there should not be an independent mechanized force to be favored by budget appropriations to the detriment of the

---

[42]Hearings: War Department Appropriations Bill, 1934 (November 28, 1932), p. 28.

[43]Ibid., p. 28.

[44]Ibid., p. 28.

training of the civilian components, but that it should be part and parcel of the various branches and through them reach its ultimate fruition and effectiveness.[45]

Collins' was not the only voice in Congress that criticized the General Staff doctrine, although perhaps the most vociferous. The Chairman of the House Military Affairs Committee, J. J. McSwain of South Carolina, sympathized with Collins' views and announced that the emphasis in military appropriations should be put on weapons and material and affirmed that he favored the "highest emphasis upon the power of aviation," which should receive the greatest possible aid, consistent with "reasonable economy" in the American scheme of preparedness. Disenchanted with the insurance theory of defense, which was behind the Army doctrine of a small regular establishment and an expansible reserve, McSwain favored more money being spent on modern machines rather than in training this skeletonized force.[46]

Influential spokesmen on military affairs throughout the country took up the cudgels for the Collins premise in the spring of 1932. Concerned over the need of providing the best defense for the least money, some military writers advocated de-emphasizing the expensive mass army, as outlined in the National Defense Act of 1920, and looked to a small force armed with the latest in scientific advancement to provide the nation with its military establishment. To these individuals not only would such a force be less expensive, but prove to be the key to victory in any future war. Hoffman Nickerson, writing in Army Ordnance,

---

[45]Hearings: War Department Appropriations Bill, 1933 (December 1931), p. 18.

[46]Army Navy Journal, February 13, 1932, p. 576.

in the spring of 1932, affirmed that the budget deficit demanded that military expenditures be cut. Tackling the question of obtaining the best organization for the least amount of money, Nickerson voiced the opinion that the National Defense Act of 1920 and its assumption of raising an improvised mass army upon mobilization was invalid. He noted that new weapons development, such as the plane and the tank, were theoretically superior to the conscript infantry levees; furthermore, the superiority of such a force armed with modern weapons made the need for a large mass army negligible, because it was unlikely that a skeleton force could be expanded by the time air power and mechanized forces had already won a devisive victory. Nickerson claimed his theories were supported by American strategic isolation from Asia and Europe and he questioned the necessity of General Staff planning for the mobilization of a large mass army, as well as the expense involved in training a skeletonized force. Favoring the proposed reduction of the officer corps and the abolition of the reserve program on the ground that a large mass army was "clumsy and expensive," Nickerson urged that limited funds be put in machine power rather than manpower and favored the adoption of a small regular establishment supported by a small National Guard equipped in modern fashion with machines supplanting men.[47] Nickerson's thesis generally ran contrary to the National Defense Act of 1920 and his radical innovations found support among the proponents of strategic bombing and an independent air force.

---

[47]Hoffman Nickerson, "Economy and the Army," Army Ordnance, XII, Vol. 72 (May-June 1932), pp. 379-383. Note: Nickerson's antipathy toward and views concerning the "mass citizen" army is outlined in greater detail in a volume by him published in 1939 on the eve of World War II, entitled The Armed Horde (New York, 1939).

The General Staff replied to its critics that any reorganization and emphasis on an independent mechanized force would be extremely unsound both militarily and financially. As indicated by General MacArthur in his testimony before the House Subcommittee on Appropriations, in which he intimated his criticism of the British emphasis on an independent mechanized force, the General Staff was resolved that, with limited funds, it could do no other than prepare for any military eventuality and not favor one modern development over basic manpower preparation. MacArthur questioned the wisdom of the British decision to emphasize an independent mechanized force in view of limited funds; tactics for such a force as well as equipment was in a state of flux and to attempt more given the present state of development would entail useless expense.[48] This meant that training and the civilian components, the latter as the skeleton of a mass army, must have first priority for the limited money available. The decisive element in warfare was man not equipment.

Because of the immense cost involved, there was no effort by the General Staff to be prepared instantaneously for a major war. Pressure for a balanced budget forced the General Staff to accomplish in peacetime, as economically as possible, those tasks which would facilitate the mobilization, training and equipment of the citizen soldier.[49] The Chief of Staff affirmed the fact that it was impossible to improve the materiel situation of the Army without increasing the size of the military budget.

---

[48] Report of the Secretary of War, 1932, pp. 81-82.

[49] Ibid., p. 86.

The underlying philosophy of the General Staff and the

> ...very basis of all armies is personnel, properly trained.... That trained manpower has to be properly equipped is a matter of common knowledge, of course; but it is easier to produce the equipment in the industrial United States than it is to get trained manpower.[50]

Military planning of the General Staff was based on the time factor involved in which men and resources of the nation could be mobilized and brought to bear during hostilities. War Department planning sought to reduce this time factor, and according to General Staff theory the greatest safety factor in the American defense strategy was the proper manning of the mobilization plan with officers and men.[51]

MacArthur resented the charge that he and the General Staff had been derelict in not providing the Army with more modernized equipment. He claimed that the Army generally was prepared to equip about two million men or two field armies with "certain essentials" from the war reserve, such as rifles, artillery, and the ammunition. This equipment was not obsolete, according to the Chief of Staff, but he noted that there were certain items of equipment, namely, tanks and other mechanized equipment, that would be lacking at the time of mobilization. This equipment would have to be developed from pilot models because "expense had made it impossible for quantity supply."[52] The Chief of Staff admitted that in view of the eonomic factors present in the country in

---

[50] Hearings: War Department Appropriations Bill, 1934 (November 28, 1932), p. 29.

[51] Charles G. Mettler, "Economy and the Army," Army Ordnance, XIII, No. 73 (July-August 1932), pp. 7-9.

[52] Hearings: War Department Appropriations Bill, 1934 (November 28, 1932), p. 27.

1932 progress toward the equipment of the Army with modern mechanized weapons would have to consist solely in the reproduction of the best in pilot models.[53]

MacArthur ruefully agreed that the materiel situation in the Army in 1932 reflected the national economic depression. Under the existing economic conditions the planned five-year program of modernization and mechanization had not been carried out as planned and funds for this activity had been eliminated from the budget for the fiscal years 1932 and 1933. In addition, the proposed 1934 budget had had $2,000,000 for this purpose eliminated. Nevertheless, the Chief of Staff claimed that progress had been made in the development of pilot models, and in research to develop new types of equipment.[54] According to MacArthur, pilot models were available for almost every type of equipment and industrial planning contemplated turning out this equipment as fast as personnel could be trained at the time of mobilization. Although the greatest materiel weakness was in mechanized equipment, the Chief of Staff believed that the materiel condition of the Army in 1932 was in "fair shape" and added that "it causes me no worry."[55]

Obviously the elimination and curtailment of budget funds for tanks and other weapons development, due to the depression, prevented large scale experimentation and testing of both tactics and equipment for modern warfare, and undoubtedly handicapped the development of military doctrine.

---

[53] Report of the Secretary of War, 1932, p. 84.

[54] Hearings: War Department Appropriations Bill, 1934 (November 28, 1932), p. 26.

[55] Ibid., p. 31.

However, this factor did not alarm the General Staff who were willing to curtail such development because of budget pressure and give first priority to manpower training.

CHAPTER VI

PROBLEMS OF REORGANIZATION AND PARTICIPATION IN RELIEF PROJECTS

Another issue that emerged during the spring of 1932 was the perennial problem of consolidation and unification of the Army and Navy. Discussion of the issue at this time was initiated by critics of the military establishment who felt that the depression and the frightening federal fiscal deficiencies made the problem all the more pressing. The proposal for a unified defense establishment, including an Air Corps on an equal basis with the older services, had been constantly before Congress in one form or another throughout the period since 1919 and was generally favored by its proponents on the grounds of economy and efficiency.[1]

---

[1]For three of the more important post World War I discussions on a unified Department of Defense see:

<u>Department of Defense and Unification of Air Service</u>, Hearings before the Committee on Military Affairs, House of Representatives, 69th Cong., 1st Sess., (Washington, 1926).

Hearings before the Joint Committee on the Reorganization of the Administrative Branch of the Government, Congress of the United States, 68th Cong., 1st Sess., on S. J. Res. 282, 67th Cong. (Washington, 1924).

<u>Aircraft</u>, Hearings before the President's Aircraft Board (Washington, 1925). This was the Morrow Board.

For the most complete summary of the entire aspect of unification see Lawrence J. Legere, Jr., <u>Unification of the Armed Forces</u> (Washington: OCMH, 1957 revision). Unpublished manuscript in OCMH Files.

As would be expected with mounting federal deficits, economy-minded congressmen in 1932 again put forward the need and urgency of the unification of the armed forces. Particularly during the early depression years, 1930-1932, public measures were judged almost entirely from the viewpoint of financial economy. Among Army and Navy leaders, with the exception of the Army aviators, the proposals for unification never had much support. During the 71st Congress the War Department stood fast in vigorously opposing any move toward unification. Secretary Hurley at that time informed congressional leaders that the administration was opposed to any such move as an attempt to economize in federal spending. Hurley added that there had been many schemes in the past for unification, ranging from a small coordinating agency set up over three independent departments, to a type of organization where all power resided in a Secretary and a Staff which would have control over all forces. According to Hurley, no scheme as yet proposed would adequately economize in military expenditures, and for the sake of economy the existing organization should be maintained.[2]

When the 72nd Congress convened in December 1931, unification of the armed forces was again revived, and regardless of the opposition of the administration hearings were opened in late January 1932 on the

---

[2]Ltr, Secretary of War to Hon. William Williamson, House of Representatives, January 26, 1931. AG 040, RG 94, NA.

unification proposal.[3] Although unification had long been a favorite topic of congressional critics of the military establishment, the Army was genuinely concerned lest Congress take "drastic action" and demand the submerging of service prejudice and the rearrangement of national defense in the hope of obtaining greater economy in government expenditures.[4]

In the face of this threat to its organizational independence and while hearings on unification were being held, the General Staff outlined its legislative strategy in order to defeat plans for unification. The Chief of Staff asked the War Plans Division for a study on the proposed legislative proposals "which would be a complete rebuttal from the economic standpoint." He admonished the staff planners that "in making our argument against the whole idea of a Department of National Defense, we should attack it first from the point of view of economy, and second from the point of view of efficiency."[5]

MacArthur's plan was to dissuade Congress from any insidious move toward unification by stressing the fact that this would build up another great echelon of command and would consequently involve additional expense. Besides reflecting its sincere concern over the

---

[3]Department of National Defense, Hearings before Committee on Expenditures in the Executive Department, 72nd Cong., 1st Sess., (Washington, 1932).

[4]Army Navy Journal, January 9, 1932, p. 443.

[5]Memo, Deputy Chief of Staff for the AC/S WPD, January 15, 1932. AG 040, RG 94, NA.

economic consequences of unification, the General Staff opposed any move which would involve the autonomy of the Air Corps and take the aviators out from under the control of the General Staff. Denying the fact that the Air Corps was not provided for by the General Staff, Secretary Hurley admonished Congress that:

> reductions in other arms and services have been made in order to provide for the existence of air support in any future conflict... These reductions, which under present conditions may have gone too far, would be entirely indefensible except on the assumptions that the air force so provided will be an integral part of the Army.[6]

Clearly the Army, having sacrificed financially in order to provide for the Air Corps, was extremely opposed to accepting autonomy for it as an economy move. The General Staff was concerned that under the false guise of economy, the long cherished dream of the air advocates was to be fulfilled and tactical air support for the ground combat arms would be lost. While viewing the proposal for unification as an additional threat to federal solvency, the Chief of Staff urged Congress to vote against the unification bill on the grounds of national defense. MacArthur cautioned congressional leaders that it was inadvisable to give serious consideration

> to this change in the face of the international situation as it now exists. The instability, the uncertainty, the loss of morale among the combatant forces that would be entailed by acrimonious discussions along this line, seems to me fraught with such peril to the government

---

[6] Ltr, Secretary of War for Hon. John J. Cochran, January 5, 1932. AG 040, RG 94, NA.

that even if everything that were said in favor of this bill by its proponents were true, I would still give my most solemn counsel to suspend action until the world has reached a condition of approximate normalcy.... Pass this bill and every potential enemy of the United States will rejoice.[7]

Warning against launching an "adventure which might involve the life of the country," MacArthur emphasized to Congress that the "ultimate cost" of unifiaation would exceed by millions any economies that could be effected

Amalgamation would represent one of the greatest debauches of extravagance that any nation has ever known... new buildings, new schools, new staffs all with additional costs.[8]

According to the General Staff the cost of a proposed independent Air Corps and unified department of defense was not susceptible to an accurate breakdown and analysis, but it claimed that it was a fact that the experience of foreign governments, who adopted such a system had been that of increased costs.[9]

MacArthur was vigorous in expounding his views in opposition to any unification and amalgamation which would entail the independence or autonomy of the Air Corps. His most telling point in attacking unification was in stressing the claim that any consolidation would require the maintenance of existing administrative organizations and

---

[7]Army Navy Journal, February 20, 1932, p. 598.

[8]Ltr, Chief of Staff for Hon. Charles H. Martin, February 18, 1932. AG 040, RG 94, NA.

[9]Ltr, Secretary of War Hurley for Senator Morris Sheppard, April 7, 1932.. AG 040, RG 94, NA.

personnel and superimpose on the existing organizations a larger "super-staff" which would be necessary in order to coordinate and administer the various subordinate branches of the armed forces.[10]

To counter the air enthusiasts argument, MacArthur pointed out that an independent Air Corps would entail increased expense because both the Army Air Corps and the Navy air arm, as they were organized in 1932, were not required to perform their own overhead duties and administrative functions. In addition he emphasized that the purchase of non-technical equipment, medical service, construction, pay, supply, and commissary were all handled through Army establishments and agencies.[11]

It is difficult to determine how much effect the General Staff's argument, that an independent Air Corps and unification of the armed forces under a single department would increase military expenditures, had on delaying and defeating the move for unification and air autonomy in the early 1930's. In any event the General Staff, alarmed over the possible loss of control over the Air Corps, found the need for economy in operation and the pressure to reduce military spending a convenient rebuttal to the claims of the Army aviators and their supporters throughout the country.

---

[10] Report of the Secretary of War, 1932, pp. 100-01.

[11] Ibid., pp. 98-99.

Faced by the intransigent opposition of the Army toward unification, both on the grounds of efficiency and economy, Congress still searched for some way in which further economies in the military establishment could be obtained with the cooperation and support of the War Department. In late February 1932, the Secretary of War was asked for his views concerning the possibilities of effecting further economies in his department. The Assistant Chief of Staff G-4, the Deputy Chief of Staff, and the Chief of Staff himself prepared Hurley's reply, and in a lengthy and important report summarized the entire problem of economy and military policy.[12] The letter prepared for Hurley's signature was the summation of the General Staff's position on the balancing of military expenditures and the maintenance of adequate defense, and gives an excellent insight into the thinking of the military during the trying depression years, and in particular the year 1932 when the Army was the target of an economy-minded administration and Congress.

The letter reviewed the National Defense Act and pointed out that this was the basic law determining military policy and that the law was "essentially American and represents the greatest and most constructive development evolved by the American government in recent years." The General Staff enthusiastically supported the provision of the National Defense Act which provided for a combination of a small professional force to act as the training cadre and a nucleus for the mobilization

---

[12]Memo, Deputy Chief of Staff for the AC/S G-4, February 29, 1932. AG 040, RG 94, NA.

of the civilian components, thus providing, in the opinion of the General Staff, for the first time in American history "more or less adequate preparation for any eventuality and at a cost within reasonable figures." According to the General Staff, the military budget was a perennial object of the most searching scrutiny

> and pressure to reduce it was constant both from the legislative and executive branches even in times of economic prosperity. As a result, possibilities for further reduction in our military expenditures, unless the essential fabric of American defense policy is to be destroyed, have been thoroughly exhausted.... Pressure for economy which has dominated the military estimates during the past several years has weakened our military establishment to a perceptible extent and has eliminated the possibilities of further economies.[13]

The General Staff refused to consider any further budget cuts, holding steadfastly that it had retreated to the last possible economic retrenchment, and voiced strong opposition to any more economic maneuvers by Congress at the expense of the Army. Noting that the budget submitted for fiscal 1933 totalled $295,000,000 for military activities, a reduction of some $38,000,000 from the previous fiscal year, the General Staff opposed any further economy moves. This figure, the General Staff claimed in strident tones, was the minimum on which the military establishment could exist for a single year: "Everything has been sacrificed in excess of the bare necessities." Bitterly the General Staff informed Congress that any material decrease

---

[13]Ltr, Secretary of War Hurley for the Hon. Joseph M. Byrns, March 26, 1932. AG 040, RG 94, NA.

in the figure before Congress would result in the sabotaging of the National Defense Act, and involve one of two alternatives: the adoption of some form of conscription or the practical disarmament of the United States. The War Department added that it was "unalterably opposed to either of these alternatives." Defending its expenditures, the General Staff noted that the budget for the military establishment was between six and seven per cent of the total federal expenditure, and that the increase in military spending since the 1918 armistice was largely due to modern equipment, such as aircraft and mechanized forms of ordnance and motive power, which contrary to popular opinion were relatively costly.

Speaking on the problem of consolidation and duplication between the Army and Navy, the General Staff affirmed that individual incidents were grossly exaggerated and claimed that between the two departments

> the most complete coordination and cooperation has been obtained. This extends to purchase, supply, and storage as well as training. Such agencies as the Joint Army and Navy Board, and its subsidiaries, the Joint Army and Navy Planning Board, and the Joint Army and Navy Munitions and Aeronautical Board are directly concerned with coordination of the Army and Navy in all phases of this work.

Of the non-military items in the War Department budget, the General Staff conceded that the situation was different and suggested that except for the administration of the Panama Canal, Rivers, and Harbors, and the Bureau of Insular Affairs, the War Department could be relieved of its non-military activities.[14]

---

[14]*Ibid.*

Under congressional pressure for the elimination of duplication and possible economies through consolidation, the Army and the Navy undertook a study of the problem. Their study, initiated by the Joint Army Navy Board, was completed in early 1933 and published at that time. The study was divided into twenty-one phases of work that were similar in the two departments. In ten of these phases there was found no overlapping, but in eleven separate categories it was found that there was sufficient evidence of possible duplication to justify a recommendation that further study be given the problem. These areas were the following: recruiting, personnel administration, health and sanitation, ordnance, quartermaster, civilian and military construction, soldiers and sailors homes, supply features of medical service, property records, and auditing. The committee noted that consolidation would bring many small savings but nothing substantial. Regardless of the "pressing necessity for retrenchment in public expenditures" the joint committee advised against any such rash move to consolidate procurement and the financial affairs of the two services.[15]

The upshot of the entire issue was the organization of the Joint Army Navy Economy Board in the fall of 1933. On October 9, 1933, at the recommendation of the Joint Army Navy Board, the joint economy board was created, and charged with the responsibility of "investigating and reporting" to the Joint Army Navy Board economies that could be

---

[15]<u>Army Navy Journal</u>, January 21, 1933, p. 419.

effected from time to time without loss of efficiency, and by the elimination of overlap and the duplication of activities.[16]

But the Air Corps was undaunted in its efforts to achieve autonomy and semi-independence from the General Staff. The Air Corps believed that adequate provision for the development of air power was not being carried out because of the fact that its budget was considered on the same basis as the requirements of the ground combat arms. In early December 1932 it requested that all procurement and budgeting functions pertaining to the Air Corps be placed under the Chief of the Air Corps and the Office of the Assistant Secretary of War for Air. This request was vigorously opposed by the Deputy Chief of Staff who advised

---

[16]Section I, General Orders No. 11, War Department, Washington, October 9, 1933. AG 040, RG 94, NA. Note: The Joint Army Navy Board had the responsibility for the preparation of strategic war plans involving joint Army and Navy forces, and might be considered the predecessor of the Joint Chiefs of Staff. "Reorganized in 1919 to correct defects that had become apparent since its establishment in 1903, the Board consisted of six members, the Army Chief of Staff and the Chief of Naval Operations, their deputies, and the chiefs of the war plans divisions of each of the services. To it came all matters that required cooperation between the two services, either by referral or on the initiative of the Board itself. It had no executive functions nor command authority and until 1939 reported to the War and Navy Secretaries. Its recommendations were purely advisory, and became effective only upon approval by both Secretaries, and, in some cases by the President himself." <u>Command Decisions</u>, prepared by the Office of the Chief of Military History, Department of the Army (New York: Harcourt, Brace & Company, 1959), pp. 4-5.

For further details of the Joint Army Navy Board and other activities relating to unification during this period see: Legere, <u>Unification of the Armed Forces</u>, particularly Chapters II and III, pp. 71-204.

the Chief of Staff:

> The budget of the Air Corps cannot be considered as a thing apart, but it must be considered as part of the military budget of the whole Army. Certainly the Air Corps must realize how the components of the Regular Army have gone to the limit in making sacrifices, not only to build up and support the Air Corps but also to build up and support the civilian components included within our military budget. Only very recently on our own initiative we squeezed an additional one million dollars out of the Regular Army, the Air Corps excepted, to enable us to continue the CMTC camps, an item that had been entirely eliminated by the Bureau of Budget...
>
> ....
>
> No arm, service or activity receives all they (sic) desire but in the final analysis the General Staff attempts to build up a well-balanced effort, remembering that their responsibility goes further into war plans employing these very same organizations. To provide for the yearly increments in the Air Corps, cuts have been made in men, money and material which otherwise would have gone to the other components of the Army.[17]

The Deputy Chief of Staff affirmed the fact that the Air Corps was given "systematic" consideration by the General Staff, and that the administration of the Army, including the Air Corps, was considered in yearly cycles. Moreover, the Chief of Staff was advised, representatives of the Air Corps were present when the annual directive for the Army activities was prepared and when it was revised, and they sat in at every meeting when Air Corps budget estimates were being considered. The Deputy Chief of Staff reminded MacArthur that in addition to the items carried in the Air Corps budget, there were many items included in the estimates of the chiefs of services for

---

[17]Memo, Deputy Chief of Staff for the Chief of Staff, undated, AG 320.2, RG 94, NA.

the maintenance of the Air Corps itself, such as pay, rations, housing and maintenance.[18]

It was at this time that MacArthur, using the excuse of economy and consolidation, was able to give a severe blow to the advocates of air autonomy. F. Trubee Davison, who had been Assistant Secretary of War for Air, and a vigorous proponent of air power, was nominated in the fall of 1932 to run on the Republican ticket for Lieutenant Governor of New York. The General Staff had never been too pleased with the Office of Assistant Secretary for Air, arguing that with air officers in their organization there was no need for a special assistant secretary in charge of the Air Corps. Hoover made no decision as to a replacement and it was felt that even if Congress would appropriate money for this office, he would be hesitant about filling the post at so late a date in his administration.[19]

When the Roosevelt Administration took over, the position was not filled. On May 23, 1933, the Director of the Bureau of the Budget wrote to Secretary of War George B. Dern and asked for "all desirable changes" in the internal organization of the War Department that the latter would recommend.[20] Dern sent the letter to MacArthur, who stated that the only change in the War Department that should be made was the abolition of the Office of the Assistant Secretary for Aviation

---

[18] Ibid. [19] Army Navy Journal, October 8, 1932, p. 101.

[20] Ltr, Douglas for Dern, May 23, 1933. AG 040, RG 94, NA.

and he directed the Judge Advocate General to prepare a draft of such recommendation for the Secretary of War.[21]

Pressure on the military establishment to attune its organization and activities so that it could accomplish noticeable budgetary reductions was a consequence of the continued economic depression and federal fiscal deficiencies. In view of the fact of constant pressure to reduce the cost of government with corresponding relief for the taxpayer, the administration and Congress were constantly seeking ways to effect greater economies in the War Department. Cognizant of these economy demands, the Army realized that it would have to "fight continually" to maintain its "procurement independence." This was essential, the Army believed, if it was to maintain its maximum efficiency in supply procurement, and the "unhampered" development of more efficient weapons and equipment.[22]

Indicative of congressional willingness to grasp at any straw in order to alleviate the financial problems of the government was the appearance of General Johnson Hagood before the Military Affairs Committee of the 73rd Congress in the spring of 1933. Hagood, long before the onset of the depression, had championed a radical reorganization of the War Department on grounds of efficiency and of economy.

---

[21]Memo, Chief of Staff for the Acting Judge Advocate General, May 25, 1933. AG 040, RG 94, NA.

[22]Lt. Colonel Earl North, "Activities of the Assistant Secretary of War in Current Procurement," Lectures Delivered at Army Industrial College, X (1933-1934), p. 32.

The reiteration of his well-known thesis at a Reserve Officers meeting in Omaha, in April 1933, brought a summons to appear before the Military Affairs Committee of the House. His remarks to the assembled committee were hardly new and the hearings consisted in the main of Hagood submitting for the record his previous statements and proposals for reorganizing the War Department. Hagood, who styled himself as a military non-conformist and an Army counterpart to the congressional "Sons of the Wild Jackass," had two main proposals to make which he claimed could achieve comsiderable economy: reorganize the Army into three main divisions: tactics, supply, and administration; and reduce federal support for the National Guard.[23]

Another serious ramification of the depression, unexmployment, also had an important impact on the Army. The continuing acute unemployment situation throughout the country gave impetus to certain schemes which would put the Army in the role of relief administrator, or at least put the Army more actively in the campaign against unemployment and economic distress. Such proposals were based on the idea that the expensive military establishment should be made to serve the welfare of the country in time of economic difficulty; besides its

---

23"General Johnson Hagood on National Defense and Reorganization of the Army," Hearings before Committee on Military Affairs, House of Representatives, 73rd Cong., 1st Sess., April 12, 1933 (Washington, 1933), pp. 11, 13. For a more detailed account of Hagood's poopösals see: Johnson Hagood, We Can Defend America (Garden City, N.Y.: Doubleday, Doran and Company, 1937). See also Hagood's The Services of Supply (Boston: Houghton Mifflin Company, 1927), Chapter XXVI, pp. 358-85.

negative role of cutting expenditures, the Army could actively participate as an instrument of the federal government in abetting prosperity. Use the Army as a vehicle of relief; the camps and barracks were ready, and the unemployed could be put in the Army and officers could give vocational as well as military training. Thus the Army would have a magnificent role in economic and social fields, and participate in social and economic activities of the country in peacetime. This idea came to fruition during the spring of 1933, when the Civilian Conservation Corps was inaugurated, and generally it received cool response from the military, who believed that any activity along these lines would weaken its efforts in national defense and serve to lay the Army open to its critics for its views on political and social matters.

In late 1930 a bill was introduced into Congress which proposed the organization of a special reserve corps for the purpose of relieving unemployment. The proposed legislation called for the enlistment of unemployed citizens between the ages of 18 - 45, for one year, and a total enlistment for the corps not to exceed 250,000. The special enlistees would receive the same pay and allowances as the Regular Army enlisted men, and in addition to their military duties, the unemployed enlistees would be given some sort of vocational training by civilian and military officials with the Secretary of War having the responsibility and authority to supervise such training.[24]

It is important to note that the proposals in 1930 gave the Secretary of War control and supervision of vocational training and educational activities. This issue became a serious point of controversy in the CCC program, with the President finally deciding that the Army should not have any control over educational or vocational training, and giving it to the Department of Interior's Office of Education. The War Department consistently opposed participating in unemployment relief and the enlistment of a special reserve corps of unemployed. Although the Army realized that this was an opportunity to broaden military training among the citizenry of the country and participate more fully in the campaign against the depression, it had serious reservations toward such a program.

The Army was willing to expedite its building program in order to alleviate unemployment, but a deviation from its policy of enlistment could not be countenanced because of the possibilities of having a deleterious effect on the morale of the Regular Army. To the Army the intermingling of unemployed enlistees and the Regular Army enlisted men was fraught with disasterous possibilities. Furthermore, the Army reminded Congress, the cost of the proposed unemployed reserve corps would total around $226,000,000 annually, an amount, which if made available to the Army could be used to secure more lasting beneficial effects both from a national defense standpoint as well as relieving

---

[24]HR 15076, 3rd Sess., 71st Cong., December 12, 1930, AG 400.38 RG 94, NA.

a greater number of unemployed. Basically the Army opposed the special unemployed reserve corps on the grounds that maintenance of the corps could only be undertaken by breaking up existing Regular Army units, thus entailing a "grave loss of efficiency to the Regular Army units and the summer training of the civilian components."[25]

Underlying these remarks was the belief of the General Staff that the fight against unemployment was not the direct concern of the Army. However, military leaders proposed the relief of unemployment by encouraging an increase in military spending. The Army claimed that if money was made available by Congress for public works and armament orders, both for Ordnance arsenals and munitions firms throughout the country, the worst effects of unemployment could be alleviated.

In the troublesome 1st Session of the 72nd Congress, during the spring of 1932, the plan of enrolling a special reserve corps of the unemployed was again proposed. Congress toyed with the idea of authorizing the enlistment of unemployed in the Army until the maximum legal enlisted strength of the Regular Army, 280,000, had been reached. Army reaction was adamantly opposed to this plan because its purpose was for the relief of unemployment, rather than the efficiency of the national defense:

> If the basic purpose of the bill is to relieve unemployment at the expense of government, it is believed the greater good

---

[25]Ltr, Secretary of War for Hon. W. Frank James, MC. January 31, 1931. AG 400.38, RG 94, NA.

> would be accomplished by utilizing men in civilian capacities on public works rather than as transient and temporary members of the military establishment.[26]

The Army was concerned that the enrollment or enlistment of unemployed in the Army would constitute a threat to the integrity and stability of the military establishment, and that the Army would be drawn into the social and political controversies of the day and thereby have weakened its efforts to remain above the political din of the nation in its tower of national defense. There were other schemes proposed for using the Army more directly in the alleviation of unemployment and economic distress and these also received a cool response from the General Staff.

However, it appears that at one time in the fall and winter of 1931-32, the Army gave some thought to the possibility of it being used as the centralized federal agency in charge of all public works. In writing to a White House official, in early 1932, the Deputy Chief of Staff, Maj. Gen. Van Horne Moseley, reminded the administration that the General Staff was not in favor of any kind of plan which visualized the acceleration of enlistment in order to absorb the unemployed citizens throughout the country: "If there is a need of an army, it is because the army must stand ready to meet the danger dominant in national and international life." At the same time, the Deputy Chief of Staff emphasized that the Army was willing to take

---

[26]Ltr, Secretary of War for Chairman House Military Affairs Committee, September 27, 1932. AG 400.38, RG 94, NA.

over control of a public works program for the Hoover Administration, and put the unemployed to work under the control of the Army Engineers. According to General Moseley:

> If the people desire the emergency handled by the Army, we will approach the problem as we do earthquakes, fire, floods, pestilence, and war. With so much money allowed for an unemployed individual, we could take charge of these people, not as part of us but as a responsibility under our care and direction.... The Army is complemented when people turn to us to solve problems, but you must let us solve it our way.[27]

If the Army was ready to solve the problems of the country, the Commander-in-Chief never gave the go-ahead, and no further plans along these lines were considered by the General Staff. The original enthusiasm of the Deputy Chief of Staff to take over public works activities for the Hoover Administration probably was not widespread throughout the General Staff nor popular with the territorial commanders of the nine Corps Areas. The Army realized that if it undertook control of public works and work relief projects it would become increasingly involved in the political and economic affairs of the country. This factor precluded any large scale planning by the General Staff actively to combat unemployment.

During the early months of 1932, Army thinking on participating directly in relieving unemployment distress and in the taking charge of relief activities apparently had finally crystallized. As late as January 1932 the Deputy Chief of Staff had intimated to the White House

---

[27]Ltr, Deputy Chief of Staff to Mr. E. P. Hayes, Chairman of the President's Organization on Unemployment, January 22, 1932. AG 400.38, RG 94, NA.

that the Army was prepared to take charge of public works, but by the spring of the year this idea had definitely been dropped. In response to a proposed Senate resolution of June 4, 1932, which would have authorized the Secretary of War to make available personnel and equipment of the Army to aid in an orhanized program for unemployment relief, the Chief of Staff voiced his sttong opposition. MacArthur pointed out that the result of such legislation would detract from the mission of the military establishment and result in numerous demands upon the Army from various sources for personnel and equipment which could not be met. The Chief of Staff noted that in order to alleviate the distress throughout the country, all Corps Area Commanders had been instructed by him to cooperate to the fullest extent with local authorities by loaning blankets and cots to charitable organizations and through the sale of salvaged clothing. MacArthur added:

> While no organized programs of unemployment relief have been presented for approval by the Secretary of War, the War Department fails to see how its personnel can be utilized for purposes of unemployment relief other than in exceptional cases when necessary in the supervision of the issuing of supplies, or in direction of work, without adding to the present situation.[28]

Proposed legislation during the summer of 1932, which would have authorized the President to employ the Army to administer relief was likewise rebuked by the Army. These proposals would have given the President sweeping powers to create a National Emergency Board,

---

[28]Ltr, General Douglas MacArthur, Acting Secretary of War to Senator Charles L. McNary, June 16, 1932. AG 400.38, RG 94, NA.

consisting of the Secretary of War and the Secretary of Labor, with the purpose of carrying out relief activities and alleviating unemployment. It was proposed that administrative and clerical personnel for the Board would come from the War Department. Voicing its "serious objections" to the proposed legislation the General Staff stressed that this would:

> take the Army away from its normal functions and employ it to administer relief.... The present economic situation is not such as to allow the use of the Army for any purposes which would weaken its effectiveness for the express purpose for which it was created and maintained.[29]

Besides being unconstitutional, the proposed bill would:

> make every Army post an asylum of relief. This is impracticable.... The presence of wayfarers would endanger property and disrupt training.[30]

Although the Army was opposed to such insidious plans calling for the use of military personnel and equipment to alleviate unemployment distress, it realized that a determined Congress could possibly push through such a proposal and the Army did formulate a vague plan based on this distinct possibility. This plan provided for a limited relief scheme, in which the Army would be in charge of feeding and supplying bedding for unemployed housed in vacant buildings in various cities and urban areas. It is important to note that local civilian authorities were to be responsible for providing housing and the Army

---

[29]Ltr, Deputy Chief of Staff to Hon. W. Frank James, Chairman of House Military Affairs Committee, July 20, 1932. AG 400.38, RG 94, NA.

[30]*Ibid*.

was to supplement their efforts. This plan was prepared in the event the Army was called upon to administer relief with special funds provided by Congress, and it included two main provisions: furnishing cots and blankets, and feeding the unemployed by organized Army mess units, with each unit prepared to feed a certain number of unemployed.[31]

The Army was concerned for purposes of morale and discipline as well as stability of organization to keep the unemployed segregated from active military organizations, and felt that in no case should the unhoused unemployed be sheltered in Army housing. This policy became more pronounced and determined as a result of the Bonus Army episode in July 1932.

During the winter of 1931-32, various Corps Area Commanders throughout the country were requested by local civic and government leaders to make available unused military housing on Army posts for the unemployed. One Corps Area Commander, Maj. Gen. Malin Craig, later to succeed MacArthur as Chief of Staff, was urged by state officials in California to make available Army housing for some 4,000 to 5,000 unemployed. Craig was vigorously opposed to this scheme but was concerned and worried that political pressure would be brought to bear and force the Army to house and take care of the unemployed.

---

[31]Ltr, Deputy Chief of Staff to Maj. Gen. Frank R. McCoy, CG 4th Corps Area, Atlanta, September 12, 1931. AG 400.38, RG 94. NA. Note: Soon after this correspondence McCoy left for Manchuria to serve as American member of the Lytton Commission. Interview with Mrs. Frank McCoy, January 10, 1960.

According to Craig

> very powerful reasons affecting morale forbids in my opinion, that these floaters should be quartered in midst or in contact with our enlisted men.... What I fear is pressure perhaps political, being brought to bear on the War Department before they have had time to consider our side of the question.[32]

Craig's fears and concern were mollified by the Deputy Chief of Staff who informed the harassed and worried Corps Area Commander that MacArthur definitely agreed with his opinions about the quartering of unemployed in Army housing, and that the latter should not be mixed in any way with the military command. Complementing Craig for his position on the matter and insuring him that he was strongly supported by the General Staff in Washington, the Deputy Chief of Staff added that there had been no policy pronouncement on the subject by the General Staff because:

> MacArthur insists upon the recommendation of the Corps Commanders being followed if it is possible to do so, for he wants to build up their authority within their commands and areas.[33]

During the spring of 1932, when MacArthur finally decided the extent of War Department participation in relief measures and Army policy on this matter, Corps Commanders were given responsibility for effecting limited Army cooperation in combating unemployment and economic distress and authorized to loan cots and blankets and salvaged

---

[32]Ltr, Commanding General 9th Corps Area to the Deputy Chief of Staff, November 18, 1931. AG 400.38, RG 94, NA.

[33]Ltr, Deputy Chief of Staff to the CG, 9th Corps Area, November 27, 1931. AG 400.38, RG 94, NA.

clothing. MacArthur's policy was for the War Department and the Army to remain out of relief activities, and if limited Army participation was required by Congress, to de-centralize this participation to the various Corps Area Commanders who would act in cooperation with local authorities. This would enable the General Staff to concentrate on its military planning and at the same time permit the Army to remain above the problems incumbent upon active centralized control of relief and unemployment.

CHAPTER VII

THE ARMY AND THE BONUS INCIDENT

One of the most controversial incidents that involved the Army during the depression years, and one which brought it into the political arena and the focus of public debate, was the use of the Regular Army to disperse the bonus marchers in Washington during the summer of 1932. The Regular Army had been used infrequently in the past to put down civil disturbance, the most recent incident which had an impact on public opinion being the use of federal troops during the Pullman Strike in Chicago during 1895.[1]

In early June 1932, with the arrival of the bonus people in Washington, Congress sought to make available to them Army cots, blankets, tents, surplus clothing, and medical and mess facilities. The War Department opposed such a scheme on the grounds that utilization of Army stocks would cause such depletion as to "require replacement with additional appropriations." By mentioning the increased cost of any proposal the Army was confident it could parry congressional importunities. Congress was told that its plans to house and clothe the bonus people with military supplies violated the

---

[1]"Federal Aid in Domestic Disturbances," Senate Document #263, 67th Cong., 2nd Sess. (Washington, 1922). Regular Army troops had been used three times between 1900 and 1932: Nevada - 1907, Colorado - 1914, and West Virginia - 1921.

"basic principles" of the War Department and the Army hoped that there would be no further discussion of the matter.[2]

In the opinion of the Army the motley assemblage of veterans congregating in Washington was hardly worthy of aid and comfort; indeed, the War Department was concerned with the possibility of serious disturbances and some anxiety that the development of close relationships between the bonus marchers and the troops would have a deleterious effect on the reliability of the latter in case they were called out for riot duty. According to one officer who participated in the eviction of the bonus people this factor made some impression on the War Department:

> Initially, the relations between the troops and the Marchers were so good as to cause some concern among War Department staff officers who, unlike the officers on duty with the troops, were somewhat doubtful about the reliability of the troops if their services were needed.[3]

MacArthur was alert to the possibility that the concentration of disaffected and unemployed people in Washington, petitioning _en masse_ before Congress, was a potential source of unrest and perhaps violence. Soon after the arrival of these people in the capital he took precautionary action to prepare the Army for any eventuality. Early in June the Chief of Staff wired all Corps Area Commanders that in case

---

[2]Ltr, Acting Secretary of War Frederick H. Payne to Hon. J. J. McSwain, Chairman House Com on Mil Affairs, June 25, 1932. AG 240 Bonus (5-28-32) Section 1, RG 94, NA.

[3]Maj Gen H. W. Blakeley, "When the Army was Smeared," _Combat Forces Journal_, Vol. II, No. 7 (February 1952), p. 28.

any bonus marchers passed through their respective Corps Areas it should be determined if any communist elements were present. The Corps Area Commanders were directed to "report in secret code" to Washington indicating the presence of communist elements and the names of the leaders of the bonus marchers with "known communistic leanings."[4] The Army felt that if it had the ultimate responsibility for the maintenance of law and order in the national capital such information was of critical value in forming a sound estimate of the situation in reference to potential trouble in Washington. But of greater significance this radiogram reflected the fact that the Army was seriously concerned over the potentiality of disturbances and violence throughout the country as a result of unemployment and the social and economic upheaval brought on by the depression. It seemed therefore to the General Staff that prudence required planning for this very real probability.

In general the replies of the Corps Area Commanders to the General Staff reflected the ignorance of the subordinate commanders in respect to the composition of the bonus marchers, and because of the lack of reliable information they were unable intelligently to appraise the social and political makeup of the various groups heading for Washington. The Corps Area Commanders had only rumors or little known facts as a basis of their replies, and obviously did not think that the presence of communists, as a source of potential violence, was a serious matter.

---

[4] Memo, AC/S G-2 for the AG, June 10, 1932, for radiogram to all Corps Area Commanders, AG 240 Bonus (5-29-32) Section 1, RG 94, NA.

From Baltimore, the III Corps Area Commander reported that there was no known information of communists within the bonus group that had left this city, but that there was a "general feeling of unrest . . . to the general effect that some serious trouble is likely to arise at an early date."[5] This was the only report from the nine subordinate territorial commanders that indicated the possibility of trouble for the War Department in Washington. In fact the general tenor of the replies was likely to soothe the concern of the beleaguered War Department in the capital. General Edward L. King reported from Atlanta that communists and troublemakers were "making little effect on southern bonus marchers."[6]

General Malin Craig wired from the Presidio that the bonus units leaving the West Coast for Washington had announced that they would not tolerate any communist elements and that to his knowledge there was no evidence of communist influence. Indeed, Craig added, among the bonus marchers from the West Coast "discipline" and "conduct were excellent."[7] In respect to the bonus people that had already concentrated in Washington G-2 reported to the Chief of Staff that of twenty-six "so-called" leaders of the Bonus Army, three were reported

---

[5]Ltr, CG 3rd Corps Area to AG, July 5, 1932. AG 240 Bonus (5-28-32) Section 1, RG 94, NA.

[6]Tel, King, Fort McPherson to AG, June 11, 45-WVR, AG 240 Bonus (5-28-32) Section 1, RG 94, NA.

[7]Tel, Craig to AG, June 14, 1932. WAG 61, AG 240 Bonus (5-28-32) Section 1, RG 94, NA.

to be communist or affiliated with communist organizations.[8]

MacArthur's concern and anxiety over the possibilities of trouble was further reflected in the fact that in early June two experimental vehicles from Aberdeen Proving Grounds, a T-4 armored car and a 75mm self-propelled gun, were ordered to Fort Myer to be available in case trouble ensued in the nation's capital.[9]

At the same time the Chief of Staff directed that the War Department's "White Plan," which contemplated the employment of the Regular Army in Washington in case of emergency, be revised. The Commanding General of the 16th Brigade, comprising the Regular Army units in and around Washington, prepared the new plan and forwarded it to MacArthur. According to this plan

> the greater part of the bonus marchers have thus far resisted all attempts of the Communists to gain control of them but there are a number of well-known Communist leaders here and they are claiming credit for the instigation of the march.
>
> Any demonstration therefore will almost certainly contain ex-soldiers without a desire for Communist affiliations and Communists themselves who will try by overt acts, possibly of violence to commit the veterans.
>
> Our operations, therefore, should contemplate giving an opportunity to the non-Communistic veterans to disperse, but of course the tactics employed must depend on the commander on the spot and the character of the emergency.

---

[8]Memo, AG for the Chief of Staff, June 12, 1932. AG 240 Bonus (5-28-32) Section 1, RG 94, NA.

[9]Ltr, Chief of Ordnance to CO Aberdeen Proving Grounds, June 4, 1932. The crews of these vehicles were told that if any person asked the purpose of the trip to Washington they were to reply that the vehicles were to be available in the capital in case anyone wanted to view the latest developments in mechanized equipment. Folder entitled: Rpt of Operations Against Bonus Marchers, 1932, Mil Dist of Washington, A46-458, RG 98, NA.

For this reason, tear gas grenades are provided which would be used in sufficient numbers to be effective if the character of the disorder did not require more drastic action at once.

The operation plan went on to direct that in case of an emergency the assembly area for the troops would be the Ellipse in the rear of the White House facing Constitution Avenue. The plan also directed that the "White House, Treasury Buildings, Bureau of Engraving and Printing and the Capitol are critical points and their protection primarily must be foreseen."[10]

Early in July Congress appropriated money for the return of the veterans to their homes and over 5,000 of the estimated 12,000 veterans then in Washington left the city. By the end of July there was estimated to be around 5,000 members of the "B. E. F." (Bonus Expeditionary Force) in Washington.[11] Congress adjourned on July 16 without passing a bonus bill and there seemed no apparent reason why the BEF should remain in the capital.

On July 21 the bonus people were informed by the Washington police that eviction of the BEF from government owned buildings along Pennsylvania Avenue, between the Capitol and the main business district of Washington, would begin within twenty-four hours. These buildings were in the process of being demolished in order to make way

---

[10]Memo, Brig Gen Perry Miles, CG 16th Brigade for the Chief of Staff, June 4, 1932. Folder entitled: Rpt of Operations Against Bonus Marchers, 1932, Mil Dist of Washington, A46-458, RG 98, NA.

[11]Blakeley, "When the Army was Smeared," p. 28.

for a proposed park, and the absence of plumbing made the sanitation problem acute. The order was postponed and the threat of a showdown between the police and the BEF forestalled. On July 27 the order was reissued and eviction began on the morning of the 28th. After one building had been cleared a scuffle between the police and some of the bonus marchers ensued and one of the latter was killed by police gun fire. News of the scuffle brought additional bonus marchers to the scene, and early in the afternoon the District Commissioners reported to Hoover that the situation was out of control.[12]

This development was followed by Hoover ordering the Regular Army to disperse the bonus marchers and presumably evict them from Washington. At 2:55 P.M. on the afternoon of July 28, the Secretary of War issued the following order to MacArthur:

> The President has just informed me that the civil government of the District of Columbia has reported to him that it is unable to maintain law and order in the District.
>
> You will have United States troops proceed immediately to the scene of disorder. Cooperate fully with the District of Columbia police force which is now in charge. Surround the affected area

---

[12]William C. White and W.W. Waters, BEF The Whole Story of the Bonus March (John Day Company: New York, 1933), pp. 175-220.
Waters claims that he was "commander" of the BEF. His account of the incident is critical toward the Hoover Administration for its efforts to force the situation after Congress adjourned and evict the bonus marchers from Washington so that it would be relieved of a political liability during the presidential campaign. Waters exonerates MacArthur and the Army but claims that the situation was never out of hand and that the Army need not have been called out to evict the BEF. For a judicious and excellent account of the incident see: Bennett M. Rich, Presidents and Civil Disorders (Brookings Institute: Washington, 1941), pp. 150 - 177.

and clear it without delay.

Turn over all prisoners to the civil authorities.

In your orders insist that any women and children who may be in the affected area be accorded every consideration and kindness. Use all humanity consistent with due execution of this order.[13]

The 16th Brigade, numbering about 600 troops from the 3rd Cavalry, 1st Tank Regiment, and the 12th Infantry Regiment were alerted at 1:40 P.M. to assemble at the Ellipse on the afternoon of the 28th. The discrepancy in the time factor between the alert at 1:40 P.M. and the order from Hurley, more than an hour later, is explained by the fact that Hoover requested the District Commissioners to inform him in writing that the situation was out of hand before orders were actually given to use Regular troops. At 3:50 P.M. General Perry Miles reported to MacArthur for orders at the Old State-War-Navy-Building at the corner of 17th Street and Pennsylvania Avenue. MacArthur showed Miles the order from Hurley, and informed him also that as Chief of Staff he would accompany the Army, "not with a view of commanding the troops but to be on hand as things progressed, so that he could issue necessary instructions on the ground." At 4:10 P.M. General Miles issued his field order at the Ellipse giving his subordinate commanders instruction for the move against the bonus marchers. At 4:30 P.M. the advance to the "affected area" began. This area consisted of portions of Pennsylvania Avenue between the Capitol and the main part of the

[13]Ltr, Hurley to MacArthur, July 28, 1932. AG 240 Bonus (5-28-32) Section 1, RG 94, NA.

Washington business district. The main BEF camp was located east of the Capitol across the Anacostia River.[14]

According to one officer who participated in the dramatic advance up Pennsylvania Avenue on that warm summer afternoon in 1932 the "affected area" below the Capitol was

> a fantastic mixture of rioters, spectators, shoppers, streetcars, baby carriages, police, infantry, and officers from the War and Navy Department in civilian clothes.
>
> The rioters, well-supplied with bricks and hunks of concrete also had considerable shelter in the partly dismantled buildings. An infantry squad with fixed bayonets quickly pushed its way into the building where the police had been resisted most successfully, ignored the rioters and went at the double up the stairs to the roof.... The cavalry, operating with drawn sabers, largely to keep the rioters from grabbing at bridles, cleared the avenue, and the long job of pushing the rioters out of the center of Washington and across the Anacostia River began.
>
> Initially, there was considerable resistence and the troops had several casualties from rock showers. The task was made more difficult by the necessity of halting before advancing to give time to innocent spectators to get out of the way. This, unfortunately, also gave the rioters time to reorganize and to get more bricks, and also time to try to get around the flanks of the troops and infiltrate with the general public back toward Pennsylvania Avenue.[15]

By 8:00 P.M. the "affected area" along Pennsylvania Avenue had been cleared and the bonus marchers had been pushed out of the center of Washington to their encampment across the Anacostia River, and the first phase of the incident had ended. At 9:00 P.M. the

---

[14]Ltr, General Miles CG 16th Brigade to Chief of Staff, sub: Rpt of Operations against the Bonus Marchers, August 4, 1932. This letter consisted of Miles' post-action report of the operation. Folder entitled: Rpt of Operations against Bonus Marchers, 1932. Mil Dist of Washington, A46-485, RG 98. Hereinafter cited as Rpt of Operations 16th Brig.

[15]Blakeley, "When the Army was Smeared," p. 29.

16th Brigade was ordered to proceed to the Anacostia Flats, the area of the BEF bivouac, and evacuate all bonus marchers from the area. Hurley's original order to MacArthur did not indicate exactly what the Army was to do after the "affected area" near the Capitol was cleared, and it appears that MacArthur gave the order to clear the Anacostia camp area at the direction of the President. According to one student of the incident it is "inconceivable that any troop movements were carried out contrary to his [Hoover's] express command."[16] The movement of the Army into Anacostia to disperse the BEF camp was one event that was most severely criticized. Hoover's critics considered that to drive the bonus people out of their only place of shelter during the night was a rather harsh measure. However, the President's decision was probably based on the realization that had the BEF been given time to organize their forces, a much more serious situation might have developed. Any appraisal of Hoover's action must take into consideration the fact that for eight weeks the city's inhabitants had been annoyed by the presence of thousands of bonus marchers.[17]

Anacostia Flats lies some two miles or so southeast of the Capitol. Here on low ground along the east bank of the river the BEF had erected its makeshift camp. Crossing the Anacostia River bridge at 11th Street the Infantry formed a line for "direct pressure" southward through the general camp area with Cavalry units

---

[16]Bennett M. Rich, The Presidents and Civil Disorders (Brookings Institute: Washington, 1941), p. 175.

[17]*Ibid.*, pp. 175-76.

covering the left flank, the right flank being covered by the river. General Miles reported the following vivid, if not too clear, account of the ensuing operation.

> The occupants of the Bonus Marchers' camp were allowed until 11:15 P.M. to remove their property and evacuate. At 11:15 P.M. the Infantry began its movement.... The movement forward was assisted by searchlights furnished by a fire truck provided by the Metropolitan Police Department. Little resistance was met in the camp except on the part of individuals, most of whom were intoxicated. When the (Infantry) Battalion reached the heights South of the camp, the right flank company was greeted with a shower of rocks. Companies K and I moved up the escarpment to the railroad track and drove the mob to the Northeast, using gas ....
>
> While this was going on the mob which had been driven off the property just south of the flats had foregathered with a crowd estimated at about 2,000 which had formed along the south edge of the flats. About this time a large part of the mob started a movement toward the Southeast part of the burning camp apparently with a view of flanking the troops.... Colonel Kunzig had also noticed the movement of the mob and had "Assembly" blown on the bugle. The Battalion reformed and the mob fell back into Anacostia. At 2:00 A.M. the troops bivouaced.

The next morning cavalry reconnaissance determined that the BEF had evacuated the Anacostia Flats area, and at noon the Army was ordered to return to Washington and evict remaining bonus marchers from areas of Southwest Washington. During July 29, success in disbursing the BEF and the "steady exodus" of the bonus people from all camps in Washington proper indicated that the Army could be returned to their regular posts during the evening. MacArthur announced that he intended to "relieve all troops by night."[18]

---

[18]Rpt of Operations, 16th Brigade.

The final report of the incident by the infantry regiment commander noted that the use of tear gas and the resulting surprise, along with a lack of leadership in the BEF, insured success for the Army. This officer noted that after the initial action by the troops there was a "barrage of profanity, the throwing of missiles and the return of tear gas grenades." He commented that many spectators joined with the bonus marchers in using "insulting language toward the troops," and that some of the BEF tried to fraternize with the regulars and get them to disregard their orders. Analyzing the participation of the troops in this sensitive duty, the officer reported:

> The troops met this duty with forebearance and restraint and throughout the operations remained calm and collected notwithstanding the resistance and insulting remarks of both Bonus Marchers and spectators. They used tactful force and were intent on accomplishing their mission effectively and satisfactorily.[19]

The report of the officer who commanded the cavalry units that participated in the incident went into greater detail. According to his report:

> Prior to the distrubance the officers, men and animals were put through a thorough course of training in anticipation of their being called upon for Riot Duty against the B. E. F. The attitude of all therefore was well defined and general. As far as this command was concerned it was purely impersonal. All took the attitude that the duty was just another job although a difficult one requiring unusual control. At no time was any sympathy shown to the Bonus Marchers.

---

[19]Ltr, CO 12th Inf Regt to CG 16th Brigade, Washington, D. C. August 6, 1932. Folder entitled: Rpt of Operations against Bonus Marchers, 1932, Mil Dist of Washington, A46-485, RG 98, NA.

It was reported that up to the time the bonus marchers showed active resistance the cavalry troopers displayed no resentment. Upon receiving the rock showers of the BEF the troops became antagonistic:

> During this fight they (the Cavalry troops) became thoroughly angry but were easily restrained after each trotting charge. The punishment and casualties received were taken as a matter of course. On the second day the general attitude was more antagonistic and the men would undoubtedly have used their permitted weapons more severely if resistance had been encountered.

Success in putting down the riotous bonus people, according to this officer, was "due to the serious intention of the regulars to handle the situation" and this led to the conviction among the BEF that it was "hopeless to oppose the regular troops...." At the same time various spectators and others obtained a "lasting lesson in the effectiveness of regular troops during disorders."

In addition, the opportunity to point out the value of mounted troops in this sort of civil disturbance was not missed. According to the report, the horse, non-toxic gas, and the saber were more effective than the rifle and the bayonet in civil disturbances, because the time interval during contact, before the latter are used as a deadly weapon, was considerably shorter compared to cavalry weapons. The report emphasized:

> Undisciplined people on foot will not withstand the advance of the mounted man and they are universally afraid of being trampled by the horse. The saber was a great aid as a punishing power. The flat of the saber was used plentifully and the point some--mainly in threatening those showing an inclination to turn during retreat.

The report concluded by urging that the Army give more publicity to its operations against the BEF on July 28-29 so that a

> conviction in the general mind that it will act relentlessly and will use at once any amount of force necessary to destroy resistance will result in its mere presence being sufficient to end many disorders.[20]

The result of this unique affair had an unfortunate effect on the Army: the use of Regular troops against unarmed civilians from a public relations point of view was a disaster. The "liberal reform" element in American political tradition, intrinsically distrustful of the professional military class, considered this display of force by the Regular Army vivid evidence of the danger of "militarism." Certainly the incident played directly into the hands of the anti-militarist and pacificist groups throughout the country.

MacArthur associated himself with an extremely unpopular and unpleasant duty and consequently received the continuing opprobrium of liberal critics. Although he was executing an order of the Commander-in-Chief, the Chief of Staff insured for himself the relentless antagonism of his critics for directing the use of federal troops against civilians. Coming at the eve of the presidential election of 1932, the eviction of the BEF from Washington served to associate in the popular mind the Army with the Hoover Administration. To those persons throughout the country who were buffeted by economic distress and unemployment the incident seemed

---

[20]Ltr, CO 2nd Sqd, 3rd Cav Regt to the CG 16th Brigade, August 5, 1932. Folder entitled: Rpt of Operations against Bonus Marchers, 1932, A46-485, Mil Dist of Washington, RG 98, NA.

cogent evidence that the Army was on the side of the "established order" that was held responsible for the economic situation of the nation. Since the Army is an agent of the Government it is by the very nature of things on the side of the established order.

If, as it has been alleged, the entire affair was the work of communist conspirators, who sought to defame and besmirch the Army in the mind of the public, their work was only too successful.[21] Regardless of the fact that the troops did not use unnecessary force and did not fire a shot, nor inflict a serious casualty, in general public opinion the Army has always been reproached and ridiculed for the eviction of the BEF from Washington in the summer of 1932.

One particular criticism of its role in the bonus episode touched the Army in a most sensitive spot. This criticism was that the Army had prepared special plans and instructions in respect to handling the bonus marchers, and thus had forced the President's hand. In a sense knowledge that the Army was prepared for any eventuality and capable of evicting the bonus people, thus relieving the Hoover Administration of a most distasteful liability, may have made it easier for the District Commissioners and President Hoover to solve their dilemma. But the Army believed that in preparing for a civil disturbance it was not forming policy, and that the formation of plans and preparations for handling riots was dictated by prudence and sound military procedure. One protest from the American Civil Liberties Union to President Hoover contained the

---

[21]Blakeley, "When the Army was Smeared," p. 26.

above criticism. MacArthur was indignant over the implication that he conspired to use force against the BEF, and denied that he had issued any special instructions for handling domestic riots. Smarting against criticism of the Army's general planning policy the Chief of Staff informed Hoover to ignore the charges of the ACLU:

> Absolutely no instructions have been issued from the War Department at any time during my incumbency of the office of Chief of Staff dealing with any riot troubles or disturbances, and any effort to show any activities along those lines due to the depression are simply fabrications.

MacArthur advised the White House to dismiss these charges and in particular the scorn of the ACLU:

> They have made frequent attacks upon the Army in every possible way. Their basic purpose, of course, is the destruction of all constituted authority. The War Department has long since made it a policy not to answer any of the communications that it receives from such a source.[22]

---

[22]Ltr, Chief of Staff to Lawrence Richey, Secretary to the President, August 12, 1932. AG 240 Bonus (5-28-32) Section 3, RG 94, NA.

CHAPTER VIII

THE DEPRESSION AND MOBILIZATION PLANS

While pressure on the Army from its congressional critics continued unabated throughout 1932 the General Staff, concerned over the need for re-evaluating its plans and programs under the impact of the depression budget, made significant moves to counteract the charges that it was not keeping up with the times. MacArthur had denied these charges and had affirmed the fact that no significant increase in the materiel condition of the Army was possible without an increase in the military budget. Nevertheless, the Chief of Staff in the fall of 1932 laid out plans for improvement by ordering strict allocation of priorities in research and development (R&D), and rearmament and re-equipment (R&R).

A directive issued by the Secretary of War on September 16, 1932, initiated a reorganization of the Army's materiel plans. The Secretary of War in his directive noted that the "non-availability of funds" had caused the amendment or cancellation of some thirty-four projects for procurement and supply, including the ten-year rearmament program for antiaircraft artillery, tractor replacement, the mechanized cavalry regiment, the 75mm howitzer, the seven-year motor vehicle replacement program, the 81mm mortar, the 37mm anti-tank gun, augmentation of the war reserves, the 4.2 inch chemical mortar, and the semi-automatic rifle. He concluded:

In view of the probability of greatly reduced War Department appropriations for the fiscal year 1934 and succeeding years in the near future, it becomes advisable to examine, restate, and bring up to date the various War Department projects in order to determine the advisable priority of the projects in hand.[1]

Thus, all the supply arms and services were directed to submit, prior to December 20, 1932, recommendations pertaining to all materiel programs under the following three main categories: research and development, rearmament and re-equipment, and augmentation and preservation of the war reserve. The branches were also informed that the projects were to be provided for in six increments spanning the fiscal years 1935-1940. Definitely the General Staff was not planning to ask the Budget Bureau or Congress for increased funds to finance its Six-Year Program, and it was Army policy that the amounts made available for each arm or service for fiscal 1934 would be considered the limiting figure for successive years. Each branch was informed that projects would be classified into one of four categories, in order of priority, and the total cost of each project in each of the four orders of priority would be approximately one-fourth of the grand total set forth in the budget estimate for 1934 for each branch.[2]

A study of the Six-Year Program indicates the influence of the depression on its conception. Caught in the pressure for a limited

---

[1] Memo, AC/S G-4 to Adjutant General, September 16, 1932. AG 111, RG 94, NA.

[2] Memo, AC/S G-4 to AG, September 16, 1932. AG 111, RG 94, NA.

budget, the Army was forced to curtail all its materiel programs both for research and development and for rearmament and procurement of new equipment. The Six-Year Program was an extremely modest plan based on the realization that additional funds would not be forthcoming. The extreme modesty of the program can be seen better in a close analysis of the reply of the Ordnance Department to the General Staff Directive. In submitting his detailed plans, the Chief of Ordnance emphasized that it was difficult to put the projects into any priority because each of the projects was of the same importance in its respective field or area, and that all items should be considered of first priority. In the field of R&R the Ordnance chief listed the following estimated funds needed to carry out the Six-Year Program:

1935 - $1,506,000 1938 - $1,480,000
1936 - $1,498,000 1939 - $1,416,000
1937 - $1,362,000 , 1940 - $1,433,000

Sizeable amounts of these figures covered the annual purchase of the semi-automatic rifle, combat cars, and artillery howitzers. The report included $250,000 for tank procurement, but only beginning in the year 1937. According to the Chief of Ordnance, this deferment had drawn the ire of the Chief of Infantry who refused to approve such a lag and urged that tank procurement begin in 1935. For the augmentation and preservation of the War Reserve the Chief of Ordnance listed the following breakdown:

1935 - $1,826,000	1938 - $2,100,000
1936 - $2,050,000	1939 - $2,135,000
1937 - $2,091,000	1940 - $2,150,000

The above figures were for the modernization and augmentation of the war reserve equipment and ammunition, and included the modernization of the 75mm gun, 155mm howitzer, and the 155mm gun that the Army had in storage, and also included the replacement and preservation of ammunition. The last category of materiel to be included in the Six-Year Program was R&D. The Ordnance Department listed its estimates for this category as:

1935 - $1,310,000	1938 - $1,310,000
1936 - $1,310,000	1939 - $1,310,000
1937 - $1,305,000	1940 - $1,305,000

Included in this estimate for R&D for the Six-Year Program were the following items: mobile artillery, artillery fire control, metallurgical, optical and acoustical research, and substitutes for strategic and critical materials. Also included each year were funds for the development of mechanized and armored equipment, bombs, grenades, artillery ammunition, and chemical warfare.[3]

According to the Chief of Ordnance, the execution of the Six-Year Program would result at the end of fiscal 1940 in the completion of the mechanization of one regiment of cavalry, and the equipment of the 1st Cavalry Division with standard armored cars, the equipment of active units of the Regular Army artillery with high-speed

[3] Ltr, Executive Officer of the Ordnance Department for the Chief of Ordnance to the Adjutant General, December 20, 1932. AG 111, RG 94, NA.

modernized equipment, and the equipment of active Regular Army antiaircraft units with standard equipment including fire control instruments, and the initiation of the equipping of the infantry with standard tanks, semi-automatic rifles, anti-tank guns, and 81mm mortars.[4]

The moderate spending program proposed by the Army, and its limited goals and aims, reflected the effect of budgetary pressure on the Army in materiel planning. Under the constant reminder that funds were extremely limited and that little relief was in sight throughout the coming years, Army plans for equipment purchasing for the years up to 1940 reflected the economic situation of the fall of 1932. Because of the fact that plans for purchases in 1940 had to be outlined in 1932, the equipment that the Army would have in its hands in the late 1930's was the product of the budgetary demands of 1932. The "time lag" -- the time interval between original purchase plans for a weapon and the time it becomes actual organizational equipment in the hands of the troops -- was extremely long during a time of economic stringency. Because of the fact that expenditures for a certain type of equipment were amortized over a number of years, in order to defer expenditures and keep spending at a minimum, the possibility was increased that when the equipment was finally in the hands of the troops it would be obsolete. It should be noted that the estimates were generally

---

[4] Memo, AC/S G-4 AOD AG, February 27, 1933. AG 111, RG 94, NA.

balanced between R&D, procurement, and augmentation of the war reserves, with augmentation of the war reserves being given slightly more funds.

Nevertheless, the Army felt: "its best interests demand that projects under R&D, under R&R and under Augmentation, Preservation and Replacement of the War Reserve be continued in a well-planned and judicious manner so as to secure from the limited funds the most benefit to the Army as a whole."[5]

One "built in" effect of the Six-Year Program that was perhaps inescapable was that it led to a competition between R&D and procurement among Army planners. Hurley had earlier in 1930 laid down his requisites for R&D, but in his coordinated program initiated in the fall of 1932, he failed to draw the clear distinction between R&D and procurement. Most of the ordnance equipment with which the Army entered World War II, such as artillery, mortars, anti-tank guns, and the semi-automatic rifle, were outlined in the Six-Year Program for procurement and not included in any special R&D program. Under budgetary pressure the Army planners naturally preferred to see some modern equipment in the hands of the troops rather than have money spent on continual R&D efforts. Except in the case of tanks and mechanized artillery, basic infantry ordnance equipment that was in the hands of the Army in 1941 was outlined for purchase as a result of the Six-Year Program in 1932.[6]

---

[5] Memo, AC/S G-4 to AG, September 14, 1932. AG 111, RG 94, NA.

[6] Constance Green, Harry C. Thomson, and Peter C. Roots, "The

With the materiel problems of the Army coming under re-evaluation and revised planning by the General Staff in the fall of 1932 because of the depression and the budgetary consequences of federal economy, manpower problems likewise came up for serious reconsideration by the Chief of Staff and his assistants. In reviewing existing manpower mobilization plans, the Chief of Staff was concerned over the fact that in the event of an emergency there would be no centralized control over an expeditionary force or field force by the Chief of Staff. MacArthur was alarmed over the fact that the military establishment was unable to become an emergency force which would weld existing units into an integrated machine capable of instantaneous response to the orders of the Commander-in-Chief. Furthermore, the Army during every past emergency was split up and the War Department and the General Staff in Washington had never been linked with the fighting elements and had been compelled to relinquish to one or more independent field commands the control of operations, while back in Washington the Department was overwhelmed with matters relating to organization, command, administration, and supply. The study of this problem led to the promulgating of the "Four Army" plan by MacArthur, which named the Chief of Staff as the Commanding General of the Field

---

Technical Services - The Ordnance Department: Planning Munitions for War," UNITED STATES ARMY IN WORLD WAR II (Washington: GPO, 1955), Chap. VII, "Research and Development 1919-40," pp. 169 -215.

Forces in time of emergency.[7]

---

[7] AR 10-15, November 25, 1921 Changed as follows: 1. Chief of Staff; duties. a. General. The Chief of Staff is the immediate advisor of the Secretary of War on all matters relating to the military establishment and is charged by the Secretary of War with the planning, development, and execution of the military program. He will cause the WDGS to prepare the necessary plans for the recruiting, mobilizing, organizing, supplying, equipping, and training the Army of the United States for use in the national defense. As the agent, and in the name of the Secretary of War, he issues such orders as will insure that the plans of the War Department are harmoniously executed by all branches and agencies of the military establishment and that the military program is carried out speedily and efficiently.

b. As Commanding General of the Field Forces. The Chief of Staff, in addition to his duties as such, is in peace and war, by direction of the President, the Commanding General of the Field Forces and in that capacity directs the field operation and the general training of the several armies, of the overseas forces, and of the GHQ units. In field operations, General Headquarters for the field forces will be established as best meets requirements. AR 1015 change was effective July 18, 1933. AG 320.2, RG 94, NA. Note: President Roosevelt was not pleased with this move by General MacArthur, and in 1936 after MacArthur was in the Philippines moved to have the regulation changed because he was emphatic that he believed that the Commander-in-Chief had the prerogative to choose his own general to command the field forces. One story that made the rounds of the War Department during the 1930's was that soon after the announcement in 1933 that the Chief of Staff would be the Commanding General of the Field Forces, both in peace and war, President Roosevelt joshed MacArthur about it one day in the White House by saying: "I don't approve of that title, Mac, but I suppose it's all right for you to have it temporarily. But just as soon as you're gone, I'm going to abolish it." Cater Files, "Interview Notes," OCMH.

MacArthur's successor, General Malin Craig, changed the old plan to have the Chief of Staff be Commanding General of the Field Forces in the spring of 1936. Graig informed the White House, in reference to the President's comment that it was undesirable to impose upon the Chief of Staff the function of Commander of the Field Force, that he was changing War Department policy. His memorandum to the White House is particularly interesting: "In the event of an emergency so serious as to warrant the establishment of a General Headquarters to command the forces in the field, the President in consultation with his military advisors will undoubtedly

Complementing radical changes in organization, the Chief of Staff also planned sweeping manpower mobilization changes. According to MacArthur, the most probable future conflict in which the United States would become involved would not require mobilization of a preponderant portion of the nation's resources:

Any World War would probably be a gradual growth, and in its initial stages, as would lesser ones, place a premium upon promptitude and expedition. Under general economic conditions, such as those prevailing, it is certain that applications for enlistment would be received promptly and in great number and in many situations would satisfy completely the manpower requirements of the Army.[8]

MacArthur, therefore, planned a three-stage mobilization effort: an initial mobilization of some one million men, a subsequent mobilization of around two million men, and a final total mobilization. According to MacArthur, the initial mobilization would include all active Regular Army units and National Guard units, and in addition, would include various inactive units which were

---

wish to make a personal selection of the officer to command the field forces, as did Mr. Wilson, when he selected General Pershing for command of the American Expeditionary Forces. He may wish to designate for the field forces the officer who at the time is Chief of Staff. If so, another Chief of Staff for the War Department should be designated, and the President will probably wish to make a personal selection in this case also.... It is my purpose to rescind such regulations as are incompatible with the foregoing ideas, and to instruct and train the General Staff accordingly." Memo, Craig for Col Edward P. Watson, Military Aide to the President, April 17, 1936. Penciled note indicates memo handed to Col Watson by the Secretary of the General Staff the afternoon of the same day. AG 320.2 (8-6-32) (I) Section 1-b, RG 94, NA.

[8] Ltr, Chief of Staff to the CG of the Field Armies, October 22, 1932. AG 320.2, RG 94, NA.

considered an essential part of the Four Army organization. The planned rate of procurement of personnel during the initial mobilization would be limited only by the exhaustion of voluntary enlistment, and would be completed by M-day plus 60, or two months after mobilization. According to the Chief of Staff, total mobilization would include the orderly mobilization of manpower and material resources of the country, and would include conscription or selective service of manpower; under a situation calling for total mobilization it was assumed that Congress would be ready with a selective service act to be in operation by a month and a half after the beginning of mobilization. The initial mobilization was planned so that the Army could be ready for an immediate effort and the emphasis was laid on voluntary enlistment.[9]

MacArthur believed that the manpower needs of the subsequent mobilization expansion, approximately two million men, could be met by the unemployed of the nation. He was enthusiastic about his Four Army plan, and thought that with effective peacetime preparation each of the field armies could be able to engage its advanced echelons in active operations almost immediately, and reach a satisfactory war footing as regards personnel and organization within six to eight weeks. Moreover, the Chief of Staff was pleased over the fact that such a mobilization could proceed with a minimum of detailed legislative authorization, and that

---

[9] Directive for the Four Army Organization, Chief of Staff to CG Armies and Corps Areas, February 6, 1933. AG 320.2, RG 94, NA.

scarcely anything was required beyond a general congressional directive authorizing the President to announce mobilization.[10]

It is definitely apparent that the depression and the resulting unemployment influenced the Chief of Staff in his plans for an initial mobilization force which could be put quickly into operations within six to eight weeks. Undoubtedly he considered the fact that during the period preceding mobilization the increase of international tensions would have brought about some increase in enlistments, thus serving to fill the ranks of the skeletonized initial mobilization force. According to MacArthur, the fallacious concept in mobilization planning had been the insistence on mobilizing a large mass army which could only be organized slowly. The Chief of Staff insisted on a moderate-sized force at the immediate outbreak of hostilities, and believed that future conflicts might not require the mobilization of preponderant resources. His plan was for the mobilization of a force in being which would have as its nucleus the Regular Army and the National Guard.

Of considerable importance in a study of MacArthur's mobilization plan is the role that he gave to volunteer enlistment in the period before enactment and implementation of selective service legislation. Influenced by the unemployment situation throughout the country, the Chief of Staff drew up his mobilization plans and gave an important role to the idea that volunteer

---

[10] Ltr, Chief of Staff to CG of Field Armies, October 22, 1932. AG 320.2, RG 94, NA.

enlistment would be the keystone for supplying the manpower needed during initial mobilization:

> The unused manpower which was stagnating the country, due to the severe economic depression then current, could in the event of a national emergency, be recruited in sufficient numbers to fill up the troop units in being and also the new units necessary to supplement those forces in the initial striking force.[11]

MacArthur's 1933 mobilization plan, which provided for the mobilization of the manpower of the country as might be necessary, was intended to cover all possible mobilizations and emphasized to a greater degree than any previous or subsequent plans the employment of intensive volunteer recruiting.

The 1933 mobilization plan has been criticized for its "unrealistic" attitude toward equipment procurement. It has been charged that it was the "unfortunate belief," not only in Congress, but in some echelons of the General Staff, that providing equipment for the initial mobilization force was no great problem because this equipment was already in the stocks of the war reserve. The General Staff and Congress are scored for the failure to realize that technology had made considerable strides since World War I and the war reserve was no longer useable.[12]

First of all, it is important in discussing this criticism of the 1933 mobilization plan to exonerate Congress. No group was more vociferous in its efforts to improve the materiel situation

---

[11] Kreidberg, History of Military Mobilization, p. 425.

[12] *Ibid.*, pp. 447-48.

of the Army than Collins and his coterie of followers in the House of Representatives. True enough, words are not actions; but congressional critics were basically unable to take action in relation to the technical aspects of military policy and affairs; furthermore, they were technically ill-equipped to determine which weapons should be developed, and deferred to the final judgment of the Army that the war reserve was adequate for "essential" armaments.

In so far as the General Staff was concerned, the basis of all doctrine and planning was the belief that man, and not weapons, was the supreme arbiter on the battlefield; therefore, it was to receive priority in the expenditure of the limited funds. The Six-Year armament plan of 1932 was a balanced program to cover current procurement, R&D, and war reserve augmentation. Budgetary pressure, coming from the White House as well as Congress, precluded the possibility of large-scale weapons development and at the same time maintain the efficiency of manpower training. The policy was one of moderation and balance in spending. None was more cognizant of the fact that obsolescence had seriously depleted the value of the war reserve than the General Staff, but it was felt that with limited funds available no one facet of the military problem, except personnel, should be favored over any other.

The General Staff itself was not too pleased with the soundness of the Four-Army Plan and the Initial Mobilization Plan that had been formulated. Strenuous doubts and concern over the "glaring" deficiencies of the plan caused the Assistant Chief of Staff of the War Plans Division (WPD) to advise MacArthur that in his opinion initial mobilization could not put into the field immediately a force capable of maneuvering operationally because of the fact that the peacetime organization of units, the organization under which units were presently set up, did not permit a sustained offensive. Furthermore, War Plans Division (WPD) pointed out that shortages in equipment, not particularly obsolescence, existed and called for a program of production considerably in excess of current appropriations if the minimum requirements of initial mobilization were to be met. According to WPD, these items of equipment consisted of motor equipment for the field artillery, and antiaircraft artillery.

WPD recommended that the Initial Mobilization Plan be broken down into three phases: the first phase would consist of an immediate effort upon the outbreak of hostilities by the Regular Army divisions of each army, and those National Guard divisions best prepared for active combat duty; the second phase would consist of balancing the forces in the field and reinforcing the additional National Guard divisions; and the third phase would consist of reinforcing the active units with inactive units, and bringing the entire force to war strength and properly balancing all units of the four armies. Concerned over the alarming shortage of personnel in the Regular Army, WPD advised MacArthur that if the existing enlisted strength of the Regular Army were raised to 165,000 men, the personnel requirements of initial mobilization would be considerably alleviated.

WPD concluded its recommendations by urging that the Chief of Staff inform the President, the Secretary of War, and Congress exactly how the reduced strength of the Regular Army affected the readiness of the nation to take effective and immediate action in an emergency, and that the Army needed an enlisted strength of 165,000 men if it were to meet the exigencies of mobilization. Besides informing the civilian leaders of the government of the manpower needs incumbent on mobilization plans, the Chief of Staff was also urged to make mention of two items of equipment which were in critical shortage, antiaircraft and motor equipment for the field artillery. Of the former, there were fourteen partially equipped regiments, and to equip them adequately would call for an additional expenditure of some $3,230,000. WPD was not concerned to any great extent with modernization, but was anxious over the shortage of equipment, and believed that possibly additional funds might be forthcoming if vigorous representation was made to the new Commander-in-Chief and to the new Congress.

In any event, the WPD was not optimistic over the ability of the Army, from a personnel and equipment standpoint, to meet the needs of the Initial Mobilization Plan. Admitting that it appeared hopeless to ask for a further increment in the strength of the Regular Army to meet the mobilization requirements, WPD advised that the situation could be helped by asking Congress to restore legislation providing for a Regular Army reserve corps: "It is believed that a large number of former soldiers would enroll therein for a small monthly pay -- say $2.00...." WPD suggested this alternative in order that the personnel needs of the mobilization force could be adequately met, for "with inadequate strength and no reserve it is difficult to proceed with any logical plan for organization and mobilization."[13]

Undoubtedly the Chief of Staff was well aware of the shortcomings of his mobilization plan, but accepted the fact that somehow the Army would have to "muddle through." The suggestions and recommendations of the WPD came right at the time when the Army was being brought under close scrutiny by the New Deal and funds appropriated for the Army for fiscal 1934 were being drastically reduced by executive decree. It would have been the height of unrealism to appeal to administration leaders, immersed in the demands of meeting the domestic economic and political problems, for additional funds to increase the strength and expenditures for the Army.

Furthermore, the Army was reluctant to make any move which would possibly alienate public opinion, such as a request for increased funds to meet the needs of the mobilization plans,

---

[13] Memo, AC/S WPD for the Chief of Staff, March 27, 1933. AG 320.2, RG 94, NA. The small monthly fee would serve as a much-needed stipend during the depression and would thereby encourage the ex-soldiers to enroll in the reserve corps. Apparently the reserve corps idea carried with it no plan for continuing and efficient training.

particularly at a time when the stress was on reducing expenditures. The Army believed that the public, by voting the new administration into office, had fully accepted the need for a radical reduction of federal spending, and to ask for an increase in military appropriations would likely cause an unfavorable public reaction against the Army. The General Staff was attuned to the need to dispel at every opportunity the charges of "militarism" which its critics leveled at the military establishment, and although an increase in the Regular Army was needed in order to meet the needs of initial mobilization, from a practical standpoint the Army was hesitant about laying such a proposal before the new administration leaders, who had little sympathy for the Army and its plans. The unsuccessful efforts of the Army to obtain Public Works funds for its needs will be dealt with in a later chapter.

In the spring of 1933 other General Staff divisions advised MacArthur against asking for an increase in military expenditures to cover an increase in the strength of the Regular Army so that mobilization plans could be more validly developed. G-1 informed the Chief of Staff:

> from a practical standpoint I believe that it would be entirely useless to propose any increase...at the present time. Furthermore, the adoption of such a course under present conditions, would, in my opinion, be likely to lead to an unfavorable reaction, and to remarks to the effect that the Regular Army is always crying for an increase in strength without any regard to conditions which prevail throughout the country.[14]

---

[14] Memo, AC/S G-1 for the AC/S WPD, April 12, 1933. G-1/12893-12, RG 319, NA.

Advising against presenting any study on the needs of mobilization to the White House G-1 counseled:

It is my feeling that to present this study to the President, Congress, and the Budget under prevailing circumstances would cause it to be regarded as Army propaganda which is being put out in an effort to counteract the danger of a reduction in the Regular establishment. I believe that it would not receive the consideration which its importance merits and that its transmission to these agencies at this time would do more harm than good.[15]

The War Plans Division of the General Staff believed that it was absolutely necessary to increase the enlisted strength of the Army if any sound mobilization plan were to be formulated. The study it submitted to the General Staff noted that the ideal number of Regular Army personnel to accomplish mobilization requirements was around 31,339 officers and some 450,000 enlisted men, a figure which WPD admitted was impossible of attaining under any possible peacetime conditions. Nevertheless, WPD strongly urged that if initial mobilization plans were to be workable and carried out rapidly, some means must be instituted to provide for a rapid expansion of the Regular Army at the time of mobilization. The only practical method in the view of WPD was to constitute a trained Regular Army reserve.

Given the fact that the maximum enlisted strength of the Regular Army that could be expected under existing conditions was 118,000, WPD advised that it was necessary to raise a reserve for

---

[15] Memo, AC/S G-1 for the AC/S WPD, April 20, 1933. G-1/12894-12, RG 319, NA.

this force of approximately 47,000 men, so that the basic requirement of a 165,000-man Regular Army would be available to meet the manpower needs of initial mobilization. WPD urged that:

> Congress and the Budget Officer be informed, along with the President, of the situation; not with the hope of obtaining immediate action, but so that those responsible for national defense will understand the true conditions and will take steps to initiate remedial action and an augmentation of the War Reserves when the financial situation permits.[16]

Along with this recommendation, the WPD urged the Chief of Staff to ask for congressional action to provide a Regular Army reserve which could be available immediately in an emergency to augment the small peacetime strength of the Regular Army.[17]

---

16 Memo, AC/S WPD for the Chief of Staff, April 28, 1933. WPD/3674, RG 319, NA.

17 Ibid. Note: The Enlisted Reserve Corps was an old concept for the General Staff, and had been studied by the War Department since 1926. It never was able to get any action because of the fact that it would take additional funds and thus the Army never saw its way clear in getting the Corps organized. In 1926, when the plan was raised, the Adjutant General and G-4 disapproved of the idea because it would call for an increase in appropriations with the resulting danger of further reductions in the enlisted strength of the active Regular Army. In 1927, the General Staff considered desirable a program of six years enlistment: 3 years active duty and 3 years in a reserve corps, but it was not approved because of the objection that it would increase expenditures. Whenever the program was introduced into Congress as a relief expedient in 1930 and 1931, the War Department informed Congress that such legislation was in conflict with the financial program of the President, and for these purposes it could not favor the reserve corps. In addition, the Army was not enthusiastic about a reserve corps which had the primary purpose of providing work relief and unemployment alleviation. Memo, AC/S G-3 for the AC/S WPD, April 17, 1933. G-3/31681, RG 319, NA.

MacArthur remained cool to the pleadings of the WPD that he take up the deficiencies of his mobilization plan, both materiel and personnel, with Roosevelt and his coterie in the White House. Hesitant about pushing defense policy matters into debate among the General Staff and still more reluctant to ask the new administration to give attention to the problems of the Army, he directed that the study of WPD be "held up until the present budgetary situation is cleared up."[18] Already the eager budget cutters of the infant New Deal were sharpening up their knives in keen anticipation of trimming the "excess" off Army appropriations that Congress and the Hoover Administration had earmarked for fiscal 1934.

---

18 Memo, Deputy Chief of Staff for the AC/S WPD, May 2, 1933. OCS/20696-15, RG 319, NA.

CHAPTER IX

THE LAST HOOVER BUDGET AND THE PROBLEM OF THE CIVILIAN COMPONENTS

While the problems of reorganization, modernization, and mobilization were increasing the pressure on the Army during the year 1932 because of the continuing economic depression, the mechanics and politics of formulating the military budget for fiscal 1934 brought new problems for the military planners. MacArthur's tentative directive for the military establishment for the fiscal year 1934 (drawn up early in 1932 at the time Collins and the House of Representatives were giving the military leaders many anxious moments over the budget for fiscal 1933) was as usual a limited and conservative estimate for activities planned two years hence. MacArthur advised the military establishment that, in formulating plans for 1934 and in making estimates for the military budget, the following items would be provided: welfare and contentment of the personnel, critically essential phases for the organization and mobilization of the Army, maintenance and training of all components of the Army, and the continuation of the housing and motor replacement programs and the provision of personnel and materiel to complete the five-year Air Corps program.[1]

---

[1] Memo, Chief of Staff to the AG, Subject: "Tentative Directive for War Department Program for Fiscal 1934," February 23, 1932. AG 111, RG 94, NA.

Although the Secretary of War had allocated a third of one billion dollars for fiscal 1934, the Budget Advisory Committee of the War Department approved a figure of $319,000,000 for submission to the Budget Bureau as the "minimum amount" which would provide a coordinated and well-balanced military program.[2] Undoubtedly the War Department budget planners took a realistic view of the money allocated by the Secretary of War and realized that the administration and Congress would never accept such a figure. They were planning for fiscal 1934 at the same time that Congress was voicing vigorous concern over the size of the 1933 budget! Prior to sending the War Department figure to the Budget Bureau, MacArthur wrote to the budget officer of the War Department, who was responsible for presenting the military estimates before the Budget Bureau, and outlined to this officer his views on the military estimates for 1934 and the points that he wanted stressed before the Budget Bureau. MacArthur emphasized that the estimates for 1934 contained the minimum figure necessary to provide for a coordinated and balanced program and he emphasized the pitiful condition into which the Army had sunk because of decreasing appropriations:

> Only by utilization of funds made available by the fall in commodity prices for the past several years and of World War stocks, and the deferment of essential activities and procurements, had made it possible to maintain the Army under the present greatly reduced appropriations.... Although it is the opinion of the well-informed that the level of commodity prices will be higher in 1934 these estimates are based on present prices only....

---

[2] Rpt of Budget Advisory Committee on Military Estimates FY 1934, August 11, 1932. AG 111, RG 94, NA.

Further deferment of essential activities such as the continuation of the Air Corps program, modernization of organizational equipment, maintenance and repair projects, and partial maintenance of the war reserve of ammunition, should no longer be continued. Certain requirements of statutory character, such as pay and allowances of military and civilian personnel involve increased expenditures which cannot be avoided. In view of these conditions, increased appropriations are essential to the maintenance of the present military establishment and to the minimum provisions for national defense....

The spirit of sympathetic cooperation which has characterized the attitude of the Director of the Bureau of the Budget, in giving the maximum degree of initiative and freedom of action as contemplated by law, and by executive policy is appreciated and its continuance is anticipated. Should it become necessary for any reason further to reduce the amount of the estimates, it is urged that the Secretary of War will be so advised and permitted to distribute such reduction within the estimates as his judgment dictates.[3]

It is unlikely that the Chief of Staff believed seriously that the Budget Bureau would acquiesce and concur in increased military spending, especially during an election year. Nevertheless, the Chief of Staff had politely cautioned the Budget Bureau that if any reduction was contemplated it should be in a lump sum, and the activity which would be curtailed should be determined by the War Department.

Any optimism that the Hoover Administration would increase military estimates for 1934 was harshly shattered in early September 1932, when President Hoover called on the War Department for further

---

3 Memo, Chief of Staff for the Budget Officer for the War Department, August 16, 1932, AG 111. OCS/20642-15, RG 319, NA.

reductions. Hoover informed Secretary Hurley that he was planning to push for a $500,000,000 reduction in the federal budget for fiscal 1934 below the current figures for fiscal 1933. Hoover added, undoubtedly with an eye on the coming elections: "Nothing will more contribute to economic recovery than a relief from taxation."[4] Therefore, it was necessary to reduce government spending. The Commander-in-Chief concluded his admonition to the Secretary of War by noting that he was aware that much of the government's activities were fixed by law and must be budgeted for expenditures. However, Hoover advised that in some cases these expenditures could be suspended with congressional approval, and the Secretary of War was directed to confer with the Director of the Budget and develop plans to prepare detailed recommendations to Congress to take such action.[5]

This obviously was intended by President Hoover as a move to reduce the ever-increasing amounts for pay and allowances and must have been received by the War Department with consternation and anxiety. Nothing further apparently was done in this regard by the Secretary of War, who was out on the political hustings throughout September and October, and perhaps he let the matter remain quiescent until his return after the election. In any event, no further action was taken by the Hoover Administration in this regard.

---

[4] Ltr, President Hoover to the Secretary of War, September 10, 1932. AG 111, RG 94, NA.

[5] *Ibid*.

The Hoover budget for fiscal 1934 was not forwarded by the administration to the Congress until after the election of November 1932. If the War Department was reluctant to give the Budget Bureau the co-operation that Hoover sought in decreasing statutory expenditures, the Bureau nevertheless went ahead and took unilateral action by sharply curtailing the funds available for the reserve program and the National Guard.

MacArthur, when informed of the proposed action by the Budget Bureau, in total disregard of his instructions to leave the disbursement of the reduction in the hands of the Army, immediately sought to bring political pressure to bear on the Hoover Administration. To the president of the Reserve Officers Association, Colonel Kemper Williams, MacArthur wired:

> While I am prepared to accept a cut of approximately thirty million dollars in estimates involving the Regular Army, I am unalterably opposed to cuts involving trained manpower of our civilian components and this includes a cut of approximately one million two hundred thousand for Organized Reserves. Am anxious to confer with you in regard to this matter. Keep confidential until I see you. /s/ MacArthur.[6]

A similar wire was sent to Maj. Gen. George Leach, Chief of the Militia Bureau, who was at that time visiting in St. Paul, Minnesota. MacArthur told the Chief of the National Guard that "disturbing information" from the Budget Bureau indicated a planned reduction in National Guard appropriations of some $7,300,000 below

---

[6] Tel, Chief of Staff to Colonel Kemper Williams, New Orleans, November 11, 1932. AG 111, RG 94, NA.

War Department requests, the main item of reduction being a fifty percent reduction in armory drills from 48 to 24.[7]

The Chief of Staff's efforts to eliminate the reduction from the War Department's budget failed and the Congress received the estimates from the executive department in December, and the Subcommittee on Military Appropriations began hearings after Congress convened. Hoover requested around $278,600,000 for military activities in fiscal 1934, a sharp reduction from the $305,700,000 the Army had received for fiscal 1933. The main reduction in the civilian components fell on the National Guard, which had its armory drills cut to 24, and the ROTC and CMTC were curtailed drastically.[8]

War Department spokesmen, although shaken by the action of the lame-duck Hoover Administration, were reluctant to make any explicit request for funds over the head of the Chief Executive, who had been soundly defeated at the polls in November. Secretary of War Hurley set the general tone of remarks when he noted that when the Director of the Budget spoke it was "my chief's word, and regardless of what my personal attitude is, I must and do support the Budget."[9] Hurley admitted that he had always testified before Congress that he favored maintaining the civilian components at

---

[7] Tel, Chief of Staff to Chief of the Militia Bureau, Maj Gen George P. Leach, St. Paul, Minnesota, November 11, 1932. AG 111, RG 94, NA.

[8] Army Navy Journal, December 10, 1932, p. 292.

[9] Hearings: War Department Appropriations Bill, 1934 (December 19, 1932), p. 649.

their present strength and training schedules because he considered them indispensable to the national defense; however, he stressed to the subcommittee that he wanted it perfectly clear that he had "acquiesced in the limiting figure of the Budget."[10] In Hurley's opinion it was not a question of what he wanted for the Army but what he was officially allotted by the Bureau of the Budget, and although he asked for more funds, the Bureau set a limit for him and it was his "official duty to support the Budget figure."[11]

If Representative Collins, chairman of the Subcommittee on Military Appropriations, was attempting to embarrass the relationship between the President and the Secretary of War by probing Hurley concerning his views on a reduction in the civilian components, he was unsuccessful; Hurley unequivocally made it clear that he supported Hoover's budget. Not so the case with some of the military officers who appeared before the subcommittee. In testimony before the subcommittee, The Adjutant General of the Army, Maj. Gen. Charles L. Bridges, who was responsible for the reserve estimates, admitted that although the ROTC and ORC programs had been curtailed by the Budget Bureau, as far as he knew this was not advocated by President Hoover. Bridges said that he was inclined to believe that the action of reducing the budget for training of the reserve components had "escaped the notice of the Commander-in-Chief." Bridges concluded his remarks by noting that

---

[10] *Ibid.*, p. 651.

[11] *Ibid.*, p. 653.

there were forces at work which sought to alter the plans of the War Department by decreasing the appropriations for the civilian components.[12] This was a clear implication of criticism aimed at Collins and his efforts to de-emphasize the reserve program, and it indicated an attempt on Bridges' part to shift the responsibility for budget decreases from the executive department to the legislative branch of the government. Collins sharply rebuked The Adjutant General and told him that he was incorrect in maintaining that the executive department and the President had not curtailed military spending, and that the military budget that was before Congress was the President's and the latter was "responsible for the transmission he makes to Congress."[13]

This byplay between Representative Collins and The Adjutant General, as well as Hurley's remarks, is indicative of the fact that throughout this period when the military appropriations were curtailed or stabilized the initiative generally did not come from the legislative branch but from the White House and the Bureau of the Budget. Except for the drastic cuts proposed by Representative Collins in the estimates for fiscal 1933, the pressure for economy and budget reduction came from the President and the Budget Bureau. Curiously enough it has been customary to blame Congress for the parsimonious condition of the Army throughout the depression years,

---

[12] Ibid., December 13, 1932, p. 503.

[13] Ibid., December 13, 1932, p. 504.

when it was executive policy to stabilize and curtail military expenditures in an effort to balance the federal budget. Congress viewed the action of the Budget Bureau as the voice of the President and from time to time questioned the capacity of the Bureau to pass on details of the military establishment. Both military officers and Congress tended to accept the estimates of the Bureau of the Budget. One student of military appropriations in the pre-World War II era has noted:

> The principal obstacle to the military establishment before World War II in getting all the money it sought was not in the War Department's backwardness in asking for funds but the administration's restriction on its requests and the indisposition of Congress to override them.[14]

Although this was specifically the case in the later Roosevelt years, because of the unprecedented power and the prestige of the White House, it was generally the case as well during the Hoover years

---

[14] Huzar, Purse and the Sword, p. 137. Note: In commenting on the problem of military policy and adequate defense expenditures in the missile and atomic age, a recent study made the following observations, which are no less relevant to the period under study:

"Citizens of a democracy must be tolerant of the fact that political parties are intensely dedicated to the winning of elections, and that it is bad electoral form to scare people about anything but the political opposition. It is difficult in a democracy to raise taxes, and ours are already pretty high. Nevertheless, it is in matters of military expenditure and foreign relations that the American people are most given to following the cues of the national administration. These are the areas in which almost any president has his greatest potential for leadership. People are usually aware how ignorant they are in these fields, and if there is one thing they devoutly wish it is a reasonably safe future for themselves and their children." Bernard Brodie, Strategy in the Missile Age (Princeton: Princeton University Press, 1959), p. 377.

because Congress was reluctant to oppose the administration's constant admonition for economy in government spending.

Action by the Hoover Administration in curtailing the reserve program, particularly the CMTC and ROTC, undoubtedly did cause some consternation and bewilderment in the General Staff, especially when less than a year before Hoover reportedly was prepared to veto any appropriations bill in which Congress would decrease personnel including the reserve components. Furthermore, during the winter and spring of 1932, Secretary Hurley was a tireless battler in the cause of preserving the reserve components from the economy moves of the House of Representatives.

The CMTC was a much maligned facet of the War Department and the first to come under the scrutiny of critics of the military establishment. The War Department admitted that the prime purpose of the CMTC was not to augment the Officers Reserve Corps, as was the ROTC, but that it had the function of offering military training to interested volunteers. In the view of the War Department the CMTC was a compromise between the proponents and opponents of compulsory military training, and served to make military training available to those youths who qualified and who volunteered. The National Defense Act authorized the Secretary of War to establish the CMTC, and to offer military training with no obligations upon the trainee for future military service. However, as the War Department felt that a lad who successfully completed four CMTC summer camps qualified for a commission, it was decided by the

General Staff to use the CMTC as a secondary source of supply for the Officers Reserve Corps, and the National Defense Act authorized their appointment as such.

With the advent of the depression and the accompanying need to economize, it was only natural that War Department critics and government economizers should look to the CMTC as one activity that could easily be eliminated from the military program without too great a damage to national defense. As discussed in an earlier chapter, there were many varied views about the CMTC program within the Army, but the General Staff, reluctant to see any of its activities curtailed, and afraid that once an activity was dropped it would be difficult -- indeed impossible -- to get it reactivated, stoutly defended the CMTC from elimination.

The General Staff claimed that the camps were extremely popular, and that the CMTC played an important role in the development of citizenship and in the moral training of youth. In addition it was claimed that during a time of depression and unemployment the CMTC served as an important source of public relief funds. In addition, the Army believed that

> because of the age and type of boy attending these camps, it is thought that the CMTC movement reaches the homes generally throughout the country more than any other War Department activity.[15]

---

[15] Memo, AG to the Budget Officer for the War Department, May 6, 1932. AG 111, RG 94, NA. Note: Section 47d of the National Defense Act of 1920 authorized the Citizen's Military Training Camps. Although the primary purpose of these camps was the instruction and training of selected civilians with a view to their appointment as

Obviously the General Staff considered the CMTC a most valuable public relations or publicity vehicle in putting the War Department and its program across to the American people, and thought it should not be sacrificed if at all possible.

Congressional criticism of the reserve program also included

Reserve Officers or non-commissioned officers, an additional purpose was to bring together young men of varied social position from all sections of the country on a basis of equality, and, under favorable conditions of outdoor life, to stimulate good citizenship by fulfilling a national obligation while at the same time improving their physical well-being through a well-rounded athletic and military training system. The young men received instruction in the elementary duties of a soldier, in the civic responsibilities of citizenship, in hygiene and physical training, and in practical leadership and character building. The idea for the CMTC emanated from the Military Training Camps Association. The responsibility for recruiting young men for the camps was assumed by this association, which established a branch in each corps area and each state under a Civilian Aide to the Secretary of War, with representatives in counties.

The first camp of this type was conducted in 1921 along the lines of the earlier "Plattsburg Plan" camps. From 1921 to 1924 inclusive, 160,391 applications from youths were received for enrollment in these camps. However, the training of but 90,624 of the applicants was practicable. By June 30, 1925, over 52,000 applications had been received in the various corps areas for camps to be held during the summer of 1925. Eleven additional posts were utilized to make a total of 40 camps. This resulted in reducing mileage costs and served partially to offset the gradual yearly increase in the per capita costs. The number of posts at which training was conducted was increased to 50 by the summer of 1926, including posts in all 9 of the corps areas and one camp in Puerto Rico. By the summer of 1928, 35,600 youths were enrolled in 52 CMTC camps from a total of 57,868 applicants.

In 1933 Congress reduced the CMTC appropriations to $1 million, less than one-half the sum granted the previous year. Necessarily, the quotas were cut to 17,536. In 1934 and 1935 the number that could be trained fell to about 16,500; however, the appropriation for 1935 permitted 31,362 to attend the camps during the summer of 1936. The camps continued through the summer of 1941, but were suspended when World War II came. To date, they have not been revived. The Army Almanac (Washington: 1950), p. 327.

the ROTC. The War Department strove mightily to defend the program as essential and necessary to national defense. Interestingly enough, MacArthur's mobilization plan for 1933 did not include any reserve units in the initial mobilization force that would be available for immediate action in the case of an emergency.[16] Provision for augmenting this initial mobilization force implied that the Organized Reserve Corps could be trained during the emergency and be brought up to a state of combat readiness. The fact that Organized Reserve units were not included in the Chief of Staff's mobilization led some observers to believe that regardless of the many protestations throughout the years by the General Staff that the ROTC was vital to a strong national defense, the Army was not convinced that ROTC products were of immediate practical use in time of an emergency. It has been charged that the general indifference of the War Department to the ROTC program, and the reserve program, was reflected in the fact that the Initial Mobilization Plan of 1932 eliminated Organized Reserve units from mobilization.[17]

MacArthur was advised against eliminating any reserve units from his 1932 mobilization plan, although as a matter of fact reserve units, which were required for initial mobilization, were

---

[16] Memo, AC/S G-3 for the Chief of Staff, February 18, 1933. AG 320.2, RG 94, NA.

[17] Gene M. Lyons and John W. Masland, Education and Military Leadership, A Study of the ROTC Program (Princeton: Princeton University Press, 1959), pp. 45-52.

discontinued as such but constituted as inactive units of the Regular Army. The Chief of Staff was warned that his action would bring a "storm of criticism" and, besides being contrary to the National Defense Act, would be harmful to the entire reserve program:

> By transforming existing Organized Reserve units to inactive Regular Army units, the plan abolishes the Organized Reserves in peace and should certainly suit some of the recent proposals in the House Military Appropriations Committee.[18]

Correspondence pertaining to MacArthur's initial mobilization plan indicates that his purpose in eliminating Organized Reserve units was not based on indifference to the reserve program, but was for the purpose of furnishing a force that could be instantaneously filled up to strength without the long and detailed problem of congressional authorization. Furthermore, units which formerly had been in the Organized Reserves and which would become inactive Regular Army units under the mobilization plan would continue to be officered by Reserve Officers, who in accordance with the law would consent to serve for more than 15 days at the discretion of the President. Because of the national economic distress and unemployment, the War Department planners envisaged no difficulty in getting sufficient Reserve Officers to consent to serve for more than 15 days in case of an emergency and the utilization of the

---

[18] Memo, Unsigned to the Chief of Staff, February 13, 1933. AG 320.2, RG 94, NA.

Initial Mobilization Plan.[19]

The general policy governing the number, assignment, and distribution of Regular Army officers on ROTC duty was based on the policy that had been formulated in 1923.[20] This policy provided that officers would be assigned in proportion to the number of students enrolled in each ROTC unit. The main difficulty encountered was that this policy did not take into account the instructional or training needs of the various units; whereas college A might have 2,000 students in ROTC, perhaps it only commissioned some 10 percent of these while college B, with only 300 in the entire ROTC unit might commission 100 percent of its enrollment. In June of 1932 there were 795 Regular Army officers assigned to ROTC. Of this number, 102 were retired officers who had continued on duty with ROTC. The appropriations bill for 1933 failed to provide for payment of these retired officers on duty with the ROTC, and as a result there was an acute shortage of instructor personnel.

In surveying the ROTC situation, G-3 advised that additional

---

[19] Kreidberg, Military Mobilization, p. 431.

[20] The 1923 policy was set forth in a G-3 memorandum, which was approved by the General Staff. This provided that for each senior ROTC unit of Infantry, Cavalry, Field Artillery, and Coast Artillery two officers would be assigned for the first 100 students and one additional officer for each additional 200 students or major fraction thereof.

For each unit of the other arms and branches, the War Department policy was to provide one officer for each senior unit having 50 to 100 students enrolled and one additional officer for each additional 150 students or major fraction thereof. Ltr, AG to all Corps Area Commanders and Hawaiian Department, sub: "Commissioned Personnel for duty with the ROTC," December 19, 1923. AG 000.862 ROTC (11-10-23), RG 94, NA.

officers of the Regular Army be assigned to ROTC in order that the total assigned to ROTC duty be raised from 566 to 675. G-3 urged this in order to prevent the rapid deterioration of training and efficiency in various units of the ROTC.[21]

G-1 concurred in general with the proposals of G-3 pointing out that the situation of the ROTC since the summer of 1932 had been serious, and that it was necessary to continue "vigorous support" of the ROTC because it was "apparent" that if the ROTC was to be kept up it would have to be given every encouragement by the War Department "consistent with the efficient administration of other activities." Particularly, G-1 felt that this was necessary in view of the fact that the authorities at many schools and colleges were faced with the problem of "pacificistic activity in the solution of which the War Department should give them every possible assistance." However, G-1 balked at the assignment of additional officers to the ROTC, and emphasized that it was impossible with the present shortage of commissioned personnel to increase the number of officers assigned to the civilian components.[22]

In the fall of 1934, the General Staff again advised the Chief of Staff that it was necessary to reappraise the policy of assigning officers to ROTC units. G-1 was alarmed over the fact that instruction had "suffered" because of a shortage of officers,

---

[21] Memo, AC/S G-3 to the Chief of Staff, April 20, 1934. G-3/33157, RG 319, NA.

[22] Memo, AC/S G-1 to the AC/S G-3, May 26, 1934. G-1/13163-7, RG 319, NA.

and was a serious situation in view of the fact that the ROTC was the main source from which well-trained reserve officers were commissioned. According to G-1, if military instruction in ROTC was allowed to deteriorate it would mean not only poorly trained reservists, but also a "general decay of the entire system due to lack of interest on the part of students and faculties." G-1 felt that a more rational use of officers assigned to ROTC could be obtained by basing assignment upon the training needs of the specific unit rather than upon an arbitrary allotment of one instructor per a certain number of students. In addition, G-1 recommended reducing the number of officers assigned to junior ROTC units (high school), the number of officers assigned to schools which did not grant reserve commissions, and the combining of duties in respect to officers assigned to National Guard detail and Reserve Corps duty.[23]

The War Department was not unconcerned with the ROTC program, as charged by its critics, but realized that along with the other items in the military program that were feeling the pinch of reduced appropriations, the ROTC would also have to be curtailed. It is interesting that in the fall of 1934, when fiscal 1936 was being prepared, the General Staff did not recommend assignment of additional officers and expansion and increased expenditures, but apparently realizing that this was hopeless, recommended a more

---

[23] Memo, AC/S G-1 to the Chief of Staff, October 30, 1934. G-1/13163-11, RG 319, NA.

rational and efficient use of what was available. In return, the War Department was charged with willful neglect and unconcern.

Although the War Department sincerely was concerned over its inability to support the ROTC program as desired by the land grant colleges, its parsimonious efforts in this regard throughout the depression only caused college administrators to become more suspicious of the Army. Budget limitations and shortages of funds, in the minds of college administrators, were only the symptoms indicating the real indifference of the War Department toward the ROTC and reserve program.[24]

Hoover's efforts to reduce the activities of the civilian components found no small opposition from National Guard authorities and from the National Guard supporters throughout the country. Although MacArthur and the General Staff refused to be drawn into a comparison or an expression of preference for any of the civilian components, National Guard spokesmen had indicated that money spent for the National Guard would be of use not only from a military point of view but also would be of value in serving as a national relief fund.[25] Maj. Gen. E. A. Walsh made this startling bid for

---

[24] Lyons and Masland, Study of ROTC Program, pp. 45-52.

[25] Representative Collins, long a critic of the Reserve components, asked MacArthur whether it would not be better to eliminate the reserve pay and allowances and use these funds for National Guard training. MacArthur replied:

"Mr. Chairman, you have gotten into a realm that is difficult for me to discuss. I consider the question from the basis of military efficiency and I cannot intelligently advise you from the standpoint of financial aspect with regard to the individuals concerned. Of

funds in his testimony before the appropriations subcommittee.

Walsh, who was not on active duty with the War Department, was president of the National Guard Association, a powerful lobby group located in Washington, and in close contact with the War Department in matters affecting the National Guard. Appearing before the appropriations subcommittee in December of 1932 as a representative of the Association, General Walsh noted that the Hoover budget for 1934 called for only 24 annual armory drills for National Guard units, one-half of what was previously authorized, and as such was "out of the question and would nullify to a great extent the training of the National Guard." General Walsh added that while his views were based on a "strictly military point of view," it should be kept in mind that during the depression the disbursement of drill money to the members of the National Guard did have an economic effect on the various communities across the country.[26] General Walsh's implications found ready sympathy in the subcommittee. Chairman Ross Collins noted that this was the most appealing thing in the entire military appropriations bill

---

course, I do not regard the pay given to the Reserve Officers or to the National Guardsmen as a military dole, if I may use the overworked term. It is necessary in order to meet the incidental expenses that those men incur because they voluntarily subject themselves to taking training necessary to fit them in time of war to defend their country." <u>Hearings</u>: War Department Appropriations Bill, 1933 (December 21, 1931), p. 8.

[26] <u>Hearings</u>: War Department Appropriations Bill, 1934 (December 6, 1932), p. 664.

and that it was

> better to give money to the National Guard scattered all over the country, even as a relief measure, than to spend money on the other forms of civilian military training, such as the CMTC.[27]

The administration's efforts to curtail the civilian components were unsuccessful and the Army had its minimum requirements reinstated into the appropriations bill. MacArthur was able to claim in the spring of 1933 that under the

> stabilized and consistently followed training programs of the recent years the civilian components have made steady progress in attaining proficiency, and thus represent considerable investment in time, effort, and money, and an asset for emergency use that should be jealously guarded.[28]

The House Military Appropriations Subcommittee reported out of committee a bill for fiscal 2934 which provided no money at all for the CMTC camps but provided some $8,000,000 above Hoover's recommendation for the National Guard. In all it called for spending some $273,000,000 for military activities in fiscal year 1934, some $4,000,000 below Hoover's requested figure.[29] The House voted to restore the CMTC funds by some $2,500,000 with the Republicans leading the plea for continuance. In addition, funds for the Officers Reserve Corps were also raised.[30] The Senate voted an amendment to increase the CMTC appropriations by some $20,000,000.

---

[27] Ibid., p. 664.

[28] Report of the Secretary of War, 1933, p. 44.

[29] New York Times, January 13, 1933, p. 2.

[30] Ibid., January 24, 1933, p. 11.

This was the Couzens Amendment which sought to use the additional funds for six months training of some 88,000 idle youths between the ages of 15-24. This was eliminated in a conference committee compromise bill which was finally passed by Congress on March 3, 1933, and War Department appropriations finally allotted by Congress for fiscal 1934 came to around $270,000,000.[31] Woefully, MacArthur noted that this amount could only permit operation of the Army on a maintenance basis, and claimed that the Army had emphasized the "inescapable dangers" which were implicit in this reduced amount:

> But the crying need for reduction in Federal expenditures impelled that body (Congress) to make the most extensive cuts it believed prudent under its constitutional duty of providing for the national defense and of raising and maintaining armies.[32]

---

[31] *Ibid.*, February 14, 1933, pp. 1-2. March 4, 1933, pp. 1-2.

[32] *Report of the Secretary of War, 1933*, p. 15.

CHAPTER X

THE NEW DEAL AND THE ARMY: PART I

While the military appropriations bill for fiscal 1934 was still the topic of strenuous debate and controversy in Congress, the Democratic Party at its Convention in Chicago nominated Governor Franklin D. Roosevelt of New York to be the Democratic Presidential nominee for 1932. Concurrent with the moves of Democratic leaders in the House of Representatives to reduce the officer corps of the Regular Army the Democratic Convention also adopted a platform which caused no little anxiety among proponents of a strong national defense posture. The Democratic platform on national defense for the 1932 political campaign read:

> A Navy and an Army adequate for national defense, based on a survey of all facts affecting the existing establishment, that the people in time of peace may not be burdened by an expenditure fast approaching a billion dollars annually.[1]

The _Army Navy Journal_ termed this plank in the Democratic platform "grotesque," and noted that total expenditures for the military and naval services, including non-military items, were

---

[1]_Army Navy Journal_, July 2, 1932, p. 1025. For the best account of Franklin Roosevelt's nomination see: Frank Friedel, "Franklin D. Roosevelt," Vol. III, _The Triumph_ (Boston: Little, Brown and Company, 1956), pp. 241-311. Also Arthur M. Schlesinger, Jr., "The Age of Roosevelt," Vol. I, _The Crisis of the Old Order_ (Boston: Houghton Mifflin Company, 1958).

actually about $600,000,000 annually.[2] Upon the conclusion of the Democratic Convention on July 2, 1932, the *Journal* noted with disgust that national defense was lucky to have been mentioned at all during the proceedings and that the platform was worded in such an equivocal manner as to appeal to the advocates of "adequate" national defense and the militant pacificist and liberal groups.[3]

National defense did not loom large as a political issue in the campaign of 1932, and both parties were disposed to accept defense expenditures as an essential federal expense which should be reduced to the lowest point consistent with safety. However, to the *Army Navy Journal*, the Republican platform was somewhat more preferable than the Democratic. According to this influential advocate for the armed forces, the Republican platform was "thoroughly satisfactory," and it was noted that the Republican Convention had shown greater interest in the problems and issues of defense. In addition, the *Journal* pointed out that the Democratic Convention gave no expression to the need of maintaining the present defense policy, based on the National Defense Act of 1920, but had thrown the door open for any interpretation of the Democratic position on national defense that anyone might wish. The *Journal* commented that the Democratic platform was so ambiguous that it left to the presidential candidate and to congressional candidates

---

[2]*Army Navy Journal*, July 2, 1932, p. 1027.

[3]*Ibid*., July 2, 1932, p. 1023.

the initiative in determining what was the Democratic position on national defense.[4]

Roosevelt opened his formal campaign at the end of July when he discussed and amplified the Democratic platform in a radio broadcast from Albany.[5] The Governor's statement that the Democratic platform was "honest to the core" brought the Army Navy Journal into the political arena with a vigorous rebuttal to the Democratic nominee. The Journal charged that the defense plank of the Democratic platform was dishonest and false, and pointed out that there was less reason for Governor Roosevelt to approve this monstrous statement than for most other politicians because of his past service as Assistant Secretary of the Navy under Wilson. It was suggested that the Democratic candidate be honest with the American public in the matter of national defense and admit that his party had made a mistake in adopting its national defense platform and announce that he favored better treatment for the armed services.[6] By mid-August the Army Navy Journal had definitely cooled toward Roosevelt. It noted that his unqualified endorsement of the platform of his party placed him in a "quizzical position" toward national defense: "In view of his former position in favor of preparedness, it is difficult to see him standing on the present platform."[7] In contrast,

---

4Ibid., July 2, 1932, p. 1027.

5Friedel, The Triumph, p. 339.

6Army Navy Journal, August 6, 1932, p. 1132.

7Ibid., August 13, 1932, p. 1147.

the Journal praised Hoover's stand toward national defense, and recommended the Republican incumbent to every "patriotic American."[8]

Roosevelt's campaign strategy was notable because of his efforts to avoid any discussion of international affairs and national defense, while striking hard on the issue of the depression as a domestic economic problem. The Governor's silence on these issues gave military observers uneasy moments. Of particular concern was the fact that one of his chief supporters, William Randolph Hearst, had advocated a unified department of defense, and his running mate, John Nance Garner, the former Speaker of the House, had worked zealously in the efforts of the House Democrats to cut the officer strength of the Regular Army during the spring of 1932.[9]

The election of Roosevelt in November and his non-committal remarks during the interregnum gave little comfort to the Army as to future military policies. The _Army Navy Journal_ noted after the election that the President-elect was confronted with the dilemma of having pledged a reduction in all appropriations by some 25 per cent, but at the same time had the political responsibility as Commander-in-Chief of maintaining support for the Army and Navy. The Journal believed that Roosevelt was opposed to any sweeping reorganization of the military establishment and new developments in

---

[8] _Ibid._, August 13, 1932, p. 1152.

[9] _Ibid._, November 5, 1932, p. 181.

national defense; it assumed that he would not act in this regard until a comprehensive survey, as pledged in the Democratic platform, was completed.[10]

One factor that undoubtedly served to increase the anxiety of the Army in respect to the advent of Roosevelt and his administration was the political alliance between the President-elect and the controversial General William "Billy" Mitchell. Mitchell, who had been court-martialed in 1926 because of his persistent efforts on behalf of the role of the Air Corps in national defense policies, was a delegate to the 1932 Democratic Convention in Chicago and had campaigned for Roosevelt during the fall of 1932. Not unexpectedly post-election rumors had it that Mitchell was in line for the cabinet post of Assistant Secretary of War for Air. In early 1933 Mitchell met with Roosevelt in New York City and outlined to the President-elect his proposals for a reorganization of the armed forces, including a unified defense establishment and an independent Air Corps.[11]

---

[10] Ibid., January 7, 1933, p. 376.

[11] During the 1932 Presidential election campaign Mitchell took the stump for Roosevelt in his native state of Wisconsin, and also in Illinois and New England. The Democratic Party thanked him for his "efficiency, loyalty, and valuable assistance to the Speaker's Bureau of the Democratic National Committee." (Ltr, Robert Jackson to Mitchell, November 15, 1932, Mitchell Papers, Library of Congress, Box 16. See also the letter James Farley to Mitchell, November 17, 1932, Mitchell Papers, Library of Congress, Box 16).

Soon after the election Mitchell apparently broached his ideas on reorganizing the Armed Forces to Roosevelt. In mid-November the President-elect informed Mitchell that he was impressed and interested in proposals for reorganization: "You gave me so many

With the inauguration of Franklin Roosevelt and the advent of the new administration, the Army was quick to realize that there would be a significant change in the relationship between the military establishment and the Commander-in-Chief. Hoover generally

---

tantalizing glimpses of a subject on which you are certainly well qualified to speak that I was tempted to set an immediate date for the talk you suggested." (Ltr, Roosevelt to Mitchell, November 19, 1932, Mitchell Papers, Library of Congress, Box 16). Mitchell replied that he could not meet with Roosevelt until after the Christmas holidays: "I shall be back home around the first of the year, and shall make myself ready to come up and see you any time and bring the data I have about reorganization of the departments and particularly about our aviation development." (Ltr, Mitchell to Roosevelt, December 21, 1932, Mitchell Papers, Library of Congress, Box 16). The meeting took place on January 3, 1933, and Mitchell presented his outline plan for reorganization. In mid-January Mitchell again wrote to Roosevelt urging consideration of his plans for reorganizing the armed forces. "Our platform," Mitchell exhorted the President-elect, "calls for a survey of national defense needs. It is highly important that this branch be reorganized, from an economy and efficiency standpoint. Our National Defense Act should be entirely revamped. In our short talk in New York the other day, I handed you a little diagram that outlined the plans that I propose for a department of National Defense. I would like very much to go into these things more in detail with you, before the convening of the special session which I think now is impossible to avoid." (Ltr, Mitchell to Roosevelt, January 17, 1933, Mitchell Papers, Library of Congress, Box 16).

There is no evidence in the Mitchell Papers that Roosevelt answered the General's entreaty for a second meeting in which the latter presumably hoped to discuss legislative strategy in respect to reorganizing the Army and Navy. Apparently Roosevelt was reluctant to adopt Mitchell's proposals, and hesitant about taking into the New Deal entourage yet another tempestuous crusader against the old order. Roosevelt's coolness toward Mitchell's proposals after January 1933 may also be due to the fact that Lewis Douglas, one of the President-elect's close advisors, had come up with a more simple plan for reducing military spending through budget restrictions.

For reports of Mitchell being considered for a cabinet post see Mitchell Papers, Library of Congress, Box 64. This box contains newspaper clippings and magazine articles pertaining to the controversial Air Corps leader during the years 1931-34. Mitchell undoubtedly would never have considered an appointment as Assistant Secretary of War for Air under the existing organization of the War Department in 1932. This would have meant serving in a position in which his views on aviation could not have predominated over the General Staff.

deferred to the judgment of the General Staff in all matters dealing specifically with military affairs and the organization of the military establishment, and generally sought not to interfere with or override decisions made by the latter. The quick response of the new 73rd Congress to the legislative demands of the new President made the Army realize that Franklin D. Roosevelt would be more than just the nominal Commander-in-Chief, and that during the coming years policy and direction would be forthcoming from the White House. Indeed, the Army Navy Journal very early in the Roosevelt Administration commented: "Nothing is more evident than the fact that the destinies of the services are in the hands of President Roosevelt."[12]

For his Secretary of War, Roosevelt selected George B. Dern. Sixty-one years old in 1933, Dern was a native of Nebraska and a former mining entrepreneur and banker who had been Democratic Governor of Utah since 1925. The new Secretary of War came to the office without any military experience. When asked by the press concerning his views on the military establishment he admitted: "I haven't any plan about anything. I'm entirely open minded. I didn't come in with any idea of putting ideas of my own in effect."[13] Dern's modesty, sincerity, and conservative views on military policy endeared him with the flamboyant Chief of Staff, and under the latters tutelage and influence he became a strong advocate of the

---

[12] Ibid., March 18, 1933, p. 576.

[13] Ibid., March 11, 1933, p. 555.

General Staff's attitude toward national defense. Dern was not a close or trusted advisor of President Roosevelt, and did not belong to the inner-circle of brain trusters or new dealers who had the ear of the Chief Executive. This proved to be a disadvantage to the military establishment in its efforts to obtain increased funds from both the Public Works Administration and from the regular administration budget.

In late March, soon after the inauguration and without any previous consultation or coordination with the War Department, the Director of the Bureau of the Budget, Lewis Douglas, directed that a cut be made in the proposed military expénditure program for fiscal 1934 of some $90,000,000. The appropriations bill for the Army had been passed by the old 72nd Congress on March 3, the day before Roosevelt was sworn in, and totalled some $270,000,000 for military activities. Douglas' cut was itemized in detail and initiated a running battle between the General Staff and the Budget Bureau over the next several months. About a month later, Roosevelt announced that he was considering a plan to furlough between 3,000 and 4,000 officers.[14]

Although he was ordered by the White House not to divulge information concerning curtailment of the military appropriations for fiscal 1934, the Chief of Staff made it known that he was "violently opposed" to any reduction of the officer corps of the Regular Army. In an appearance before the House Military Affairs Committee

---

[14]New York Times, April 21, 1933, p. 6.

concerning the plan to furlough officers, MacArthur emphasized that such a development was unspeakable and would engender in the Army a feeling that it was being treated unfairly, and as a consequence there would be a breaking down of the faith, morale, and discipline of the Army. Voicing his anxiety over the activities of the new administration, MacArthur stressed to Congress that he had not been consulted concerning cuts in the officer strength, and by way of criticism added that while the Hoover Administration discussed such proposals with the War Department, such apparently was not the policy of the new administration.[15] The Army reacted to these economy moves of the new administration with "consternation." Many officers in Washington ominously believed a reduction of officer personnel by at least 2,000, along with the elimination of the CMTC, ORC, ROTC, curtailment of National Guard activities, and the consolidation of the Regular Army in a few large cantonments was "inevitable."[16] The Army Navy Journal blasted the New Deal in an editorial when it charged that moves were "being made by the Administration in power to destroy even the inadequate security the nation now possesses."[17]

Already early in the first months of the Roosevelt administration the seeds of suspicion and distrust had been planted between

---

[15] Army Navy Journal, April 22, 1933, pp. 689, 691. See also The New York Times, April 27, 1933, p. 7.

[16] New York Times, April 12, 1933, p. 2.

[17] Army Navy Journal, April 8, 1933, p. 636.

the Chief of Staff and the Commander-in-Chief. Viewing the early months of the New Deal, historians have focused their attention on the CCC, AAA, NRA, and other dramatic episodes of the famous "100 days," but have given little discussion to the bitter struggle by MacArthur to hold the line against New Deal efforts to reduce the Army to a caretaking establishment.[18]

In the Army there was bitterness over the fact that Roosevelt would curtail military activities, including training, arsenals, and civilian employees, all for the sake of economy in government expenditures, and at the same time establish labor camps and pay the "unemployed and vagrants" a dollar a day for a 40 hour week as against the 60¢ a day the private soldiers, sailors, and marines received.[19] This pique on the part of the Army reflected its anxiety that the new administration was out to pursue basic political, social, and economic goals at the expense of the military

---

[18] The best account of MacArthur's difficulty with Roosevelt over the matter of the military budget for fiscal 1934 is found in Frazier Hunt's The Untold Story of Douglas MacArthur (New York: Devin-Adair, 1954), pp. 147-160. Surprisingly enough, the recent work by Walter Millis, Arms and State, Civil-Military Relations in National Policy (New York: The Twentieth Century Fund, 1958), omits any reference to this early budget battle, and notes only that "against his strongest New Deal supporters, the President pushed steadily though cautiously for larger annual appropriations for the services." p. 23. It is surprising to note that in his recent work on the New Deal, Arthur M. Schlesinger, Coming of New Deal (New York, 1959), omits any reference to this issue.

[19] Army Navy Journal, April 8, 1933, p. 636.

establishment.[20] Thus there was engendered early in the Roosevelt Administration little sympathy by the Army toward the New Deal. At the same time, the various new dealers and brain trusters in Washington became antagonized with the Army leaders over the latter's refusal to cooperate in economy and reform measures. Between March 28 and June 10, the Chief of Staff was constantly exerting pressure on the administration leaders to reinstate the former appropriations figure that had been passed by the 72nd Congress for fiscal 1934. As a result, relations between the White House and the War Department deteriorated. MacArthur, determined to avoid further cuts in the military budget, forced interviews with Douglas and with the President, and argued vehemently that funds would have to be reinstated. MacArthur's final effort was to threaten Roosevelt that if he refused to reinstate the curtailed funds, the Chief of Staff would resign his commission and take the issue to

---

[20]A recent study on the theory and politics of civil-military relations points out that "reform liberalism" of the early decades of the twentieth century, including in its intellectual lineage populism, muckrakers, new freedom, and new deal, vigorously opposed professional military groups. "In the reform lexicon, militarism was virtually coexistive with all evil; it was incompatible with the democratic premises of American society." Reform liberalism's attack on professional militarism took two general forms: It looked upon the military profession as backward and primitive, and military expenditures as wasteful. "In sum, the reformers viewed military professionalism as economically wasteful, socially useless, and ethically backward." Samuel P. Huntington, _The Soldier and the State_ (Cambridge, Massachusetts: Harvard University Press, 1957), pp. 291-292.

the public in a series of speeches across the country.[21]

The first public announcement of the struggle over the threatened budget reduction was made by Secretary Dern, who on Easter Monday, April 17, revealed that reductions in the military appropriations for fiscal 1934 had been "mapped out" by Budget Director Lewis Douglas, and that it was proposed that War Department expenditures be curtailed by some $144,000,000, with a reduction of approximately $90,000,000 planned in military activities.[22] During all his bitter struggles at the White House and with the Budget Bureau, MacArthur was under direct orders to handle the matter secretly; he was not permitted even to discuss items that were to be reduced with his branch and arm chiefs or those vitally interested in the planned reduction.[23]

Throughout the months of April and May, MacArthur found support in his efforts to seek reinstatement of the budget cuts from Secretary Dern.[24] This was a difficult position for Dern to take in view of the fact that as a newly appointed member of the cabinet he wanted to appear as a staunch and loyal subordinate of the

---

[21]Hunt, Untold Story of MacArthur, p. 152. Further reference to this episode is found in a series of interview notes taken by Dr. Harold Cater in preparation for a work on the history of the General Staff. This reference is cited hereinafter as: "Interview Notes," Cater Files, OCMH. Ltr, Maj. Gen. Van Horn Moseley to writer, January 18, 1960

[22]New York Times, April 18, 1933, p. 1.

[23]Army Navy Journal, July 8, 1933, p. 898.

[24]"Interview Notes," Cater Files, OCMH.

President, and one eager to cooperate in activities that pertained to his department. Dern, coming into the department with little concept of the requirements of the Army, came under the influence of the Chief of Staff and the latter's views concerning the needs of the Army. On May 16, in a radio broadcast, Secretary Dern defended the War Department appropriations bill and noted that military expenditures consisted of only 6 per cent of the total federal budget. Reiterating the General Staff argument, Dern told the American public that national defense necessarily costs money and that this fact did not justify neglecting the reasonable demands of defense. However, Dern added that the Roosevelt Administration and the War Department were putting forth every effort to reduce expenditures and still maintain an adequate defense.[25] Dern's efforts to placate the administration leaders and at the same time support the Army in its efforts to obtain the funds that were scheduled for reduction brought forth criticism from the Army Navy Journal. At the same time it was realized that Dern was not a

---

25Dern Papers, Library of Congress. Radio speech, NBC, May 16, 1933, "Problems of the War Department." Note: There are five boxes of the private papers of George B. Dern in the Manuscripts Division of the Library of Congress containing the late Secretary's speeches and general correspondence from 1933 to his death in 1936. There is little of value to be found in his papers pertaining to policy and problems of the War Department during his tenure of office, and even less concerning Dern's relations with the White House. It appears from his published speeches that are contained in the Library of Congress collection that Dern over the years became a stout defender of the Army and its views concerning national defense. No official War Department correspondence is in the Dern collection.

close confidant of the President, and that he was faced with a problem of which he knew little and for which he had no experience.[26]

The outcome of the struggle between the War Department and the White House was that Roosevelt directed that the matter of military expenditures for fiscal 1934 be reconsidered by the Budget Bureau, and military appropriations for fiscal 1934 were finally raised from the original White House figure of around $196,000,000 to $225,000,000. Furthermore, the entire plan to furlough Regular Army officers was dropped. No evidence in the Army files or correspondence throws light on Roosevelt's decision to change his original plan to reduce military appropriations by some $90,000,000. But, being a consummate pragmatist and political tactician, he undoubtedly realized that he would need the Army's support and willing cooperation to bring off the CCC program successfully. In addition it would be confusing to public opinion if he were to furlough 2,000 Regular Army officers and then bring them back on active duty to administer the CCC program.

The date on which the Army appropriations figure was settled

---

[26]Army Navy Journal, April 22, 1933, p. 669. The Army Navy Journal admonished Dern to stand up for the Army, and used as an example the story told of Harding's Secretary of War, John Weeks, who, when informed that the President wanted to decrease the officer corps, replied with the following: "Am I worth a thousand officers to the Administration?" enquired Mr. Weeks. "What's the matter, John?" replied President Harding. "I merely want to know if I am to run my department?" "Of course," replied President Harding. "Then there won't be any cut," Weeks decided. And there wasn't. Unfortunately for the Army, Dern was no John Weeks, and more significantly, Franklin Roosevelt was no Warren Harding.

at $225,000,000, June 10, 1933, corresponds with the general period in which the Army was becoming more and more involved with the CCC, and it was apparent to Roosevelt that if this unprecedented project was to be successful it would be necessary to bring in the Army to a greater degree than was originally planned. Roosevelt perhaps realized that a retreat by him on the appropriations issue would insure the Army's support and cooperation on the CCC, and he would stand to gain politically more in the end if the CCC, under the Army's administration, was a success.

In mid-June 1933, Secretary Dern notified the Army that the military budget had been set for fiscal 1934 by "executive action" at $225,000,000. According to Dern: "Every effort has been made to absorb the cuts so as to minimize the impairment of national defense."[27] Dern did not deny that the reduction of military appropriations from $270,000,000 to $225,000,000 had not impaired national defense; he indicated that the War Department was taking action so as to reduce this impairment in order to "drive for the greatest retrenchment in our history." Dern warned that curtailment would be related to living expenses, materiel, training activities, and overhead civilian personnel. Furthermore, reduction was planned by omitting Regular Army field training, including target practice, flying training, the suspension of activities pertaining to the arsenals and depots of the Ordnance Department, re-equipment programs,

---

[27] Army Navy Journal, June 24, 1933, p. 849.

and R&D. The National Guard was scheduled to retain all its personnel and conduct field training, but its armory drills were to be reduced to between twelve and twenty drill periods annually. The ROTC program likewise was listed by Dern for curtailment, and only one-third of its personnel were to receive summer training.[28]

---

[28]New York Times, June 18, 1933, pp. 1 - 8. Dern's public statement on War Department expenditures noted:

"All components of the Army of the United States will have less funds. However, each is retained without reduction in its fighting personnel. The regular army will omit its normal field training, suspend many of its supply, arsenals, and depot activities, its research and development studies, its re-equipment, including aircraft and its armament activities as well as certain curtailment in its motor and animal procurement programs.

"The National Guard will retain its existing personnel and be able to conduct all field and partial armory training. While the National Guard will have to suspend some of its activities, it is estimated that the funds available will permit two weeks field training and at least twelve, and probably twenty, armory training drills.

"ROTC camps will be maintained, but with curtailment in supplies, uniforms, equipment and also with about one-third reduction in its summer training camp activity.

"The Organized Reserve is now associated with the CCC work in so far as there is a shortage of regular army officers for this work. As most of the Reserve Officers associated with the Civilian Corps are of junior grades, some funds have been reserved which will permit the training of a few of the key field officers of the Reserve Corps in accordance with the annual program of training the Organized Reserves.

"The CMTC will be held as scheduled, but with a reduction in attendance to meet the limited funds available. This reduction will limit all training to candidates who have had previously one summer's training in the CMTC.

"The Army school system, which provides schooling for all components including West Point and air cadets, will continue.

"Field training and target practice, for the regular army will be suspended during the fiscal year 1934, except that recruits will fire such courses as are deemed necessary to become reasonably proficient in the use of small arms...."

Although this reduction by the Roosevelt Administration was a "severe blow" to the Army, the *Army Navy Journal* admonished its readers to remember that the original figure freely mentioned as the objective of the administration was a $90,000,000 cut; furthermore, the number of Army personnel had been preserved intact.[29]

In reviewing the move of the Roosevelt entourage to reduce military spending, the Chief of Staff in his annual report vigorously excoriated such efforts. He denounced the administration's original plan to reduce military spending beyond the $270,000,000 figure that had been appropriated by the 72nd Congress: "This sum ($270,000,000) was approximately $65 million less than that made available for similar purposes for fiscal year 1932 and provided for sharp contractions in activities essential to permanent efficiency of the Army."[30] MacArthur claimed that the $270,000,000 figure was the minimum amount necessary for a single year's maintenance, on a depression basis, for the military establishment. He noted that although this fugure was below the amount believed prudent by the Army, the latter was preparing to put it into effect with the least possible damage to national defense when, on March 28, information was received from the Bureau of the Budget that an additional cut of some $90,000,000 was to be made. MacArthur noted: "This was a stunning blow to national defense."[31] He added that if the White

---

[29]*Army Navy Journal*, June 24, 1933, pp. 849, 867.

[30]*Annual Report of the Secretary of War, 1933*, p. 15.

[31]*Ibid*.

House had succeeded in this move, it would have meant the "scrapping of the system prescribed in the National Defense Act, and the reduction of the American Military Establishment to the status of a Federal constabulary." MacArthur admits that he "vigorously contested" the reduction that the administration planned on the grounds that it was inadequate for the Army, and that the adjustment of the requirements of the Army was the subject of "continuous and intensive study by the War Department, and of written and oral presentations to the Director of the Budget."[32]

To the Army one of the most alarming features about the Roosevelt reduction of June 1933 was the fact that this action in curtailing funds for fiscal 1934 would have a serious effect on the military arsenals operated throughout the country by the Ordnance Department. Military spokesmen had urged repeatedly that these plants be continued in order to maintain their technical standards, and to prevent the deterioration of equipment. Even after Roosevelt had set the budget figure at $225,000,000, the Ordnance arsenals were faced with their most critical curtailment since World War I. Military appropriations for fiscal 1932 had been $335,000,000, for fiscal 1933 the figure was $285,000,000, and for fiscal 1934 Congress had approved some $270,000,000. This was a drop in a two year range of $65,000,000, and now the new administration had ordered the figure for 1934 to be set at $225,000,000, a further reduction

---

[32]*Ibid.*, p. 17.

of $45,000,000. This new figure meant that Ordnance arsenals and depots would have to curtail activities and reduce operating personnel by approximately 7,700. Besides the deterioration of plant equipment and the loss of investment, the Army was concerned over the fact that this move would increase unemployment and present a possible loss of technically trained personnel.[33] This dangerous situation was alleviated only after the most urgent protestations to the administration and the allocation of $6,000,000 of emergency public works funds for Army arsenal operations during the summer of 1933.

As outlined by Secretary Dern, the revision of the War Department expenditure estimates from $270,000,000 to $225,000,000 necessitated a study of the new figure by Army planners in order to prepare an expenditure program for fiscal 1934 that would meet the new allocation limit. According to General MacArthur, after he received the revised figure from the Budget Bureau on June 10, he called a meeting of the General Council of the War Department

> and invited representatives of the National Guard and Reserve Officers Association. I explained how the budget had been arrived at and the conferences between the Budget Bureau and the War Department, and invited recommendations and required also that if they recommended increases in some items they would have to recommend corresponding decreases in some other items.... I myself, on my own volition, made certain changes; I sweated from the Regular Army a million dollars to permit the CMTC to function to a limited extent. I raised the amount for the reserve components; I provided

---

[33]"Our Arsenals and Their Personnel," Army Ordnance, XIV, No. 79 (July-August 1933), pp. 44-45.

for the National Rifle Association. I took from the depleted Regular Army in order to preserve the threatened civilian components.[34]

As expected, recommendations were made to the Chief of Staff urging increased appropriations for the coming fiscal years in order to make up for the consequences of Roosevelt's reduction. MacArthur, of course, realized that the arguments advanced for increased funds were sound from the military point of view and

> really understate the necessities of the case. Even to the most anti-militarist mind of the country they could only, in my opinion, seem to be modest.... I am still hopeful that as the fiscal year goes on some condition or situation will arise which will make it possible to revert to the appropriations originally made by Congress and that the figures we now have to envision may not be final.[35]

Undoubtedly the Chief of Staff's optimism over the possibility of increased military expenditures, which was expressed to the entire General Staff and War Department branch and bureau chiefs, was based on his confidence that funds from public works appropriations would soon be forthcoming for the Army. In notifying the General Staff that the withdrawal of funds for fiscal 1934 would be limited by the President's instruction that only $225,000,000 would be available, MacArthur laid down the following principles to govern spending for fiscal 1934: (1) arsenals, manufacturing plans and repair facilities would be reduced in operation; (2) R&D would be

---

[34] Hearings: War Department Appropriations Bill, 1935, p. 26.

[35] Memo, Chief of Staff to the AG, June 16, 1933. OCS/20642-46, RG 319, NA.

curtailed and re-armament and re-equipment would be restricted to those items considered necessary for emergencies; (3) expenditures for the procurement of aircraft would be now less than one-fourth of the original estimate, and, in addition, the actual operation of aircraft would be reduced to below the minimum amount formerly prescribed; (4) Regular Army training would be limited to drill on posts and camps and existing facilities would receive no funds except for emergency repair and maintenance; (5) target practice would be suspended, except for new recruits; (6) all branch and special schools would be continued provided they could be financed within the total limiting budget figure allotted to each respective branch; (7) the National Guard would hold their annual two weeks training in the field and not less then twelve armory drills throughout the year; (8) funds would be made available from other sources to maintain a restricted reserve training program.[36]

Difficult times had indeed befallen the Army if funds were inadequate to hold target practice and rifle marksmanship. One can well imagine the reaction within the Army to this development when it is recalled that the one thing that General Pershing demanded as the essential in training troops for battle in 1917-18 was capability and proficiency in rifle marksmanship. Although things were indeed bleak in the early summer of 1933, MacArthur could console himself over the fact that he had succeeded in

---

[36]Memo, Deputy Chief of Staff to AC/S G-4, June 16, 1933. OCS/20642-46, RG 319, NA.

obtaining $225,000,000 from the tight-fisted new dealers who had originally planned to decrease the military budget to a figure well below $200,000,000.

Not unexpectedly the National Guard, which had prevailed over attempts by Hoover and Democratic congressional leaders to cut its activities, violently opposed Roosevelt's parsimonious treatment of its armory drill schedule. Pressure by the National Guard Association on the White House resulted in having the regular schedule of forty-eight armory drills reinstated into fiscal 1934. The decision on this matter was announced by the Budget Bureau on July 6, after a lengthy meeting between Roosevelt, Lewis Douglas, and spokesmen from the National Guard Association. Douglas was ordered by Roosevelt to increase National Guard funds from $18,000,000 to $24,000,000, an increase which would allow the Guard to hold forty-eight drills instead of twelve as originally planned.[37] Understandably, MacArthur was irked over the action of the National Guard in going over his head and pressuring Roosevelt into giving them increased funds.[38] MacArthur was perturbed over the fact that he had been seeking diligently throughout the spring to have funds for the National Guard maintained and, in several sessions with the President and the Director of the Budget, the National Guard lobbyists had succeeded where he had failed.

---

37 Army Navy Journal, July 8, 1933, pp. 889, 904.

38 "Interview Notes," Cater Files, OCMH.

Reflecting on this incident, MacArthur must have realized that his position as Chief of Staff and head of the military establishment had been derogated. MacArthur's pique at the action of the National Guard in going to the Commander-in-Chief was not based on his reluctance to see the civilian components receive more money, but on the implication given by Roosevelt that in all matters pertaining to military affairs he would be the court of final decision. MacArthur had never tired of championing additional funds for the civilian components even at the expense of the Regular Army, and Roosevelt's action in increasing funds for the National Guard without consultation with the Chief of Staff was bound to have the effect of weakening the authority of the General Staff over the civilian components and their spokesmen. The incident was another early indication by Roosevelt that he would be no mere nominal Commander-in-Chief, but would exert the final authority in regard to the peacetime Army. If the various civilian components had a direct channel straight to the White House, what would prevent an independent minded Air Corps chief from gaining the influence of the Commander-in-Chief and overstepping official Army channels and the Chief of Staff?

The administration's efforts to cut back funds for the Army, MacArthur's threat to resign and take the issue of national defense to the people, the President's action in approving increased funds for the National Guard without notifying or consulting MacArthur, all added fuel to the enmity between the Chief of Staff and the

White House.[39] On July 24, not long after the National Guard lobby had swung into action and pressured Roosevelt into granting it more funds, a delegation from the Reserve Officer's Association called on the President and requested more funds for Reserve Officer training. Three days later the Secretary of War was informed by the Director of the Budget that the President had directed an additional million dollars be allotted to the ORC. This additional money would permit a fifteen day training period for 7,000 more reserve officers,

---

[39]Underlying MacArthur's concern over Roosevelt's action was the attitude of the President that the Army was his personal domain to do with as he chose. In discussing the War Department activities during the early Roosevelt years, one member of the General Staff described the Roosevelt-MacArthur relationship as a clash of personalities: "Each was a Hamlet and there was no place on the stage for two Hamlets." Besides a difference of opinion on important policy matters there occurred insignificant incidents which the sensitive Chief of Staff took as further indication that the President considered the Army his personal domain. For example, MacArthur became perturbed over the President's ordering the Army to transport Mrs. Roosevelt's horses to and from Hyde Park and Washington and stabling them at Fort Myer. Another incident was Roosevelt's ordering the Army to store his daughter's personal household furniture at Fort Myer during the period between her divorce and second marriage. "Interview Notes," Cater Files, OCMH.

MacArthur's antipathy and suspicion toward Roosevelt was reciprocated. According to Rex Tugwell, a close New Deal confidant of the President, Roosevelt considered that the two most dangerous men in the United States in the early thirties were Huey Long and Douglas MacArthur. Tugwell notes that Roosevelt was of the opinion that MacArthur was the potential "man on horseback" that gave "realism to the dreams of conservatives. There was none so well endowed with charm, tradition, and majestic appearance as MacArthur; and the Nazi-minded among American leaders recalled with approval that incident that had seemed to all liberals so reprehensible--that, of course, was the battle of Anacostia Flats, in which unemployed veterans had been dispersed with tanks and tear gas when they had organized a protest march to impress President Hoover and the Congress." Rexford G. Tugwell, The Democratic Roosevelt (Garden City, N. Y.: Doubleday & Company, 1957), p. 349-350. Tugwell's remarks are indicative of the splenetic distrust of the New Deal toward MacArthur.

with the provision that the funds would be restricted to provide training for only company grade officers and graduates of the ROTC.[40] The ease with which the ROA and the National Guard obtained their increased funds from the White House might have encouraged the mistaken idea that MacArthur and the General Staff were insouciant toward providing the civilian components with adequate funds.

The problem of expenditures for the military establishment for fiscal 1934 had subsided during the summer of 1933 when another issue came to the fore which impinged on the relationship between War Department officials and the civilian leaders of the new administration. Lewis Douglas, Roosevelt's Budget Director, who had been in the thick of the struggle over budget reduction, came up with the idea that it would save the federal government millions of dollars if the Army was regrouped into several large cantonments. This plan originally was conceived by Harold Ickes, head of the Public Works Administration, who devised the scheme in order to reduce the amount of funds allotted to the Army for buildings at its various posts, camps, and stations. The idea appealed to the White House coterie, and Roosevelt was reported to have "definitely in mind" the abandonment of a large number of Army posts.[41] No decision was reached by Roosevelt during August, but the question was to be answered at the same time the allotment of PWA money to the

---

[40] Army Navy Journal, July 29, 1933, p. 950. This brought the total of Reserve officers scheduled for training for fiscal 1934 to 11,000.

[41] Ibid., August 19, 1933, p. 1010.

War Department for housing was decided.[42] What angered the Army was the fact that it did not receive any correspondence requesting its views or recommendations on this plan, nor was it asked which camps should be retained and which closed down. Furthermore, instead of relying on the War Department for advice on an issue of particular and important interest to it, Roosevelt took his advice from Douglas and Hugh Johnson, the head of the National Recovery Administration (NRA).[43] In mid-September Roosevelt "let it be known" that he planned to redistribute the mobile land forces of the Regular Army, and that his proposals contemplated abandoning 50 or more posts. Foreseeing a flurry of protests, the administration did not disclose the names of the posts that were to be abolished. In all there were a total of 210 camps in the continental United States; some 60 of them were listed on a "caretaking basis" with no military activity and only 150 were employed as troop concentration points.[44]

Without indicating any plans to abandon Army posts or concentrate the Army at a fewer number of installations, the administration announced on September 20 that the PWA had approved an allotment of some $54,000,000 to the Army for construction and

---

[42]New York Times, August 17, 1933, p. 3.

[43]Army Navy Journal, August 19, 1933, pp. 1010, 1016.

[44]New York Times, September 14, 1933, p. 9.

reconditioning work at 32 posts in 19 states.[45]

It was almost a month after the first public reports that the administration was planning to regroup the Army and close certain camps as an economy move, as well as to improve the over-all military posture of the country, that the War Department was officially informed of the scheme. On September 25, 1933, Lewis Douglas advised the Secretary of War that he had tentatively selected 15 posts at which he planned to concentrate the Regular Army. The Secretary of War was advised that if he did not concur in the list he might submit an alternate list.[46] MacArthur quickly advised his civilian superior to stand fast against such an insidious plan and that the War Department

> Should set forth its vigorous opposition.... The matter and location and abandonment of posts is one in which Congress is vitally interested and any changes as contemplated by the Bureau of the Budget would surely result in Congressional investigation.[47]

Besides stressing to the Secretary of War that the move would not bring about economy, but rather would be an extravagance, MacArthur implied that he might not be unwilling to have the matter brought up before Congress, thereby obtaining congressional support for the

---

[45] Ibid., September 21, 1933, p. 20. Note: The original War Department request was for $135 million for construction and reconditioning of its posts, camps, and stations.

[46] Ltr, Director of the Budget to the Secretary of War, September 25, 1933. G-4/29778, RG 319, NA.

[47] Memo, Chief of Staff to the Secretary of War, October 6, 1933. G-4/29778, RG 319, NA.

War Department's position.

In a formal letter of reply from the War Department to the Budget Bureau on the matter of closing the Army camps, Secretary Dern voiced vigorous resentment over the fact that the "decision to concentrate the Army was made without any consultation with the War Department."[48] Douglas was warned that the War Department wanted its position clearly understood in case there developed a congressional investigation overthe issue of abandoning military posts. Dern emphasized the fact that new construction would be required to meet the proposed concentration and that this would total more money than could be saved by such a move. Furthermore, additional funds would be required for the travel of civilian components to the new permanent encampments for training and, instead of realizing economy, the plan of Douglas would increase military appropriations.

Dern's letter then outlined the history of posts and encampments and noted that the origin of the idea of concentrating the mobile Army into a few large posts was based on the proposals of the former Secretary of War, Newton D. Baker. According to Dern, Baker's plan, drawn up after World War I, visualized a Regular Army of about 500,000 men, with no appreciable civilian components, and for such a large force a small number of division-size encampments was ideal. Baker's plan was superseded by the National

---

48Ltr, Secretary of War to the Director of the Budget, October 12, 1933. G-4/29778, RG 319, NA.

Defense Act which placed the main reliance for national security on the civilian components whose training was one of the main responsibilities of the small Regular Army. For such training, the War Department stressed to Douglas, scattered posts were infinitely superior and less costly, and made for efficient contact between the Regular Army and the civilian components. The scattered posts were, in effect, the schools for the peacetime training of the entire civilian components; the greater the number of posts, the better the Regular Army could accomplish its mission of training the reserves and National Guard.

After this detailed analysis of the War Department position, Secretary Dern emphasized that the entire program of posts and encampments had been studied in great detail by the General Staff ten years before and, as a result, the existing program had been developed. A building program had been initiated and more than $100,000,000 had been expended over the years. Dern concluded by noting that it was a "misconception" on the part of the Budget Bureau that there were useless and expensive posts in the present set-up and that Douglas was looking for a problem that was non-existent.[49]

Significantly Dern's letter to Douglas on the issue of the economy and efficiency of closing certain Army posts reflected the adamacy of the General Staff against curtailing any of its

---

[49]*Ibid.*

activities on the ground that the consequence would be the weakening of the potentiality and capability of the civilian components. The War Department did not become a pleader for the Regular Army during the depression, but was, in effect, a lobbyist for the civilian components: the National Guard, Officer's Reserve Corps, ROTC, and CMTC. This fact suggests the difficulty of accommodating the expensive provisions of the National Defense Act of 1920 which indicated that the civilian components would serve as the backbone of the American military establishment. This proved to be too expensive a defense luxury to be accommodated adequately by the limitations of peacetime budgets, particularly with the exigencies of a depression budget when the emphasis was on reduction and curtailment. The War Department had long emphasized that the National Defense Act required a relatively large budget because of the civilian components and not because of the Regular Army. If significant budget reductions were the goal by administration and congressional leaders an overhauling of the 1920 legislation would be required.

The role of President Roosevelt in all these issues pertaining to the Army in the early days of his administration is enigmatic. One critic of the President claims that he was opposed to the military program of the General Staff and personally directed the policies which the Army felt were a threat to its viability. Roosevelt, it is claimed, gave authority and orders to Douglas to cut the Army budget for fiscal 1934, and indicated that he would back his budget chief in the latter's decisions.[50] The influential Army Navy Journal did not signal out the President for attack but struck out at his advisors, particularly Douglas and the power he wielded as Director of the Bureau of the Budget. Douglas, the Journal warned, "has wielded virtually the power of life and death over the government activities, including the National Defense."[51] The Journal emphasized that advocates of national defense were concerned over the fact that in addition to formulating the budget for the next fiscal year (1935), Douglas was overseeing the execution of all government expenditures for the current fiscal year and had the "power to discontinue any activity which he regarded as unnecessary or which can be suspended in his judgment without inconvenience or loss to the public...."[52]

Another issue that exacerbated the relationship between the Army and the new administration was the President's Executive Order Number 6166, dated June 10, 1933. The order in essence specified that the

> function of the disbursement of moneys of the United States exercised by any agency is transferred to the Treasury Department ... the head of which shall be a chief disbursing officer.[53]

At the same time Roosevelt asked Congress for approval of his

---

[50]Hunt, Untold Story of MacArthur, p. 151.

[51]Army Navy Journal, August 19, 1933, p. 1019.

[52]Ibid., September 23, 1933, p. 68.

[53]Executive Order 6166, June 10, 1933, AG 404, RG 94, NA.

government reorganization plan, which would provide this central procurement bureau and a central disbursing officer in the Treasury Department.[54]

The Army took this order as a direct threat to its command responsibility and authority and, following almost immediately upon the settlement of the appropriations issue, it was viewed by military leaders as an attempt on the part of the civilian entourage at the White House to weaken the autonomy and independence of the military establishment. The order, in effect, would make all disbursement of funds for military spending the function of the Treasury Department. It would mean abolishing the Finance Department of the Army and the transfer to the Treasury Department of the General Staff's responsibility for the disbursement of military appropriations.

In July 1933 Roosevelt ordered the plan postponed until January 1934. In late December the Army succeeded in obtaining further postponement with the understanding that conferences would be arranged with Treasury Department officials in order to work out some sort of a compromise. In urging the Secretary of War vigorously to oppose this move by White House officials, the Chief of Finance advised that unless strong and "affirmative action" was taken to excuse the Army from the provisions of the Executive Order, the distribution of Army funds would be "transferred to the complete supervision and control, and thereafter

---

[54]New York _Times_, June 11, 1933, pp. 1, 3.

operate as an activity of the Treasury Department."[55]

In early February 1934, a conference between War Department and Bureau of the Budget officials was unsuccessful in settling the dispute, and both sides held to their position. The Army flatly opposed any act which it viewed as a threat to its independence and authority; the administration officials claimed the move was essential for economy and for centralized disbursement of government funds, and that if the Army was exempted from the order, the Post Office Department and other departments would also have to be excused. On February 12, 1934, the Chief of Finance outlined the Army's position in a lengthy letter to the Treasury Department. He emphasized that the Army was basically different from the civilian activities of the government, and that any removal of any cog from the military machine damaged the whole.[56] The Chief of Finance claimed that the Army was more than willing to cooperate in bringing about true economy of government, but because of the unique mission of the military establishment, its machinery and organization was too delicate to be tampered with for reasons of doubtful economy:

No matter how small a part of the disbursing function is placed under civilian control, to that extent there is a detraction from

---

[55]Memo, Chief of Finance to the AG, December 2, 1933. AG 040, RG 94, NA.

[56]Ltr, Chief of Finance to Commissioner of Accounts and Deposits, Treasury Department, February 12, 1934. AG 040, RG 94, NA.

the supreme control over military operations which should be solely vested in military commanders.[57]

The reluctance of War Department officials to cooperate with efforts to place the financial mechanism of the government on a more rational and efficient basis, and the claim of Army officers for autonomy and independence, undoubtedly irritated the eager New Deal planners now ensconced in the other government agencies. During the spring of 1934, the issue remained unresolved. Finally, in late May, President Roosevelt revoked those parts of his executive order applicable to the disbursing functions of the armed services. No explanation was given for the Chief Executive's revocation in this regard, but evidence of increasing War Department involvement in the disbursement of CCC and PWA funds may have influenced Roosevelt, It was obvious to the President that such a program as the CCC depended largely on the experienced supply and procurement officials of the War Department. At the same time, Lewis Douglas, the controversial Director of the Budget who had led the vanguard in the effort to bring Army fiscal affairs under more direct control by the Bureau of the Budget and the Treasury Department, was becoming increasingly disillusioned with the

---

[57]Ibid., the Chief of Finance"s letter reflected the view of the War Department that the mission of the Army inherently placed it above the day to day political and economic issues of the civilian government apparatus: "The paramount consideration of national defense is the most vital function of Government and nothing should be allowed to interfere with its full, complete, and independent action."

Roosevelt New Deal, and he finally resigned in August, 1934.[58] In a marginal note penciled to a copy of Roosevelt's revocation order that was forwarded to the Deputy Chief of Staff, the Chief of Finance indicated the delight of the War Department in the successful defense of its financial autonomy:

> Dear Drum-- I have worked 8 months for this result. It is very gratifying. The integrity of the High Command is maintained, and command and responsibility continue to go hand in hand. Without this the civilian disbursing officer of the Treasury would have completely dominated the High Command. I know you will be pleased with this. Yours, /s/ Coleman.[59]

---

[58]Douglas' defection from the New Deal was precipitated his basic view that "government retrenchment and a balanced buuget were necessary not only for recovery, but for human freedom itself." Arthur M. Schlesinger, Jr., "The Age of Roosevelt," Vol. II, The Coming of the New Deal (Boston: Houghton Mifflin Company, 1959), p. 289.

[59]Marginal Note to Executive Order, May 29, 1934. "Revocation in Part of Section 4 of Executive Order No. 6166, June 19, 1933. AG 040, RG 94, NA. Note: General Coleman was The Chief of Finance.

CHAPTER XI

THE ARMY AND THE NEW DEAL: PART II

The Army, angry and aghast at the activities of the Roosevelt Administration in economizing by curtailing military expenditures, was still optimistic over the possibility of obtaining funds through the Public Works Administration for military projects. One of the last and most important provisions of the Roosevelt legislative program that encompassed the famous "one hundred days" was the National Industrial Recovery Act, better known as the NRA. Attention has been given to this legislation and the provision it made for the organization of industry and business in order to obtain their cooperation in matters pertaining to prices, wages, hours of unemployment, unfair competition, and production. Of importance to the Army was the provision of the bill to spend $3.3 billion in public works, and Section 202 of Title II of the NRA bill which provided that the Federal Administrator of Public Works, under the President

> shall prepare a comprehensive program of public works, which shall include among other things the following: ....
> ....
> (e) and if in the opinion of the President it seems desirable, the construction of naval vessels within the terms and/or limits established by the London Naval Treaty of 1930 and of aircraft required therefor and construction of such Army housing projects as the President may approve, and provision of original equipment for the mechanization and motorization of such Army tactical units

as he may designate: Provided, however, that in the event of an international agreement for the further limitation of armament, to which the United States is signatory, the President is hereby authorized and empowered to suspend, in whole or in part, any such naval construction or mechanization and motorization of Army units.[1]

Immediately after passage of the NRA, the General Staff was ordered to prepare studies on Army needs that could be fulfilled through the expenditure of public works funds. The Army realized that its program and estimates for funds would have to be moderate in order to be accepted by the Public Works Administrator, Harold L. Ickes. The estimate studies encompassed general motorization, mechanization, motorization and modernization of field artillery, motorization of anti-aircraft artillery (AAA), housing, ammunition, and aircraft.

The original G-3 study on mechanization was addressed to the problem of determining to what extent mechanization should be initiated through the use of public works funds. G-3 noted that under mechanization (defined as the application of motor vehicles to the battlefield as actual weapons) the total number of units scheduled for mobilization consisted of nine light tank regiments, three medium tank regiments, two mechanized cavalry brigades, thirteen armored car squadrons, and fifty light tank companies for the various infantry divisions. Realizing that this total was

---

[1] HR 5755, 73rd Congress, 1st Session, May 23, 1933. "A Bill to encourage National Industrial Recovery, to foster fair competition, and to provide for the construction of certain useful public works, and for other purposes." AG 508 I.R. (5-1-33), RG 94, NA.

impracticable of being financed by any public works funds, G-3 suggested that "wisdom and preparedness would indicate the procurement of sufficient tanks...to equip the units to be mobilized in the Initial Mobilization period."[2]

In forwarding the G-3 study on the use of New Deal funds for the mechanization of part of the initial mobilization force to MacArthur, the Deputy Chief of Staff, General Drum, noted that there had been general agreement among interested chiefs of the War Department relative to the types and kinds of equipment. However, Drum remarked, objection was made to the number of armored car squadrons that were scheduled

on the grounds of the number of regiments of cavalry (2) that would have to be dehorsed for this purpose and the lack of experience in utilization of squadrons. The majority were of the viewpoint that instead of squadrons there should be seven (7) troops

....

Some discussion took place as to whether or not we were sufficiently advanced from the technical and organizational viewpoint to start on the expenditure of the money set forth in the project herewith. The majority of the members of the council believed that we were prepared to launch this project. However, practically all agreed with the G-3 recommendation that the project be limited to the fourth priority, which includes:

1 cavalry brigade
1 regiment of medium tanks Infantry
1 regiment of light tanks Infantry
7 troops armored cars
7 companies division light tanks
1 battalion Field Artillery

at a cost of approximately $23,000,000.[3]

---

[2] Memo, AC/S G-3 for the Chief of Staff, subj: "Organization and Cost of Mechanization," May 24, 1933. AG 537.3 I.R. (5-24-33), RG 94, NA.

[3] Memo, Deputy Chief of Staff for the Chief of Staff, subj: "Mechanization Project," May 26, 1933. AG 537.3 I.R. (5-24-33), RG 94, NA.

From the Drum memorandum that was sent to MacArthur it is apparent that within the Army there was reluctance to push ahead boldly with a mechanization program, and even if more funds were forthcoming, some individuals were cautious over such development. The alarm of the War Department chiefs over the "dehorsing" of cavalry regiments reflected the conservative "wait and see" approach to military organization and equipment. It is interesting to note that the General Council of the War Department, although deciding on fewer armored car units, approved generally the same estimate as the G-3.[4]

With the G-3 study on the use of public works funds for mechanization, G-4 forwarded its study pertaining to motorization. G-4 estimated the need of the Army to complete motorization of active units at $37,000,000 ($17,000,000 for the Regular Army and $20,000,000 for the National Guard). In supporting this figure G-4 emphasized that it would complete and extend all motorization projects and replace World War I vehicles and thus effect economies through the replacement of animals and the reduction of maintenance

---

[4]Note: A squadron in the old cavalry usually consisted of a headquarters troop and two or more troops of cavalry. In order to have organized 3 squadrons of armored cars, as outlined in the G-3 memo, the cavalry would have been required to break up existing horse units in order to organize not only the line or combat troops of the new units, but also, and perhaps more important, would have had to organize additional headquarters, supply, and overhead units. By listing armored car units as troops instead of squadrons, the cavalry need furnish less personnel for overhead and headquarters duty, and at the same time the basic number of combat personnel and equipment would be essentially the same.

and repairs of old equipment. The total of 8,456 vehicles that G-4 requested be procured through public works funds did not include motor transport for the Anti-aircraft Artillery units, which was included in estimates for the combat equipment for that arm. G-4's estimate noted that there were 6,348 motor vehicles on hand in the Army as of May 1933 of which 4,432 were manufactured during the First World War.[5] General Drum, as Deputy Chief of Staff, went over the estimates on motorization with the General Council and he informed MacArthur that there had been conflicting views, some for complete motorization of all artillery and others opposed to this plan. Drum recommended that one-half of all Regular Army divisional artillery of each division be motorized and the other half retained as horse or animal drawn, while all National Guard units be motorized. The total request for PWA funds for motorization that was recommended to MacArthur was around $38,000,000.[6] Again it is evident that there was no unanimous enthusiasm among military leaders to motorize; perhaps this was not based on any recalcitrant and conservative attitude to maintain the old methods and equipment but, to a concern that after the first flush of federal funds to alleviate the equipment problem in the Army, the civilian leaders of the government and congressional

---

[5] Memo, AC/S G-4 for the Chief of Staff, May 24, 1933. AG 537.1 I.R. (5-17-33) Section 1-C-1933, RG 94, NA.

[6] Memo, Deputy Chief of Staff for the Chief of Staff, May 29, 1933. AG 537.1 I.R. (5-17-33) Section 1-C-1933, RG 94, NA.

economizers would fail to maintain adequate funds for the maintenance and repair of the equipment. The obsolescent rate for military equipment forced military officers of the early nineteen thirties to be conservative in requesting funds; equipment scheduled in fiscal 1932 for procurement in fiscal 1934 might be obsolete by the time it came to be issued to combat units. Thus the Army, with limited funds available, was hesitant about moving rapidly toward mechanization and motorization.

G-4's study on ammunition covered the needs for training and for the war reserve and estimated the needs of the Army in this category at $274,000,000. The figure covered a five priority project for the augmentation and preservation of the war reserve and training ammunition required for all components for two years.[7] In reviewing this study, General Drum doubted if "any amount of money approaching this large sum can be expected." Drum recommended that all that could be expected would be around $11,000,000 for training and for the preservation of stocks of the war reserve on hand.[8]

The G-4 study on the cost of providing the ordnance equipment needed for all active units of the Regular Army and the National Guard gave a total of approximately $5,200,000. Of this

---

[7] Memo, AC/S G-4 for the Chief of Staff, May 23, 1933. AG 471 I.R., RG 94, NA.

[8] Memo, Deputy Chief of Staff for the Chief of Staff, May 29, 1933. AG 471 I.R., RG 94, NA.

total the Regular Army was scheduled to receive less than a million for the procurement of an infantry mortar to replace the old Stokes mortar of World War I vintage and a late model of the 37mm infantry gun. The National Guard in the G-4 study was allotted $4,500,000 in order to complete its organization equipment. Reflecting the concern of the General Staff over the possibility of domestic strife in 1933, G-4 noted that "gas masks were needed to enable the National Guard to cope with serious situations arising in connection with civil disorders."[9]

In another study pertaining to the estimated cost of modernizing field artillery units, G-4 informed the Chief of Staff that it contemplated equipping two regiments of 75mm pack howitzers, providing wheeled guns for the cavalry division, and changing the carriages of the 75mm and 155 mm guns on hand so that they could be towed by trucks at greater speeds and the guns themselves traversed and elevated to better advantage. The program was outlined in five categories of priority and totalled $35,000,000.[10] In a handwritten note appended to the last page of this study, the Deputy Chief of Staff wrote that he doubted if he would be able to include this program for forwarding to Congress but that G-4 should

---

[9] Memo, AC/S G-4 for Chief of Staff, subj: "Mobilization Equipment," May 24, 1933. AG 471 I.R., RG 94, NA.

[10] Memo, AC/S G-4 for Chief of Staff, "Modernization of Field Artillery," May 24, 1933. AG 471 I.R., RG 94, NA.

keep it handy as a last priority![11]

The G-4 study concerning the use of public works funds for the re-armament and re-equipment of mobile anti-aircraft artillery was developed in conjunction with G-3 and the WPD. The study covered the estimate of cost necessary for the rearmament and equipment of AAA regiments of the Regular Army and National Guard, and for establishing a portion of the War Reserve in the principle items of equipment for all AAA regiments in the proposed initial mobilization, a total of thirty-five regiments. The program was separated into five priorities, the first priority included the active Regular Army and National Guard units and the total estimated cost of these units was listed as $17,400,000 and the total cost of the entire program was estimated at $34,600,000.[12]

The estimated cost of the needs of the Air Corps was outlined by G-4 in a program totaling $39,500,000. This figure contemplated the requirements necessary to complete and maintain to the end of fiscal 1935 (June 30, 1936) the Air Corps Act of 1926 which provided for 1800 aircraft. The G-4 estimate involved the procurement

---

[11] Handwritten note accompanying above memo. Initialed by General Hugh A. Drum for the Chief of Staff. Note: Drum's comment that he doubted his ability to present this program to Congress is perplexing because of the fact that the PWA program was not scheduled to go before Congress for approval. Congress had voted the funds to the administration and Harold Ickes and President Roosevelt rather than Congress decided on the project.

[12] Ltr, AC/S G-4 for Director Federal Employment Stabilization Board, June 6, 1933. AG 580 I.R. (6-6-33) Section 1, RG 94, NA.

of 1034 aircraft including 372 pursuit and 132 bombardment aircraft.[13]

The unrealistic nature of the post-World War I defense legislation is indicated in this request which did not contemplate anything except meeting the requirement of laws already on the books. The Air Corps Act of 1926, with its plan of having 1800 serviceable aircraft on hand after a five-year period ending in June 1932, was impracticable of attainment because of the fiscal and political tenor of the nation at the time of its passage, and it was further emasculated by the financial policies of the Hoover and Roosevelt Administrations. The difficulty of financing modern weapons of war is vividly exemplified by the fact that, in order to keep 1800 aircraft serviceable, the Air Corps estimated that it was necessary to have 2057 aircraft on hand! This figure was based on actual experience during the early 1930's. The Air Corps also warned that a further reduction of manpower authorized for depots and air bases would increase the number of aircraft required on hand as the time factor involved in repairs and overhaul would increase due to shortage of personnel and cause the number of serviceable aircraft to be reduced.[14]

The General Staff, conforming to the instructions of the

---

[13] Ltr, AC/S G-4 for Director, Federal Employment Stabilization Board, June 6, 1933. AG 580 I.R. (6-6-33) Section I, RG 94, NA.

[14] Memo, Deputy Chief of Staff for the Chief of Staff, June 2, 1933. AG 580 I.R. (6-6-33) Section I, RG 94, NA.

Secretary of War, had brought forth an interesting estimate. The enormity of the request that was forwarded to Ickes and his PWA Board was a reflection upon the state of the Army and the fact that due to fiscal limitations imposed by national policies, both political and financial, the Army was ill-equipped for modern warfare. In recommending the estimates the Chief of Staff noted that the items were "deemed essential for modern efficiency and a well balanced program of preparedness." The total estimate forwarded to the PWA Board came to around $304,000,000, and included $135,000,000 for housing, $23,000,000 for mechanization, $35,000,000 for modernization of Field Artillery, $39,000,000 for the Air Corps, $39,000,000 for the general motorization of the Army, and $33,000,000 for the modernization of the antiaircraft equipment. This figure represented the General Staff's estimate of the Army's deficiency of modern weapons and equipment in 1933.[15]

In the limited military budget that was given to the Army every year, priority had to be given to the detailed and costly provision of the civilian components, and as a consequence, materiel suffered. Except for a small amount for R&D the Army materiel program had been held down rigidly in appropriations since the 1918 armistice. It is significant to note that throughout the entire series of studies prepared by G-4 and G-3 concerning the equipment needs of the Army the National Guard was seldom ignored.

---

[15] Report of the Secretary of War, 1933, p. 19.

In every category, except mechanization, high on the list of units scheduled to receive funds were various National Guard units. The General Staff stressed the fact that in the construction and building program, the National Guard and other civilian components would benefit as much as the Regular Army.

Of course estimating the needs of the Army and forwarding the request for funds is another thing from having the funds allotted and expended. Unquestionably the Army was hardly confident that it would receive funds anywhere near the $300,000,000 that it had requested. The $300,000,000 figure was probably for the benefit of the civilian administrators in the PWA to be used as a guide to calculate the amount necessary to bring the Army up to date with modern equipment, and the Public Works Board could determine from this figure a compromise sum, which, although considerably less than the original figure, would be willingly accepted by the Army. Army spokesmen pointed out that the figure was not too preposterous, when one kept in mind that almost one-half of the figure -- $150,000,000 -- was for housing and technical construction and was not in the direct sense, armaments and equipment. And orders for equipment in 1933, at a time when all World War I stocks were obsolete or obsolescent, would be economical in the long run and benefit national defense and aid economic recovery through the stimulation of industry.[16]

---

[16] Army Navy Journal, June 24, 1933, pp. 849-50.

That the Army was realistic about the $300,000,000 request is evident by the fact that in his appearance before the Public Works Board in July 1933, Secretary Dern planned to make a verbal request for only $173,000,000. Dern's appearance before the Public Works Board, and his submission of the military program was the cause of a misunderstanding between the Secretary of War and Harold Ickes, which, unfortunately for the Army, perhaps prejudiced its future chances of obtaining New Deal funds for building up the military establishment. Omitting any reference or mention of the Army program, Ickes announced on July 14 that he had allotted $115,000,000 for the first public works projects. Earlier Roosevelt had approved $400,000,000 of federal roads money to the states and $238,000,000 to the Navy for ships.[17] When asked the result of the Army request, Ickes claimed that Dern had withdrawn his estimates during his appearance before the Public Works Board and would submit it later. Ickes claimed that at a meeting of the Special Board of Public Works, Dern had presented the Rivers and Harbors estimates and that they were adopted. Ickes added:

> I then asked him whether he had any other proposals to make and he promptly replied that the other one that he had in his hand he would withdraw.[18]

---

[17] Army Navy Journal, July 15, 1933, p. 927.

[18] "The Secret Diary of Harold L. Ickes," Vol. I, The First Thousand Days, 1933-1936 (New York: Simon and Schuster, 1935), p. 68.

Dern became enraged over Ickes' remarks to the press and the derogatory implication that the Secretary of War had refused to stand up for the Army and its estimates for PWA funds. On July 19, Dern denounced Ickes' statements as "misleading" and stated that he had withdrawn the Army estimates because:

> I was not satisfied with the action that I anticipated was about to be taken by the board and, therefore asked that further consideration be dropped until a subsequent meeting.[19]

The Army Navy Journal claimed that Ickes was prejudiced against the Army, and his assertion that the Army's request for PWA funds was "not socially beneficial," caused Dern to ask that further consideration of the Army's requests be dropped until a subsequent meeting. Included in Dern's $173,000,000 request was $100,000,000 for military housing, $50,000,000 for motorization and mechanization, $13,000,000 for Ordnance, and $10,000,000 for aircraft.[20]

The issue of the Army estimates before the PWA Board did not

---

[19] New York Times, July 19, 1933, p. 9. Dern also pointed out to the press that he had no plan or thought of enlarging the Army, but was in "favor of making it the most modern and effective military organization possible in the interest of national defense. To that end I think we ought to be given substantial sums for these purposes. Comprehensive plans were prepared under my direction and submitted to the Board of Public Works weeks ago. The projects are ready to start; hence, men could be put to work immediately and a goodly share of the employees would belong to the building trades. The construction of airplanes, besides enabling the Army to complete its five-year program, would give work to a great many highly specialized workers in an industry that is vital and that has been having a hard time to keep going."

[20] Army Navy Journal, July 22, 1933, pp. 929, 948.

serve to improve the relationship between the Army and the New Deal. Certainly Ickes became more suspicious of the Chief of Staff as the Bete noire behind a naive and gullible Secretary of War. Ickes describes the President's position on the entire affair as in support of the Director of Public Works against the cunning machinations of the War Department:

I had an appointment with the President at Noon today (Friday, July 21, 1933). He was still in bed, and for forty minutes I went over the public works matters. He brought up the matter of Secretary of War Dern by telling me that Dern had allowed himself to be put in an unfortunate position by the Chief of Staff, General MacArthur. I didn't go into the Dern matter except to say that I thought his interview given to the papers was unfortunate and that it wasn't based upon the record. The President went on to tell me how he had to sit down on General MacArthur pretty hard himself on one occasion, and he expressed the opinion that MacArthur was running the War Department.

....

The President asked me to wait until after the press conference because Assistant Secretary of War Woodring had put up a matter to him that he wanted to discuss with me, so after the press conference the three of us met in his office. Woodring wanted him to sign an Executive Order allocating $13 million to the War Department out of the public works funds in order to keep the munitions factories going. He said the factories could not open on Monday unless this allocation was made. I objected on the ground that it would set a bad precedent if the President, without consideration by the Board of Public Works, or recommendation from it, should assign a sum to any Department by Executive Order. I said that while it might be a hardship for the men employed in the munitions factories to be laid off for a week or two, they wouldn't be in as bad a case as people who had been unemployed for two years or more. I also said that if this matter had not been passed upon by the Board and submitted to the President, the fault lay with the War Department and not with the Special Board for Public Works, but he did agree, after asking me whether it would be all right so far as I was concerned, that the War Department should give out a statement that $6 million had been assured for the continuing of the munitions factories and that they would operate as usual on Monday.[21]

---

[21] Ickes, First Thousand Days, pp. 68-69. On July 22, Ickes

No better example of the ability of President Roosevelt to appease antagonistic factions in his administration can be presented than the dexterous manner in which he comprised the issue of public works funds for the Ordnance arsenals. Ickes left the conference with Woodring and Roosevelt confident that his Chief had supported him in his efforts to bring the Army into line; Woodring undoubtedly was elated in his ability to obtain funds for the Army by going over the head of the hostile and obstinate Board of Public Works and appealing directly to Roosevelt.

MacArthur, as Acting Secretary of War during Dern's absence from Washington, was invited to attend the Board of Public Works meeting on Thursday, July 27, 1933, to present the Army's estimates. Ickes' scorn and repugnance toward the military establishment and its Chief of Staff is best illustrated by the "Old Curmudgeon's" account of MacArthur's appearance before the Board;

I had asked Chief of Staff MacArthur to come in on some Army projects. He had presented a very large list running into the hundreds of millions, out of which the President allowed him $6 million for coast defenses in the Canal Zone and Hawaii, in addition to $6 million previously allowed for ammunition. MacArthur is the type of man who thinks that when he gets to Heaven, God will step down from the great white throne and bow him into His vacated seat, and it gave me a great kick to have him in and break the news

---

informed the War Department that an allotment of $6 million had been made to the Army for "the manufacture and/or reconditioning of munitions in government arsenals." Ltr, Ickes to Secretary of War, July 22, 1933. AG 471, I.R., RG 94, NA. In the expenditure of this money $4.8 million was applied to procurement and $1.2 million for preservation of ammunition. Memo, AC/S G-4 for Chief of Staff, August 2, 1933. AG 471 I.R., RG 94, NA.

to him. While he was here, though, two or three of the members foolishly asked him some questions which gave him a chance to deliver a lecture on the subject of the necessity for the little old peanut Army posts that we have scattered around the country.[22]

Throughout the summer of 1933, the failure of the Public Works Board to approve the Army requests did not cause too great concern within the Army. It was felt that, regardless of Ickes' recalcitrance and antagonism to spending money on any military project, the President wanted concessions made in regard to the Army estimates. The *Army Navy Journal* believed that Roosevelt was willing to grant some funds for motorization and mechanization but would make no decision on the matter until after the close of the Geneva Disarmament Conference in the fall of 1933.[23] In September Secretary of War Dern outlined to Ickes the necessity for favorable action concerning the Army's request for PWA funds. His remarks were a curious blend of an apology for being so bold as to write to the Administrator and also a special plea for the Army and the need of preparedness. Noting that action on the mechanization program of $23,000,000 was still pending, Dern stressed the urgency of funds for this purpose by noting that mechanization of the Army had barely been kept alive since 1918 because of the lack of funds and the desire to perfect a pilot model before attempting quantity production. Present design, according to the Secretary

---

[22] *Ibid.*, p. 71.

[23] *Army Navy Journal*, July 29, 1933, p. 967.

of War, was now "sufficiently satisfactory" to justify procurement of enough vehicles to equip units required for the task of developing the tactics and techniques of mechanized units. Dern pleaded that PWA funds were the only foreseeable source of money for the mechanization plans of the Army: "The prospects of obtaining appropriations for this project doubtless are slight because of budgetary limitation."[24]

At the same time Dern wrote to Ickes urging favorable action on the other Army requests: motorization, AAA, and modernization of the field artillery. The complex and technically involved military programs may have deterred the PWA Board from taking a more favorable view toward the military estimates. Certainly the possibility in the Army programs of duplication, the loss of close supervision by the PWA over the expenditure of funds on military projects, combined with the deep seated suspicion of the military establishment on the part of Ickes, did not augur well for the Army in their attempts to obtain PWA money.

Dern urged Ickes to grant funds for motorization by pointing out that the $38,000,000 motorization program was urgently needed, and it was pointed out that by spending the money 38,335 men could be employed in the automotive industry for three months and approximately 126,000 other workers in allied industries.[25] Dern also

---

[24] Ltr, Dern to Ickes, subj: "Mechanization of the Army," September 5, 1933. AG 537.3 I.R. (5-26-33) Section I-B, RG 94, NA.

[25] Ltr, Dern to Ickes, subj: "Motorization," September 5, 1933. AG 537.3 I.R. (5-26-33) Section I-C, RG 94, NA.

referred in this letter to the $33,300,000 request for motorization of the AAA, and noted that the inadequacy of ground defenses against air attack prompted favorable action on this "moderate" project; he reminded Ickes that the stringent budgetary limitations in prospect for the future and the considerable time required for the manufacture of this equipment in an emergency, indicated the wisdom of including this project in the PWA program.[26]

The third letter that Dern wrote to Ickes on September 5, concerning the Army's request for PWA funds was in reference to the motorization and modernization of the field artillery. The Secretary of War stressed the fact that this program was not in duplication of the general motorization program of $38,000,000, and again pleaded with Ickes that the PWA funds were the only hope of the Army: "unless this project is included in the Emergency Public Works, our field artillery weapons will never be modern."[27]

Undoubtedly, the complexity of the Army estimates as well as the size of the $300,000,000 request deterred the PWA Board from giving more sympathetic and capable analysis. Disregarding Ickes' unsympathetic attitude toward MacArthur and his "peanut" Army, the PWA Board was technically ill-equipped to study and to judge the suitability and necessity of Army appropriations. Dern's three

---

[26] Ibid.

[27] Ltr, Dern to Ickes, sub: "Field Artillery Modernization," September 5, 1933. AG 537 I.R. Section I-C-1933, RG 94, NA.

letters to Ickes on September 5, were the first attempt by the Army to inform the PWA Board of the detailed requirements of the Army, and that the money was needed for urgent and necessary projects. Dern's efforts in this regard were timely and wise. The PWA Board felt that if they had the responsibility and authority for spending PWA funds it was necessary to know in more detail how the money was to be spent and was understandably hesitant to serve as a rubber stamp for passing money to the General Staff.

The Army was aware of this fact, and therefore not too confident that the Board would approve its requests. However, Dern realized that in the end "everything depends on Mr. Roosevelt."[28] Therefore, if Dern could impress on the President the necessity of the Army obtaining public works funds perhaps a part of the Army's request would be granted. Dern reminded the President that this was a timely method of killing two birds with one stone: modernize the Army and whip unemployment. In early September Dern rather optimistically announced:

> the decision on all matters is in the hands of the President.... We have felt that this was a good time to bring the Army up to date by using Public Works money. It would be pretty hard to get some of these things through Congress under ordinary conditions. Now is quite a good time to get up to date and do it in such a way as to fit in the Army ideally with Public Works, acting as a recovery measure. After all, that's the primary object; not primarily a construction measure but a recovery measure.[29]

---

28 Army Navy Journal, July 1, 1933, p. 872.

29 Ibid., September 2, 1933, p. 19.

In mid-September Roosevelt decided to approve a $50,000,000 allotment of PWA funds for Army housing.[30] As a result, the Army was hopeful that an appreciable remainder of its program might gain consideration from the Commander-in-Chief.

War Department plans and dreams of obtaining PWA funds, after being held in abeyance throughout the summer and early fall, were shattered on October 25, 1933, when one of Ickes' assistants telephoned a Major Tompkins, who served as liaison officer between the General Staff and PWA, and informed him that the President had approved allotting to the Army $10,000,000 for motorization and mechanization, and $7,500,000 for aircraft.[31]

Although the Army did not expect anything in the neighborhood of $300,000,000, it had hopes of getting around one-half of this total or $150,000,000. In Ickes' account of the final decision on granting PWA funds to the Army, it was Roosevelt himself who decreased the Army allotment after Dern had pushed through the Public

---

[30] New York <u>Times</u>, September 21, 1933, p. 20. Note: The Times commented that the "long continued battle for adequate housing" had partly been won, and that the allotment of $54.7 million for construction and reconditioning of 32 camps was only part of the original request by the Army of $135 million. "It is generally understood that there is little chance of the full allotment being made."

[31] Memo, Maj. W. F. Tompkins to the AC/S G-4, October 25, 1933. AG 537.3 I.R. RG 94, NA. Note: The public announcement that the PWA was going to allot some $25 million for national defense to the Army and Navy was made on October 21, 1933. New York <u>Times</u>, October 22, 1933, p. 15. The times noted that the award of $15 million for new aircraft was "only a small part of the total asked, but supporters of a larger air force were certain that the first allocation was only a forerunner of other awards to follow."

Works Board an allotment of some $170,000,000. Ickes implied that Dern had deceived the Board and influenced it toward approving the Army's estimate by stating that Roosevelt had concurred in the $170,000,000 figure. According to Ickes:

> I lunched with the President today (Friday, October 20, 1933) to take up a number of matters with him, but he had so many things he wanted to talk about that I didn't really get through. However, he did scrutinize the list of public works that I submitted to him. On the Army list that Secretary Dern got us to adopt yesterday on the theory that it had the prior approval of the President, he did just what he said he would do. He allowed $15 million for aviation for both the Army and Navy, and $10 million for motorization and mechanization for the Army. This was quite a contrast with the $172 million that Dern had had us put through for the Army alone. He also disapproved a considerable allocation for coast defense purposes.[32]

The action of Roosevelt in reducing the Army allotment to some $17,500,000 must have come as a shock to Dern, who had good reason to believe that Roosevelt was willing to grant the Army a more sizeable sum. In early October, before the announcement of the award of the $17,500,000 to the Army for aircraft, mechanization, and motorization, Dern claimed that Roosevelt had directed him to re-submit the War Department estimates to the PWA Board.[33] Dern evidently took this to mean that if the Army could come up with a more modest request than its original $300,000,000 figure, it stood an excellent chance of having the estimate approved.

The new Army estimate forwarded to Ickes on October 18, 1933,

---

[32] Ickes, First Thousand Days, p. 111.

[33] Ltr, Dern to Ickes, October 18, 1933. AG 537.3, I.R., RG 94, NA.

was broken down into two categories, Class A and Class B, and totalled around $170,000,000. Class A category totalled approximately $95,000,000 and included funds which the Army termed "fundamental and immediately necessary." Class B category covered projects that were desirable but which could be postponed to meet budgetary requirements. Class A category included $22,800,000 for mechanization, a figure almost identical with the original request, $11,000,000 for AAA, $3,600,000 for motorization of Regular Army and National Guard units, and $11,200,000 for aviation. Dern emphasized, when he forwarded the revised estimate to Ickes, that the request was being re-submitted at the direction of President Roosevelt for "immediate consideration."[34]

The final allotment that was approved by President Roosevelt in October made it incumbent for Army planners to revise their planned spending program. In accordance with the resolution of the Special Board of Public Works, before any money was actually transferred to the War Department, the latter was required to furnish a breakdown of how the allotment would be spent geographically by state and by project. In the revised project for the spending of $10,000,000 for mechanization and motorization forwarded to the PWA Board on December 1, 1933, the General Staff visualized expending some $7,000,000 for general motorization, $64,000 for modernization of field artillery equipment on hand,

---

[34] Ibid.

$924,000 for AAA, $656,000 for mechanization (tanks), and $1,250,000 for spare parts for all of the above items. Of the total of $10,000,000 granted by Roosevelt, the Regular Army was scheduled to receive around $8,000,000 and the National Guard approximately $2,000,000.[35]

The allocation of the $7,500,000 for Army aviation was presented by Roosevelt to the Army planners. The Army Air Corps had reluctantly accepted the original revised figure of October, although it was decidedly dissatisfied with the planned procurement of only 20 bombers. The Air Corps advocated spending the final $7,500,000 which Roosevelt had granted on the procurement of a long-range amphibious observation plane which could also serve as a bomber. This apparently was an endeavor to get around the General Staff's reluctance to procure long-range bombers. The General Staff was aghast at the proposal and vigorously opposed it on the grounds that the amphibian was not fully developed and was intended for naval purposes. The General Staff emphasized that the $7,500,000 be limited to fighting planes available for purchase at that time.[36] It was not until late in April 1934 that the revised aviation program was finally submitted to Ickes. The final

---

[35] Ltr, Dern to Ickes, December 1, 1933. AG 537.3 I.R. RG 94, NA. Note: The program was submitted by the General Staff to MacArthur for approval on November 27, and was forwarded to Ickes on December 1, 1933.

[36] Memo, Deputy Chief of Staff for the Chief of Staff, November 10, 1933. AG 580 I.R. (6-6-33) Section II, RG 94, NA.

revision differed from the original revision proposed by the General Staff in that, in deference to the Air Corps, it omitted pursuit planes and utilized this money for the procurement of additional bombardment aircraft. The total aircraft procurement program planned by the Army with $7,500,000 PWA funds included 64 bombers at $83,000 each and 30 attack planes. The program came to $7,500,000 with the addition of radio equipment for all aircraft.[37]

While revision of the motorization and mechanization program was taking place in the General Staff, Dern, who was chagrined over the failure of the President to appropriate more money, made a further plan to Roosevelt for funds for the mechanization program. On November 7, in a lengthy letter, Dern pleaded with Roosevelt for additional funds for the procurement of tanks:

> our military leaders point to the necessity of maintaining in peace a sufficient supply of these weapons to insure sound tactical and mechanical development and such knowledge by our industrial plants so as to provide an early and adequate supply in case of emergency. Our program is a modest one, designed only to meet the above requirements.[38]

According to Dern, the tank procurement program visualized by the General Staff with PWA funds encompassed one brigade of mechanized cavalry, two regiments of medium tanks, and one battalion of field

---

[37] Ltr, Chief of the Air Corps to the AG, April 21, 1934. AG 580 I.R., RG 94, NA.

[38] Ltr, Dern to Roosevelt, November 7, 1933. AG 537.3 I.R. (5-17-33), Section II, RG 94, NA.

artillery, the total number of mechanized combat vehicles coming to approximately 600. Concluding his letter, Dern informed Roosevelt that the $23,000,000 estimate from the Army for tanks "has been approved by the Public Works Board and only waits your decision."[39] Dern's efforts to change the Chief Executive's mind were to no avail and the Army went ahead on its revised allotment of $10,000,000 for both mechanization and motorization.

The planning of the General Staff ran into difficulty over the problem of how to use the small sum made available. MacArthur was dissatisfied with the General Staff's revised plan because it did not meet the "most urgent requirements" of the Army's combat units. In his view, too much of the limited funds were going into vehicles assigned for maintenance and administration. The first priority, according to the Chief of Staff, was to enhance the mobility of the fighting units of the Army and the main purpose should be to assure the maximum readiness of the tactical units. In MacArthur's view, the service units of the Army could rely on improvisation in case of an emergency and use equipment that could be readily available from civilian organizations whose functions ran generally parallel to non-combat Army service units. MacArthur did not want the Army to buy motor equipment indiscriminately, but be specifically related to improving the combat capacity of the tactical units. The Chief of Staff wanted to procure the following

---

[39] Ibid.

equipment with PWA funds: (1) all items of motor equipment needed for the mechanized cavalry regiments, except possibly tanks; and (2) complete motorization of the 1st, 2nd, and 3rd Divisions, including all of their combat trains and artillery. MacArthur felt that such a program would provide a possible expeditionary force "homogeneously" equipped.[40] Other members of the General Staff were dubious about MacArthur's vigorous assertion that it was necessary to motorize the Regular Army combat units. Brig, Gen. Hugh A. Drum, the Deputy Chief of Staff, pointed out that the Regular Army must be prepared for any emergency, and operations could involve a country where good and sufficient roads were non-existent. A compromise solution was adopted by the General Staff and the Chief of Staff whereby the Army would motorize all of the 1st Division, with all mounts and animal-drawn vehicles belonging to the infantry and artillery headquarters being retained, and providing for motor transport to carry these mounts and vehicles in trucks.[41] This was an ingenious compromise; the horse soldiers kept their horses and the advocates of motorization got their trucks. How efficient and sound the compromise was is another question.

Basic to the entire question of allotting public relief funds for military projects was a fundamental divergence of views concerning the purpose of relief spending between the New Deal and the

---

[40] Memo, Chief of Staff for the Deputy Chief of Staff. AG 537.3 I.R. (5-17-33) Section 1-C-1933, RG 94, NA.

[41] Memo, Deputy Chief of Staff for the Chief of Staff, November 22, 1933. AG 537.3 I.R. (5-17-33) Section 1-C-1933, RG 94, NA.

General Staff. This was reflected in the allotment of money for the motorization program rather than for the mechanization program. A total of 7,776 vehicles were scheduled for procurement by the Army with PWA funds and the Army was directed to make every effort to get the work into the hands of manufacturers as early as possible so that the objective of providing employment relief could be hastened.[42] To the relief administrator, the Army was to use the funds to hasten economic recovery, never minding the detailed technical requirements needed for combat vehicles. The Army, although eager to spend the money, had its own requirements for vehicles which at times precluded rapid contract and procurement. G-4 urged that the motorization program should reflect tactical needs and the organization of combat units; the number of passenger cars should be reduced and substituted with pick-up trucks or station wagons.[43] G-3 agreed with this proposal but was skeptical of the Army's ability to change the procurement program: "the emphasis of the whole program is not on exactness of detail that peace-time expenditure programs usually call for but speed is desirable and is still the fundamental reason governing the spending of money."[44] Reluctantly, MacArthur affirmed later that the entire amount of money

---

[42] Army Navy Journal, December 16, 1933, p. 305.

[43] Memo, AC/S G-4 for Chief of Staff, December 20, 1933. AG 537.3 I.R. (5-17-33) Section 1-C-1933, RG 94, NA.

[44] Memo, AC/S G-3 for the Chief of Staff, December 20, 1933. AG 537.3 I.R. (5-17-33) Section 1-C-1933, RG 94, NA.

made available for the Army was primarily for the purpose of providing work relief and that the projects were determined by officials of the PWA. He added that the funds were not allotted in strict accord with the Army's most critical needs.[45]

Another example of the basic conflict between military planners and relief administrators in the expenditure of funds for military projects arose in late 1933. Ickes had allotted approximately one million dollars of PWA funds to the Bureau of Aeronautics of the Department of Commerce so that this Bureau could foster cheap commercial and sport aviation throughout the country and thus aid as a subsidization of the light aircraft industry. At a meeting at the Labor Department in December with representatives of the PWA, War Department, Navy, and Commerce it was hoped to arouse enthusiasm of the Army and Navy in the project in the interest of national defense. It was proposed to use military aviators as instructors, with the money distributed by the Commerce Department to local flying fields and to the aircraft industry. The Chief of the Air Corps, in contrast to the Navy representative, was cool to the entire idea and emphasized that the Air Corps had already submitted "priority projects" to the PWA of greater importance and which had not been met in this entirety.[46]

---

[45] Report of the Secretary of War, 1935, p. 53.

[46] Memo, Chief of the Air Corps to the Deputy Chief of Staff, December 19, 1933. AG 580 I.R. (6-6-33) Section II, RG 94, NA.

The Department of Commerce sent its plan to Dern in early January 1934, and requested his views on the project. In advising Dern, the Air Corps pointed out that the program was based on a bill that Senator Bingham had introduced in 1932 which was based on the idea of training 100,000 reserve pilots on commercial airdromes throughout the United States under the supervision of Air Corps officers. Funds for aircraft and facilities would come from PWA funds distributed by the Department of Commerce. Maj. Gen. Westover, the Chief of the Air Corps, was flatly opposed to the idea on the grounds that the plan was unsound and the spending of the money was of no value to the national defense. Westover added that a further initial outlay of $250,000,000 was required for additional training to make the program useful and another $150,000,000 annually was necessary to keep the pilots trained. He added that this figure was "so prohibitive that no support from Congress could ever be expected."[47] G-4 concurred in the Air Corps position and emphasized the fact that the scheme of subsidizing established and reputable aircraft factories might be satisfactory but "not as a project of the War Department as a means of furthering the ends of national defense."[48] Dern in turn informed Ickes that the War Department did not want any part of a relief program

---

[47] Memo, AC/S G-4 for the Chief of Staff, January 12, 1934. AG 580 I.R. (6-6-33) Section II, RG 94, NA.

[48] Ltr, Dern to Ickes, January 15, 1934. AG 580 I.R. (6-6-33) Section II, RG 94, NA.

in which the benefits to national defense would be of a secondary or subsidiary nature.

The War Department believes that every effort should be concentrated toward rounding out effectively the Five-Year Air Corps program authorized by Congress, and that any dispersion of federal funds on less essential projects is unwarranted except for the primary purpose of fostering commercial aviation.

If the project was not primarily directed to benefit national defense, the Army was unenthusiastic and cool about participating. The War Department felt that it could not endorse any plan as a measure of defense in which the allocation of funds would come through another agency but at the same time involve the peripheral expenditure of limited War Department funds not directly contributing to the development of national defense.[49]

---

[49] Ibid. Note: Dern in his letter to Ickes noted that various bills had been considered during the past two years on the problem of providing reserve pilots to meet the emergency. In general, according to Dern, the problem was not one of personnel but equipment, and at the outset of an emergency the Air Corps was confident it could train new pilots as fast as aircraft were produced. The Bingham Bill involved the training of 100,000 aviators over a period of five years with the government furnishing the funds for purchase and maintenance of aircraft and the Army furnishing instructors. Another plan presented by the American Eagle-Lincoln Aircraft Corporation called for training of 40,000 youths with the objective of fifty hours of instruction under the direction of the War Department, who would be obliged to purchase 1,000 light planes. Dern emphasized that the Army was opposed to all these schemes because of the "enormous annual drain on Federal funds which would be necessary to carry out such programs." One would think that the Army would have been eager to cooperate in such a venture in which the Army and its aviators would receive increased publicity and exert their influence to a greater degree throughout the country. It is surprising that the Army Air Corps was opposed to a plan which undoubtedly would have been to their long range benefit. Three basic reasons can be given for this opposition: (1) the reluctance to become involved in a scheme in which the Army would be open to the charge of seeking to spread

The War Department was conservative in its philosophy of government spending; it was reluctant to support any program that appeared to be unsound and which was for the primary purpose of economic and unemployment relief and only secondarily of benefit to national defense. The Army believed in spending not for the sake of spending, but for a program that had been planned and outlined by the General Staff for stated needs and vital requirements, and which would come under the specific control and responsibility of experienced War Department fiscal officers. War Department projects that came before the Board of Public Works were the "crystallization and reflection of various studies which had been made by the General Staff,"[50] and not quickly devised schemes to get the General Staff into the public treasury and "prime the pump." The Army always stressed in their request for PWA funds that their plans were for national defense and a resulting by-product would be unemployment alleviation and aid to industry.

"militarism"; (2) the determination not to spread its activities and programs thinner by participation in a questionable project; (3) the suspicion that once initiated, Congress, as in the 1926 Air Corps Act, would not support the program adequately and the Army would be embarrassed again and have to plead and beg for support as in the ROTC and CMTC programs.

[50] Ibid.

CHAPTER XII

MOBILIZATION OF THE CIVILIAN CONSERVATION CORPS (CCC)

The Army during 1930 and 1931 had voiced its opposition to congressional leaders concerning various proposals to bring the Army into the fight against unemployment by using military facilities and military personnel to organize and supervise some sort of an unemployed corps. Before the 72nd Congress adjourned in March 1933, it brought up again a proposal to use the Army to alleviate unemployment by organizing a special corps. In January 1933, there was introduced into Congress the Couzens Bill which conceived of using the Army to feed, house, and clothe the unemployed throughout the country; the original figure mentioned was around 300,000. Immediately MacArthur set his staff to studying the proposals of the Couzens Bill "so that in the event" he was called on to submit recommendations he would have an answer. Furthermore, a lengthy study would be of possible future value in case the new Roosevelt Administration planned any such project.

The War Department study was made by G-3, and was concurred in by the other general staff divisions. The study was unenthusiastic about the Army participating in a relief scheme and noted several serious factors militating against Army participation. Primarily the General Staff stressed the fact that the Army could not house more than 67,000 men in available military housing and furthermore this housing was in the southern part of the country far removed from the areas of acute unemployment. The staff added, that if the Army was to rent shelter and housing in urban areas, and house the unemployed, the maintenance of discipline over men not enlisted in the Army or subject to military law would be so great as possibly to discredit the Army.

The very idea of military control over such shelter arrangements would be apt to arouse individual resistance and foment riots which the Army would be forced to suppress. The use of National Guard armories for shelter would present great disadvantages.[1]

The General Staff recommended that because of considerations of economy, in order to keep the unemployed in "stable conditions" in areas where their final adjustment must be made, and to prevent the massing of discontented men, the solution of the problem was more direct federal relief through civil relief agencies. However, the Army was willing, if Congress was determined to bring the military establishment into the fight against unemployment, that the best interests of the government could be served by: (a) limiting the number of unemployed aided by the Army to 68,000,

---

[1]Memo, AC/S G-3 for Chief of Staff, January 24, 1933. G-3/31340, RG 319, NA. Note: This memorandum was submitted and signed by Colonel Duncan Major, Acting G-3. Colonel Major later became the War Department Representative on the CCC Advisory Committee. His original opposition to any work project and his favoring of some sort of military training are interesting points when it is realized that Colonel Major was responsible for liaison between the War Department and the other departments during the operation of the CCC.

the number which could be housed adequately on military reservations; (b) follow the CMTC as a model and train the individual rather than give him employment on federal construction projects; (c) require an oath of the unemployed trainee, but one which specified that United States Government did not seek his services but only offered relief; (d) secure legislation authorizing increased pay for the Regular Army enlisted men who would assume new duties and responsibilities and also request permission to utilize Reserve Officers; (e) provide a small monthly fee for the unemployed trainee.[2] Secretary Hurley's formal reply to Senator David Reed, Chairman of the Senate Committee on Military Affairs, reiterated the main points against the scheme as in the G-3 memo, and in addition, emphasized the fact that the organization of an unemployed corps would necessitate dipping into the War Reserve to provide the necessary supplies and equipment needed for the undertaking. In contrast to the G-3 recommendation that if Congress was determined to go ahead with such an undertaking it should be modelled after the CMTC and organized at Army posts in available housing, Hurley advised a different solution. Undoubtedly reflecting the Chief of Staff's view, the Secretary of War informed the Senate that the only feasible way that the Army could be brought into the scheme, would be through the utilization of facilities available in the urban areas where unemployment was acute and have

---

[2] *Ibid.*

Army personnel supervise the messing, housing, sanitation, and control of the unemployed organization. Members of the proposed relief bodies would be required

> to conform to certain rules and regulations, including prescribed exercises, and governing personnel from the Regular Army, as they circulated among the unemployed and dealt with them would have many opportunities to make a right impression upon the unemployed group and do much good work of this kind, which would go far in moulding a better morale throughout the men so housed, to the end that criminal tendencies might be lessened and respect for government augmented.[3]

It is obvious that the Army's views on participating in unemployment relief were not crystallized in early 1933. The G-3 memo, although opposed to the general idea, proposed the possibility of a special reserve corps along the lines of the CMTC. Hurley's letter, written several days later, incorporated the views of the General Staff in general opposition to any Army participation in unemployment relief, but instead of admitting the possibility of a special reserve corps on military posts, accepted the feasibility, under certain conditions, of the Army participating in urban areas by organizing shelter and messing facilities. The strong reservations of the Army toward participation in unemployment relief had been voiced before the Bonus Army episode in July of 1932, but undoubtedly the reference in Hurley's letter to "criminal tendencies" and "respect for government" reflected the trepidation of

---

[3]Ltr, Hurley to Senator David Reed, January 27, 1933. G-3/31340, RG 319, NA.

military leaders in dealing with the unemployed. Although Hurley's letter and his characterization of the unemployment problem demonstrated how far Army thinking was divorced from the social and economic problems of the country, it also reflected the Army's unfortunate experience with the Bonus Army in the summer of 1932.

During the lame duck session of the 72nd Congress, the Senate passed a proposal to increase the War Department appropriations by $24,000,000 in order to enroll 80,000 unemployed between 18 and 21 in the CMTC. This amendment died in House-Senate conference late in the session.[4] Related to this Senate proposal, MacArthur wrote to General Fox Conner, Commanding General of the 1st Corps Area in Boston, and advised the latter of his views and ideas on the subject of possible CMTC expansion. Although this had been the original proposal mentioned in the G-3 memo on January 27, 1933, Hurley's letter to Senator Reed had opposed such a scheme, and referred instead to the possible participation of the Army in messing and sheltering the unemployed in urban areas stricken by acute unemployment. MacArthur informed Fox Conner that in case the CMTC was expanded into some sort of unemployed corps, it would include vocational training, military training, the teaching of grade school subjects, and citizenship training. Vocational training, according to the Chief of Staff, could be achieved during regular Army post routine by selecting men from the unemployed corps for training in

---

[4]New York <u>Times</u>, March 4, 1933, pp. 1, 2.

telephone exchanges, carpenter and blacksmith shops, tailorshops, barbershops, and bakeries. Military training would consist of basic infantry training with the objective of inculcating "cohesion, obedience, teamwork, and discipline." MacArthur also visualized that Corps Area Commanders would be given wide discretion to act when their judgment dictated action contrary to War Department instructions or regulations.[5]

The tenor of MacArthur's letter to General Fox Conner reflected the fact that the Army was aware that an organization of unemployed was a distinct possibility under the new administration that would take office in March, 1933. MacArthur's letter indicated that regardless of its recommendations and reservations against participation in such an organization, the Roosevelt Administration would likely set up some sort of unemployment relief organization and require the Army to administer it. Already in MacArthur's mind was the plan that, in this event, Army participation would be de-centralized and responsibility and authority for administration would rest with the nine corps area commanders.

Soon after his inauguration, President Roosevelt presented to the War Department the problem of formulating a plan, whereby with the assistance of the Army the Federal Government could alleviate unemployment. The Deputy Chief of Staff, Brig. General Hugh A. Drum, had ready by March 9, the War Department's outline program

---

[5]Ltr, MacArthur to Fox Conner, undated. G-3/31340, RG 319, NA.

and Secretary Dern took the plan to the White House that afternoon. the plan that Drum formulated for the President in its detail, completeness, and thoroughness, suggests that the War Department General Staff had given the subject of an unemployed corps vigorous study since late January, and was prepared to cooperate to a limited extent with the Roosevelt Administration in such a scheme. The Army was convinced at this time, according to a member of the G-3, that no matter how earnestly organized labor, the Department of Labor, and other civilian groups might advise against the use of the Army in the fulfillment of Roosevelt's scheme in order to avoid such criticism as regimentation of labor, militarism, and the like, there was but one way to accomplish the rapid and efficient establishment of the labor camps and that was to bring in the Army.[6]

According to the project outlined by General Drum, reforestation, national park development, surveying and mapping, irrigation projects, flood control, and reclamation presented possible fields of mass federal employment. In view of the legislation already on the books, projects of this kind were readily available because the Employment Stabilization Act of 1931 required the federal departments to maintain plans for construction projects six years in advance. Drum also emphasized that inherent in any scheme of mass induction of the unemployed into a federal organization was the

---

[6] Army Navy Journal, July 8, 1933, p. 893.

need of administration and supply; he noted that none of the federal departments except the Army were capable of administering the needs of the number of citizens that Roosevelt's scheme visualized. Drum proposed the following two plans: (1) all federal departments immediately develop projects with a view of employing about 500,000 men; (2) under call of the President the Army would "induct into the Federal employment" various classes of unemployed men and organize them into units suitable to meet the requirements of various federal projects. The Army would use its camps for the purpose of organizing the men into units and after induction and organization the Army would send the men to areas as requested by the federal departments. Thereafter the full responsibility for the administration, supply, finance, and discipline of these units would rest with the federal department under which they were working. General Drum, alluding to the possibility of the future involvement of the Army in actual camp administration, informed Roosevelt:

> if the foregoing is believed to be impracticable, it may be necessary for the War Department to create and function a system to meet these requirements (camp administration). However, this step should be avoided in view of the possible conflicts resulting from dual control.[7]

Drum clearly informed the President that the Army was against the

---

[7]Memo for the President, prepared by Brig Gen Hugh A. Drum, Deputy Chief of Staff for the Signature of the Secretary of War, March 9, 1933. AG 400.58, RG 94, NA.

actual running and administration of the camps and he cautioned the Chief Executive of the two special considerations to keep in mind pertaining to the Army. Primarily, Roosevelt was advised that the Army could take care of mobilizing about 100,000 men by April 15, and could expand this number by June 1 to 200,000. The time period estimated before the first group of 100,000 actually left for the work camps was about six weeks. Secondly, Drum was concerned that in participation in the CCC the Regular Army would be weakened in carrying out its main effort of national defense, and the Deputy Chief of Staff urged that some units of the Regular Army be maintained "intact and available for immediate use in emergencies."[8]

On March 21 Roosevelt asked Congress for authorization of the CCC for the purposes of reforestation and unemployment relief and Congress pushed the measure through in ten days by voice vote.[9] In speaking to the press two days after the introduction of the measure in Congress, Secretary Dern sought to disarm the anti-militarists critics of the proposal who were concerned over the fact that the Army was involved. Dern emphasizedc the fact that the sole responsibility of the Army was to organize the works units and send men from the conditioning camps to the work camps:

---

[8]Ibid.

[9]James MacGregor Burns, Roosevelt: The Lion and the Fox (New York: Harcourt, Brace and Company, 1956), p. 169.

It has been pretty definitely worked out that this activity will not be confused with the military establishment in any sense of the word. The Army has the personnel, officers and men, who could do this work (organizing the units) without additional expense to the government. It has posts, buildings and so forth that might well be used for this purpose. It is the cheapest way to do this and will give the Army a peacetime activity of a social nature. I think more or less of a new departure.[10]

Four days after the introduction of the bill in Congress, March 25, the War Department sent all Corps Commanders a radiogram informing them of the impending task and the quotas of men that were tentatively assigned to each corps area for induction into federal employment. Instructions also emphasized the fact that the Army would enroll the men after they had been certified for selection by the Labor Department and that this enrollment would take place at local Army recruiting stations. The men would then be transported to the nearest Army camp, where after four weeks of preparation, including physical examinations and physical training the men would be transported by units to work camps and the control of the men would be transferred to representatives of the other agencies. The Corps Area Commanders were specifically instructed that while under military control, training would be limited to building up "physique and unit esprit."[11]

The March 25 message was of necessity very sketchy and quite

---

[10]Army Navy Journal, March 25, 1933, pp. 589 - 90.

[11]Memo, AC/S G-3 to the AG, March 25, 1933. (For Radiogram to all Corps Area Commanders). AG 324.5 CCC (3-25-33) Section L, RG 94, NA.

general. It was to serve only to alert the Corps Commanders of what was going on in Washington, and assured the subordinate commanders in the field that detailed instructions would be forthcoming as soon as the War Department and other related agencies had agreed upon the exact program and the President had given his final approval. The final order which outlined the Army's participation in the CCC was drawn up on April 5, and approved by the President the next day. On the same day Roosevelt issued an Executive Order directing participating departments to appoint a representative to constitute an Advisory Council to the Director of the Emergency Conservation Work (CCC). As Acting Assistant Chief of Staff, G-3, Colonel Duncan Major was verbally directed by MacArthur to prepare the necessary regulations for the War Department's role in the CCC. On the morning of April 3, he was told to report to Roosevelt's secretary, Louis McH. Howe, for further instructions concerning the preparation of CCC regulations.[12]

The final regulations, approved by Roosevelt on April 6, were forwarded to all Corps Area Commanders and published as an Army General Order. This Order noted that consistent with its "traditional

---

[12]Memo, War Department Representative on the Advisory Council to the Chief of Staff, June 15, 1936. AG 324.5 CCC (6-6-36). Note: For Director of the CCC Roosevelt selected Robert Fechner, at that time head of the Machinists Union. According to Frances Perkins, Roosevelt selected a labor leader as Director on the theory that organized labor would be "well disposed" toward the CCC. Roosevelt had come to know Fechner during his tenure as Assistant Secretary of the Navy during the Wilson Administration. Frances Perkins: The Roosevelt I Knew (New York: Viking Press, 1946), p. 180.

conduct and desire to serve the nation in all relief emergencies" the Army would cooperate in the CCC program. Army posts would be used as reception centers for the enrollees and once the CCC units were turned over to another department at the work camps "the mission and responsibility of the United States Army would cease." The Order provided several main guidelines for the Corps Area Commanders in carrying out their duties; and because of its uniqueness and significance, it will be discussed in some detail. The territorial Army commanders were informed: (1) They would be responsible for the "supervision, administration, and supply of all members and units of the CCC" within their respective corps area while under Army control. (2) The principle of de-centralization would govern, and within limitations local commanders would determine appropriate action in problems that arose; whenever it was necessary to act contrary to War Department instructions, the Corps Area Commander would be expected to follow "unhesitatingly the dictates of his own judgment making a full review to the War Department as soon as possible." (3) The acceptance of the enrollees certified by the Labor Department was to be made at Army recruiting stations or other places designated by the Corps Area Commander, and physical examinations would be given at this place or at the reconditioning camps. (4) The reconditioning camps were planned to serve the dual capacity of reception and replacement centers. These camps would be determined by the Corps Area Commanders and would perform the function of receiving new arrivals, classifying enrollees into specific work units, conditioning the men physically, and providing them with necessary supplies and clothing. (5) The work units would be organized in the reconditioning camps into distinct and autonomous units with cooks, mess orderlies, clerks, aid men, bakers, tailors, carpenters, and other overhead positions. These personnel were to be furnished or developed from within the members of the work unit. The basic size of the unit was to be based on the contemplated employment of the unit, but the average size was planned to be around 250 men. The Corps Area Commanders were authorized to fix the tables of organization of the work units to suit local conditions and work requirements through information made available to them by the Corps Area representative of the federal department that would be in charge of the actual work. The basic work unit would be a company and no higher units were planned to be formed.

The regulations specified that members of the CCC, while under Army control, were not members of the military establishment, but would be required to comply with orders and instructions issued by proper authority, and continued violation of orders or regulations would be a cause for dismissal from the CCC; the final decision in each case would be made by the Army commander in charge of the reconditioning camp.[13]

---

[13]War Department Regulation (Provisional), April 5, 1933. By Order of the Secretary of War, Douglas MacArthur, Chief of Staff. AG 324.5 CCC (3-25-33) Section 1, RG 94, NA. Note: Penciled note accompanying the regulation and initialed by the

Throughout the first few days of April it was the intention that the Army control over the CCC units would terminate at the time that the units were turned over to the work project superintendent at the railhead near the work camp. This was the desire of the civilian agencies of the government involved in the CCC, such as the Forestry Service, and Agriculture Department soil conservation officers, as well as the wish of the War Department.

> In all prior interdepartmental conferences no more had been asked of the Army. The earliest possible termination of Army contact had been sought. This was in complete accord with the Army's hopes and purposes and interferring at a minimum with its mission under the National Defense Act.[14]

However, the White House quickly realized that without more complete and continuing participation of the Army it would be impossible to administer the work camps effectively and insure the success of the entire CCC program. Consequently, on the night of Saturday, April 8, the War Department Representative of the CCC Advisory Council was called to the White House and it was proposed to him that the Army expand its participation to include control

---

Deputy Chief of Staff indicates that the President gave final approval to the above regulations on April 6.

[14]Army Navy Journal, July 8, 1933, p. 893. Note: Colonel Major, Acting AC/S G-3 and the WD Representative on the CCC Advisory Council, wrote an account of the initiation of the WD participation in the CCC for the July 8 edition of the Army Navy Journal. The article naturally was quite laudatory over the accomplishment of the Army and reflected the idea of the poor, despised Army coming to the help of the floundering and frustrated civilian departments of the government.

over all matters of work camp activity except the actual technical supervision of the work itself. Colonel Major, who was the War Department Representative on the Advisory Council, claims that he argued against any increase in the Army's role in the CCC and that a decision was reserved until Monday, April 10, when the Secretary of War would discuss the matter and make the final decision. On Monday, Secretary Dern accepted the increased role for the Army, and the General Staff, who had been alerted to the situation on Saturday evening, had drawn up over the weekend a set of regulations and estimates of cost. These latter studies had to be approved by Mr. Robert Fechner, the Director of the CCC, and discussed at numerous conferences with the representatives of the Departments of Labor, Interior, and Agriculture and all matters of controversy had to be referred to the White House for final decision.[15]

---

[15]Ibid., April 15, 1933, p. 649. See also Order to Corps Area Commanders in Memo, Chief of Staff to AG, April 12, 1933. AG 324.5 CCC (3-25-33) Section 1, RG 94, NA.

Army estimates of cost of CCC:

A. Initial estimate per individual:

Transportation to Camp	$10.00
Transportation to Work	25.00
Clothing	38.00
Medical Inspection	5.00
Shelter	15.00

B. Daily cost per man in reconditioning camps:

Subsistence	.33
Medical	.07
Equipment and Supplies	.08
Motor Transportation	.02
Pay	1.00

(Memo Acting AC/S G-3 for AG, April 7, 1933). Estimates of cost after departure from reconditioning after the above estimates:

Cost of clothing, food, shelter, pay $2.02 per man per day. (Memo, Acting C/S GS-3 for AG, April 13, 1933). AG 324.5 CCC (3-25-33) Part I, RG 94, NA.

On Wednesday, April 12, the War Department informed all Corps Area Commanders that the Army was to broaden its participation in the CCC program and would be "responsible for all matters incident to command of the camps and their supply, administration, sanitation, medical care, hospitalization and welfare." Furthermore, the camps were to be "established under the supervision of Regular Army personnel who may be replaced at the discretion of the Corps Area Commander by Reserve Officers." The Corps Area Commanders were authorized to call to active duty for six months the following personnel for each 1,000 of CCC enrollees: three medical officers, and for each forestry camp, three line officers (one captain and two lieutenants).[16]

Realizing that the Corps Area Commanders were soon to be overcome by the sheer weight of supply and administrative matters, now that the Army was becoming more involved, and in order to insure more "flexibility" of organization, the General Staff directed the organization of a subordinate district headquarters, which would be set up under the Corps Area headquarters for the purpose of de-centralizing the multitudinous problems of command, administration, and other details. The General Staff directed that in most cases each work camp would consist of one CCC company which would have initially the following military personnel: one Regular Army officer as company commander; three commissioned

---

[16]Memo, Chief of Staff to AG, April 12, 1933. AG 324.5 CCC (3-25-33) Section 1, RG 94, NA.

officers from the Reserve on active duty; one Regular Army noncommissioned officer (NCO) as company first sergeant; one Regular Army NCO as supply sergeant and clerk; one Regular Army NCO as mess sergeant; and one Regular Army enlisted man to be cook. The district and company commanders were charged with "complete responsibility" for the camps, personnel administration, and welfare of the men including shelter, clothing, feeding, discipline, morale, sanitation, and medical care. According to directives of the General Staff the company commander would decide in situations where the welfare of the men was concerned, whether or not work was to be performed by the individual. Furthermore,

> except when it is necessary to fulfill responsibility and conform with regulations prescribed by the Director of Emergency Conservation, the district and company commanders will not interfere with the time, place, or manner of labor prescribed by technical advisors. Where it is impossible for the district and company commanders to adjust their problems with representatives of other departments in the field, they will promptly report the situation to the next higher authority.[17]

These instructions, amending and supplementing the regulations sent out by the General Staff a week before on April 5, are significant in the fact that they were very general. It was MacArthur's plan, even after the Army became involved in the actual operation of the work camps, that the Corps Area Commander would have as much discretion and autonomy as possible. The General Staff in Washington would lay down the general policy, but

---

[17]Memo, Acting AC/S G-3 for AG, April 13, 1933. AG 324.5 CCC (3-25-33) Section 1, RG 94, NA.

the subordinate Corps Commanders would implement the general regulations to fit their specific problems. Perhaps of all factors aiding the success of the Army's role in the CCC, the policy of MacArthur to de-centralize control of actual operation had the greatest import. Besides insuring a low bureaucratic overhead at the top of the organization, de-centralization of responsibility meant expeditious handling of supply bottlenecks and decisive and quick action in relation to all personnel and other administrative problems.

The effectiveness of the policy of de-centralization was vividly confirmed in early May when President Roosevelt ordered the Army to enroll and assign to the work camps the entire CCC complement of 274,000 men by July 1. The directive, with its sense of urgency, interjected a dramatic element into the CCC affair. This rapid mobilization and the consequent hum of excitement and the intensification of effort undoubtedly served as an adrenalin to the Army's morale, and coming right at the time of the bitter budget controversy with the New Deal leaders, and the question of whether military expenditures were "socially beneficial," gave the Army further impetus and incentive to bring off successfully the requested mobilization of some 250,000 men in approximately seven weeks. Here was a unique opportunity to hoist the New Deal critics on their own petard and show to the administration and the public the efficiency of the "peanut" Army; a chance to galvanize the rambling and diversified military establishment into one dynamic effort to achieve the goal of the President and confound the critics of the Army! The drama and the excitement that the CCC mobilization brought to the routine day-to-day activity of the General Staff is well illustrated by the account of the Acting G-3, Colonel Major:

> It was a momentous day (May 10, 1933). In a few hours more had been accomplished than in a previous month. A clear cut decision on a definite plan to fulfill a task, the complete definition of which was positively ordered, electrified the whole effort. The old order changed. That afternoon all Assistant Chiefs of Staff and Chiefs of Services met in the Office of the Deputy Chief of Staff. The new mission was given, stirring everyone. Plans and action for the field were required by the next morning. That night instead of a stray light here and there the War Department's windows were ablaze. The big machine was rolling in a war effort. The Army was under test but what a grand opportunity the task offered.[18]

Roosevelt was dissatisfied with the slowness of the CCC enrollment. On May 10, 1933, the date he ordered the Army to get the CCC into the work camps by July 1, there was a total of 52,000 men enrolled; 43,500 of these were under the Army in the reconditioning camps, and 8,500 were actually in work camps and on the job. There had been a daily average enrollment of 1,530.[19] The President's announced goal of having 250,000 boys in the woods by the first of July was clearly behind schedule.

On May 10, 1933, Mr. Robert Fechner, the Director of the CCC,

---

[18] Army Navy Journal, July 8, 1933, p. 895.

[19] Memo, War Department Representative on CCC Advisory Council to Mr. Robert Fechner, Director Emergency Conservation Work, May 12, 1933. AG 324.5 CCC (3-25-33) Section 1-B, Part I, RG 94, NA.

requested members of his Advisory Council to submit in writing their plans of how to step up the CCC enrollment so that 274,000 members could be in the camps by July 1. The Army replied that the War Department contemplated the reception by June 7 of 222,000 men at an average daily rate of approximately 8,540 beginning on May 12, and the complete organization and equipment by June 23 of 1,200 CCC companies, a rate of some 27 per day. The War Department claimed that they could have all the men in their place of work by July 1 if the last contingent of CCC enrollees had been certified for enrollment by the Labor Department by June 7.

The War Department admitted that with men coming into the CCC at a rate of some 8,000 per day supply would be the critical factor in keeping the flow of men continuing with no delays. Consequently, the Army requested permission for requisitioning supplies through open market purchase and the elimination of bids, contracts, and other time-consuming peacetime procurement practices.[20] Another important requirement that the Army demanded from the Director of the CCC was the authority to provide increased pay and grade for a definite number of foremen or "leaders" from among the CCC enrollees in order to de-centralize command and authority in the work units while mobilization was under way. Furthermore, the Army claimed that the "application of disciplinary methods similar to those of the 104th Article of War" were

---

[20] Ibid.

necessary because the mobilization of the CCC "parallels an Army in the field." In addition, the Army pointed out that complaints will come into Washington, but investigation should be waived and delayed because of the fact that "the Corps Area Commander will need all the help that can be given him and should be harassed as little as possible."[21]

According to MacArthur, the mobilization of the entire planned CCC enrollment by July 1 intensified the responsibility and need of authority by the Corps Area Commanders; and in his radiogram of May 13, sent to all Corps Area headquarters informing them of the mobilization effort, MacArthur stressed that the War Department in Washington was aware of the fact that the task required wide "discretion and authority, which is accorded you. Where questions arise not covered by instructions, or when necessary to change such instructions, you are authorized to act."[22] G-4 advised that a total concentration of the Army's effort was necessary if the mobilization of some 220,000 men by July was to be successfully completed. Success, the G-4 emphasized, depended on speeding up the work of supply. Consequently, the summer training program of the Army would have to be suspended, and the entire resources of the Regular Army personnel, supplies,

---

[21]Ibid.

[22]Memo, Chief of Staff to AG, May 13, 1933, for radio to all Corps Area Commanders. AG 324.5 CCC (3-25-33) Section 1-B, PART II, RG 94, NA.

transportation, and shelter must be made available for the effort.[23]

In order to insure concentration of effort and expeditious handling of CCC affairs, the Chief of Staff ordered that all offices concerned with CCC matters should be temporarily divorced from other duties and set up as an independent section. Furthermore, all CCC problems would be handled directly between individuals involved through telephone or personal conversations, and all written documents should be avoided. All questions from the field regarding CCC matters were ordered to be answered within 48 hours, and a daily supply bulletin would be issued by G-4 to the field so that all decisions on questions of supply could be promptly circulated.[24]

Besides the problem of supply and administrative bottlenecks, the most exigent situation that developed for the Army was the problem of personnel. On May 14, 1933, immediately after the executive order to mobilize the CCC by July 1, G-1 proposed that control over officers serving in the CCC be decentralized to the Corps Area Commanders by directing them to use at least 50% of all Regular Army officers now on duty under their control before calling to active duty any reserve officers, except medical officers and chaplains. G-1 urged that this include all Regular

---

[23]Memo, AC/S G-4 to the Deputy Chief of Staff, May 13, 1933. AG 324.5 CCC (3-25-33) Section 1-B, Part I, RG 94, NA.

[24]Memo, Deputy Chief of Staff for all Chiefs of Arms and Services, May 16, 1933. AG 324.5 CCC (3-25-33) Section 1-B, Part I, RG 94, NA.

Army officers on duty with the civilian components. In addition, in order to meet the officer demands of the CCC, G-1 proposed that the Command and General Staff School, the Special Branch Schools of the Infantry, Field Artillery, Coast Artillery, Engineers, Cavalry, Signal Corps, and Medical Corps be closed on May 22. G-1 proposed that 60% of the Staff and faculty of the branch special schools be used for CCC duty.[25]

About a week later, G-1 estimated that for mobilizing 250,000 CCC enrollees it would require a total of around 4,900 officers, other than medical and chaplains, and that there would be available by June a total of 4,171 officers, leaving a shortage of around 418 officers. With the approval of the President some 1,500 reserve officers were to be called to active duty to meet the need for trained leaders and supervisors.[26] During this period G-3 submitted a study on the need of officers required for full time duty with the CCC after the transition period or mobilization period ended on July 1. G-3 estimated that approximately 3,500 regular officers would be needed to man the camps and district headquarters and 850 more would be needed with the CCC program at depots, Army posts, and corps headquarters. As plans stood, G-3 estimated that each work camp called for a minimum of

---

[25]Memo, AC/S G-1 for Chief of Staff, May 14, 1933. AG 324.5 CCC (3-25-33) A Section 1-B, Part I, RG 94, NA.

[26]Memo, AC/S G-1 for C/S May 25, 1933. AG 324.5 CCC (3-25-33) Section 1-B, RG 94, NA.

four Regular Army enlisted men, and with the addition of men required for headquarters, the total came to around 5,700 and the total enlisted strength estimated to meet all needs of the CCC coming to approximately 7,000.[27]

Another problem that faced the War Department was the fact that approximately 155,000 of the 220,000 men that were to be mobilized had no work projects available in their states of residence. According to War Department plans, the center of mass of this group of 155,000 men was in Ohio and the center of work was in Nevada. Thus, besides organizing 220,000 men, 155,000 of them would have to be moved approximately 2,200 miles, a prodigious logistical problem.[28]

On July 1, 1933, MacArthur reported that the mobilization was completed on schedule; within seven weeks the assembly of 220,000 men had been accomplished and units were organized and at work at 1,315 camps throughout the country.[29] Viewing the entire affair as a mobilization test and as an exercise of mobilization plans, MacArthur was satisfied and highly pleased with the Army's performance, and readily pointed out the wisdom of General Staff planning which had insured the satisfying results. In contrast

---

[27]Memo, AC/S G-3 for Deputy Chief of Staff, May 18, 1933. AG 324.5 CCC (3-25-33) Section 1-B, Part I, RG 94, NA.

[28]*Army Navy Journal*, July 8, 1933, p. 901.

[29]*Report of the Secretary of War, 1933*, p. 6.

with the "cost, confusion, delay, and inefficiency" of the 1917 mobilization, MacArthur claimed that the 1933 exercise was carried out expeditiously, economically, and efficiently. The Chief of Staff emphasized that the causes for this contrast were discernible in the changes wrought in defense planning by the National Defense Act of 1920. According to MacArthur the first and "most important" factor that insured the success of the CCC mobilization was the number and efficiency of the Regular Army officers available for the emergency in 1933 compared with the figure available in 1917 Secondly, the Officers Reserve Corps, which had been almost wholly lacking in 1917, was well equipped to supply reinforcements for the regular officers. Thirdly, the supply and equipment available in war reserve stocks made it possible to issue to the CCC organizational and individual equipment without going through expensive and time consuming procurement and manufacture.[30]

MacArthur, proud of the accomplishment of the Army, felt that the success in the CCC mobilization was an irrefutable answer to the pacificist and anti-militarist critics of the Army:

> To epitomize the military lessons of the 1933 mobilization, it has given renewed evidence of the value of systematic preparation for emergency, including the maintenance of trained personnel and suitable supplies and the development of plans and policies applicable to a mobilization. Particularly, has it served to emphasize again the vital need for a strong corps of professional officers and for an efficient body of commissioned Reserves.[31]

---

[30] *Ibid.*, p. 6-7.

[31] *Ibid.*, p. 8.

On June 30, MacArthur wired congratulations to the Army on achieving the mobilization of the CCC and its distribution to the various work camps by July 1. Reviewing the task and its accomplishment, the Chief of Staff exaltedly claimed that the mobilization of the CCC "represented the greatest peacetime demand ever made upon the Army and constituted a task of character and proportions equivalent to emergencies of war." Furthermore, the Army success was indicative of

> the superior standard of professional fitness of the Army. Only high morale, a spirit of cooperation, pride of service, and devotion to duty could have accomplished such splendid results. I extend to you and all members of your command my sincere appreciation of this great accomplishment. It was well done, Army. /s/ MacArthur.[32]

In writing to the Director of the CCC on June 30, the War Department Representative on the CCC Advisory Council, Colonel Duncan Major, who was also Acting G-3, vigorously pointed out to the civilian Director that the Army had successfully carried out its mission. He emphasized that the following conclusions could be drawn from this success on the part of the Army: (1) The General Staff had justified itself as a planning agency. (2) The organization of the United States into territorial Corps Area Commands had proven sound, and the decentralization of effort with the General Staff supervising and coordination, but delegating

---

[32]Memo, Chief of Staff for the AG. June 30, 1933. AG 324.5 CCC (3-25-33) Section 1-C, June 1933, Part I, RG 94, NA. The message was to be read at all posts and stations within the continental limits of the United States at the first formation after receipt.

execution of all details was a sound policy. (3) The necessity of maintaining stocks of equipment on hand in reserve had been vividly demonstrated. (4) If the Army was to meet successfully any emergency, it must have the means and authority to execute its mission, and have protection for all interference by other departments of the government.[33]

Colonel Major's four conclusions are significant in the fact that they appear to have been meant more as guidelines to the future relationship between the Army and the civilian officials of the government involved in the CCC program than as lessons of purely military validity. After the conclusion of the mobilization phase, and the transition to a more routine administration of the CCC, the Army was aware of the fact that future problems would include touchy and sensitive questions related to civil-military relations. Colonel Major's memorandum to Fechner suggests that he was clearly admonishing the latter that if he wanted a successful and efficient CCC, it would be necessary to accept control by the Army over the many facets of the CCC without interference from his office or other civilian officials and departments.

---

[33]Memo, Acting AC/S G-3 to Fechner, June 30, 1933. AG 324.5 CCC (3-25-33) Section 1-D, Part I, RG 94, NA.

CHAPTER XIII

THE ARMY AND THE CCC: PROBLEMS OF ADMINISTRATION

MacArthur emphasized with considerable cogency in his annual report for fiscal 1933 that the employment of the Army to meet the emergencies of peace, although important and within its legal jurisdiction, did not justify the continued neglect of its fundamental mission.[1] In particular, MacArthur stressed the fact that the assignment of some 3,000 Regular Army officers to the CCC meant the sharp curtailment of several essential activities of the Regular Army, including the training of the civilian components, the operation of special branch schools, and the training of the Regular Army itself. Implied in the Chief of Staff's report for 1933 was the message that it was necessary to get the Regular Army out of the CCC as soon as possible. MacArthur noted that allotments of officer personnel to the service schools had been cut some 50%, from the usual 8% of commissioned personnel of the respective branch allotted to school duty to 4% of officer personnel. In addition he had noted that of the 1,600 officers assigned to duty with the civilian components, withdrawals to meet the demands of officers for CCC duty had reduced this number to approximately 700.

---

[1] *Report of the Secretary of War, 1933*, p. 8.

As for the Regular Army itself, MacArthur stressed the fact that the lack of officers had brought training to a standstill, a condition which was the very "antithesis" of what should prevail. As a result of this condition MacArthur recommended the assignment of additional Reserve Officers to duty with the CCC.[2]

The Army, cognizant of these problems, felt that with completion of the mobilization phase of the CCC, it was exigent to get the Regulars out of the woods and back to the troops and their normal military activities. Army spokesmen stressed the serious impairment of national defense that would result from the Regular Army officers continuing to administer the CCC. The Army Navy Journal noted that because Regular Army officers were being used for the CCC, for the "first time in the history of many units" training had been suspended and the normal maintenance and increase of military efficiency had been curtailed. In addition, the training of the ROTC summer camp units without regard to budget allocation, was being suspended. Five of the nine corps areas had cancelled ROTC summer camp for 1933 because of the shortage of Regular Army officers who had been assigned to the CCC.[3]

Thus it was that in late July the War Department notified all Corps Area Commanders that Regular Army officers on duty with the CCC, whose normal assignment was with the civilian components

---

[2]Ibid., pp. 9-10.

[3]Army Navy Journal, July 10, 1933, p. 818.

and service schools, either as student or faculty member, were to be replaced as soon as possible with reservists. All students and instructors at the Command and General Staff School, and all service branch schools were ordered to report to their respective schools by September 1. All officers assigned to ROTC and National Guard units were to report to their organizations by October 1. Corps Area Commanders were authorized to call to active duty such reserve officers as necessary to replace the regulars. However, the War Department made it clear that with each CCC Company and each CCC district headquarters there would be one Regular Army officer on duty to instruct and aid the reserve officers in the problems of camp administration.[4]

It is significant to note the order of priority that the War Department gave to the replacement of Regular Army officers assigned to the CCC. Primary consideration was given to the school system and the civilian components; the curtailment of the activities of units of the regular establishment could be tolerated, but the War Department held that it was of the prime importance that the Army school system and the training and the efficiency of the civilian components be maintained. This order of priority was the general policy throughout the depression years in respect to budget allocation, and was reflected in the War Department's release of officers assigned to the CCC. However, due to the multitude of

---

[4]Ibid., July 29, 1933, p. 949.

various problems faced by individual Corps Area Commanders it was found that it would be extremely difficult to carry out the general policy of having all Regular Army officers assigned to the civilian components replaced by reservists before the winter of 1933-34.

On September 12, 1933, the War Department informed all Corps Area Commanders that the replacement of Regular Army officers, whose normal assignment was other than to the civilian components, was "indeterminate." According to the General Staff, it was planned to perform the CCC mission and resume other "normal obligations" by calling to active duty an ample number of reservists. This policy, in the thinking of the General Staff, was consistent with the basic theory of "mobilization in war," whereby the citizen soldiery would in an increasing degree be called upon to assume the responsibilities of an emergency. Thus the General Staff conceived the CCC program as a mobilization training exercise. Reserve Officers called to CCC duty would obtain the necessary training and experience under the guidance of Regular Army officers, with the ultimate objective being to recall all regulars on CCC company duty. The General Staff reaffirmed its policy of giving Corps Area Commanders discretion in determining when the services of regulars should be terminated, and advised that it might be necessary, at district headquarters and Corps Area headquarters, to have regulars remain for an indefinite period. It was planned by the General Staff that Reserve Officers would continue on CCC duty until the termination of the Army's participation in the program.[5]

In reviewing this policy in October, G-1 reflected the concern that various Corps Area Commanders were not moving fast enough in replacing Regular Army officers with reservists and were keeping the former on duty with the CCC to insure a high degree of efficiency in the program to the detriment of the basic mission of the Army. G-1 proposed that the War Department inform all Corps Area Commanders that it was not contemplated to retain Regular Army officers "indefinitely" with the CCC, and that in the main reservists had demonstrated their fitness to conduct the camps under the supervision of a small number of regulars. G-1 recommended that the subordinate territorial commanders be admonished that War Department policy called for the retention of Regular Army officers with the CCC until the spring of 1934, when it was hoped that all could be returned to their normal assignments. Concluding his recommendations to the Chief of Staff, G-1 emphasized the importance of relieving the regulars from the CCC, and the necessity of maintaining high training standards of the civilian components.

Reduced funds for the Reserves, even making allowance for opportunities of certain reserve officers on active duty with the CCC, are only sufficient to give field training to less than half of the number given such training during recent years. Thus inactive training of the civilian components becomes increasingly important. With a reduced number of instructors the inactive training,

---

[5]Memo, AC/S G-1 for the AG, September 12, 1933. AG 324.5 CCC (3-25-33) Section 1-F, RG 94, NA.

conferences, and extension school work, cannot be carried on adequately. If the full number of Regular Army instructors are not returned to their normal duty in the near future, much of the work will be completely disorganized and some of the important activities cannot be carried on at all.[6]

The General Staff division which was most closely involved with the planning, administration, and liaison of the Army with the CCC program was the G-3 division. G-3 did not concur with the general urgency of the G-1 proposals, and favored the idea of allowing each Corps Commander wide discretion in deciding the date on which to relieve Regular Army officers from CCC duty. Referring to the fact that the first six months enrollment period would be up at the end of October, and that the second enrollment period would be during the fall and winter of 1933, G-3 wanted as many regulars as possible to remain with the CCC. G-3 was of the opinion that no definite date should be set for the relief of regulars assigned to the CCC, except that all Corps Area Commanders be advised that relief should be as soon as possible when the situation in each Corps Area warranted. G-3 warned the Chief of Staff that the coming months would be a "period of flux" in the CCC camps throughout the country, and the replacement of regulars would hamper the Corps Area Commanders in the administration of the camps and was inadvisable.[7]

---

[6]Memo, AC/S G-1 to the Chief of Staff, October 4, 1933. AG 324.5 CCC (3-25-33) Section 1-G, Part I, October 1933, RG 94, NA.

[7]Memo, AC/S G-3 for the Chief of Staff, October 7, 1933. AG 324.5 CCC (3-25-33) Section 1-G, Part I, October 1933, RG 94, NA.

The main difference between G-1 and G-3 recommendations appears to have been that the latter believed that the CCC program took precedence over other missions of the Army at that particular time, and that Corps Area Commanders, who were primarily responsible for carrying out the CCC mission, should not be confused and harassed by instructions from Washington concerning the relief of Regular Army officers. G-1 seems to have been in general agreement on the latter point, but believed that the relief of the regulars should be expedited, and that execution of the basic War Department mission of national defense must not be deferred.

MacArthur apparently sought a compromise solution to the problem for on December 5, 1933, the War Department informed all Corps Area Commanders that Regular Army officers whose normal duties were with the civilian components would be relieved of duty with the CCC not later than January 1, 1934, and all other regulars as soon as the situation warranted.[8]

If the problems raised by Regular Army officers participating in the CCC were extremely onerous for the War Department, from the point of view of having a deleterious effect on the training and efficiency of the military establishment, the issue of Regular Army Enlisted Men (EM) was no less difficult. In the original instructions and regulations covering the Army's participation in the CCC, it was provided that four EM would be detailed to each

---

[8]Memo, AC/S G-1 for the AG, December 5, 1934. AG 324.5 CCC (3-25-33) Section 1-J, December 1933, RG 94, NA.

CCC company, and the Corps Area Commanders were instructed at the same time not to assign any Regular Army EM to duty with the CCC whose pay was not equal to or in excess of that received by members of the CCC. Immediately it became obvious that the number of EM in the Regular Army receiving pay equal to or in excess of the amount paid to enrollees in the CCC, and who could be spared from their normal military duties, was limited. In practice Corps Area Commanders, using the wide discretion allowed them by the Chief of Staff in the administration of the CCC, went ahead and assigned to CCC duty as many Regular Army EM as necessary, regardless of the equality of their pay with the CCC enrollees.

By September this situation was causing an alarming problem of morale throughout the Regular Army. At that time G-1 warned the Chief of Staff that it was "essential to the morale of the Army" that all EM on duty with the CCC have a pay increase or be released from duty with the CCC at the earliest possible date. According to G-1, attempts to provide for an increase in pay for these EM would be disapproved by the Bureau of the Budget, and the inevitable result would be, as was being demonstrated throughout the Army, a falling off of the re-enlistment rate, transfer applications, and desertions. G-1 emphasized that the record of EM assigned to the CCC reflected:

great credit on the loyalty of these men who in spite of conditions which are bound to be damaging to their self-respect and belief in fairness, have carried out their duties.[9]

The G-3 division of the General Staff, reflecting its concern over the efficient functioning of the CCC camps, did not concur with the G-1 proposals, and advised that the War Department should not harass the Corps Area Commanders with directives on this problem. G-3 believed that the Corps Area Commanders were aware of the problem and were taking "proper action to return Enlisted Men to their regular organizations as consistent with efficiency and local conditions."[10]

The issue was finally resolved in the fall of 1933, when Colonel Duncan Major, the War Department Representative on the CCC Advisory Council, returned from a field trip to various CCC camps and Corps Area Headquarters and reported that there was general agreement among Corps Area Commanders that Regular Army EM receiving less pay than the CCC enrollees should be relieved from CCC duty. Colonel Major informed MacArthur that all Corps Commanders were desirous of carrying out the directives of the War Department on this matter as soon as possible, and not later than the early spring of 1934. Colonel Major, Concerned over this unwholesome situation, noted that in his opinion the relief could be made

---

[9]Memo, AC/S G-1 for the Chief of Staff, September 16, 1933. AG 324.5 CCC (3-25-33) Section 1-F, RG 94, NA.

[10]Memo, AC/S G-3 for the AC/S G-1, September 20, 1933. AG 324.5 CCC (3-25-33) Section 1-F, RG 94, NA.

without detriment to the various CCC projects no later than the first of the year.[11]

MacArthur, satisfied that all Corps Commanders were in harmony on this policy, did not take any further action. He realized that any positive directive in this regard might unduly hamper the Corps Area Commanders, who needed Regular Army EM to carry out the burdens of CCC administration and supply regardless of the differential in pay between the enrollees and the Regular Army personnel. MacArthur had voiced his concern over the wholesale use of Regular Army EM in the CCC,[12] and was dissatisfied with the idea of the poorly paid enlisted man coming in contact with the higher paid CCC enrollee. In discussing the comparison between the cost of a CCC enrollee and the cost of an enlisted man in the Army, before the House Appropriations Subcommittee on Military Appropriations in January 1934, the Chief of Staff indicated his bitterness for what he considered was wanton disregard for the soldier who organized and administered the CCC. The Chief of Staff noted that a comparison in cost was generally a standoff in such items as food, training, and equipment, but that there was a "differential" against the soldier of 43% in pay; the pay of a private in the Army was around $18 a month, and an enrollee

---

[11]Memo, WD Rep on CCC Advisory Council to Deputy Chief of Staff, November 27, 1933. AG 324.5 CCC (3-25-33) Section 1-F, RG 94, NA.

[12]Report of the Secretary of War, 1933, p. 11.

in the CCC received $30 a month. To the Chief of Staff this was an "immutable" factor that caused the cost of the CCC to be more and would "always stand out."[13]

The controversial aspect of the quality of the Officer Reserve Corps participating in the CCC program was one of the principal factors that caused "liberal" critics of the Army to urge that the military establishment be withdrawn at an early date from the CCC. Robert Fechner, the CCC Director, was also quite concerned over the War Department plans to substitute reserve officers for regulars, and after returning to Washington in mid-January, 1934 from a visit to various CCC installations throughout the South, he told his Army advisor that he "wished the War Department could have left one regular officer with each CCC company." Fechner was politely but firmly reminded by the War Department Representative on the CCC Advisory Council that the:

> Army had dropped everything last spring to put the CCC over; that we had closed our schools, depleted our troops of officers and key non-commissioned officers; that due to our efficient and well organized army, the situation could continue for a short time without harmful results but not for long, and for that reason, the Chief of Staff was very anxious to return officers to their normal duties.[14]

---

[13] Hearings: War Department Appropriations Bill, 1935 (January 25, 1934), p. 32.

[14] Memo, WD Rep on CCC Advisory Council to the Chief of Staff, January 15, 1934. AG 324.5 CCC (3-25-33) Section 1-K, Part I, January, 1934, RG 94, NA.

The Army believed that because of the indefiniteness of the entire CCC program, and the harm that was consequent to the military establishment, it was necessary for the Regular Army officer to be replaced.

Perhaps the most controversial aspect of the Army participation in the CCC, and one which brought it under the sharpest criticism was the issue of "militarism." The term militarism is defined here to mean any aspect of disciplinary procedure or indoctrination that the Army believed was necessary for a smooth functioning of CCC. This would include various minor disciplinary activities to training in subjects directly related to military activity.

The original plan of the Army was to have its control over the administration of the CCC "guided" by the 104th Article of War, giving the commanding officer summary court authority over the enrollees. This procedure was to guide the Army in its original plan to administer the CCC only as long as it was responsible for the enrollees in the so-called reconditioning camps and until the Army turned the enrollees over to the other departments at the work camps. With the expansion of the Army's role to cover the administration of the camps, it was necessary to adopt a less militaristic procedure for discipline.

On June 9, the General Staff adopted a "penalty system" to be used for minor offenses that was considered by G-3 to be comparable to penalties customarily imposed by "management of industrial enterprises in order to maintain efficiency of production." Under the "penalty system" it was planned to include the conduct of hearings governed by rules of evidence and each hearing was to be a matter of record. Penalties would include "admonition, suspension of privileges, substitution of duties within camp instead of work and deduction of not to exceed three days cash allowances per month."[15] At the same time that it promulgated these directives, the War Department informed the Corps Area Commanders that for the purpose of "rewarding energetic effort and recognizing outstanding leadership," there would be established within the CCC the position of leader and assistant leader with pay of $45 and $36 a month respectively. Five per cent of the total company strength were to be assigned to "leader" rank and eight per cent of the strength were to be given the rank of "assistant leader." These appointments which would facilitate the decentralization of control and responsibility would be made after arrival at the work camp by the Army officer commanding the company in sonsultation with the work superintendent representing the technical service in charge of the work project assigned to the CCC company. In all cases of disagreement in appointment between the Army officer and the work superintendent it was planned that the matter would be handled as the Corps Area

---

[15]Memo, Acting AC/S G-3 for AG, June 3, 1933. AG 324.5 CCC (3-25-33) Section 1-C, June 1933, Part I, RG 94, NA.

Commander might direct.[16] It is evident that the War Department, desirous of obviating a plethora of complaints and problems from being sent to Washington, and thereby diverting the attention of the General Staff from its purely military mission, gave to the Corps Area Commanders wide authority and discretion in handling the CCC.

On June 19, 1933, the War Department notified all Corps Area Commanders of detailed instructions concerning revision of previous regulations; the only major revision gave the camp commander authority to discharge an enrollee from the CCC. The new regulations emphasized that all members of the CCC had civilian status and for crimes and offenses which constituted a violation of civil laws, members of the corps would be turned over to civil authorities. The Army officer in charge of the CCC camp was given authority to discharge a member of the CCC for refusal to work, continued or serious misconduct, and unwillingness to abide by the rules and regulations prescribed. The new revisions also indicated in greater detail the conduct of hearings, emphasizing that they would be conducted in a "fair, patient and firm manner, and in accordance with the rules of evidence."[17]

In late July, the War Department published regulations concerning the appeal of decisions rendered by the camp commander.

---

[16]<u>Ibid</u>.

[17]Memo, AC/S G-3 for AG, June 13, 1933. AG 324.5 CCC (3-25-33) Section 1-C, June 1933, Part I, RG 94, NA.

These regulations provided that the accused had the right to appeal to Mr. Robert Fechner, the civilian Director of the CCC in Washington, if dissatisfied by the camp commander's decision and punishment. The appeal would be made in writing within two weeks of the original decision and would be routed by the camp commander through the district and corps commanders to the War Department for transmittal to the Director.[18] It is surprising that the War Department agreed to this proposal and that it was approved by the General Staff, because this provision intrinsically provided that a civilian would have the right to review the decision of the military commanders and meant that there would be a terrific backlog of cases awaiting Fechner's review. No sooner had this provision been approved than the Army urged its repeal. Fechner was sympathetic to the Army's position that the Corps Area Commanders should have final review authority of all cases in their respective Corps areas, but nevertheless felt that an enrollee given a dishonorable discharge should have some way in which he could appeal his case to a civilian authority.

The War Department was adament that Corps Area Headquarters should be the final court of appeal, although it might be possible to accept a compromise and send to CCC headquarters in Washington for a review of those cases in which the Corps Area Commander did

---

[18]Memo, AC/S G-3 for AG, July 26, 1933. AG 324.5 CCC (3-25-33) July 1933, Part I, RG 94, NA.

not sustain the decision of the camp commander.[19] The War Department proposal on the problem of appeal was outlined the next day by Colonel Major in a letter to Mr. Fechner. The Army proposed that because of the threat to discipline and in view of the fact that Fechner did not have enought time to review all appeal cases, the Corps Commanders be delegated the authority to pass on appeals. Their decision would be final and based upon a thorough investigation by a "disinterested officer" after careful review at Corps Area headquarters. Colonel Major emphasized that approval of this proposal would "place responsibility for discipline on the shoulders of the Army where it belongs." Furthermore, it would tend to provide greater justice to the government and enrollees, and result in prompt "adjudication of disciplinary cases and maintain a disciplinary control admittedly slight in which a continuation of the present method must eventually wreck."[20] On March 7, 1934, the War Department informed Corps Area Commanders that Fechner had approved the change in regulations and gave Corps Commanders final responsibility and authority in cases of appeal.[21] The Army hailed Fechner's approval of this change in the disciplinary

---

[19]Minutes, CCC Advisory Council Meeting, February 28, 1934. RG 35, Records of CCC, NA.

[20]Ltr, War Department Representative on CCC Advisory Council for Mr. Robert Fechner, March 1, 1934. AG 324.5 CCC (3-25-33) Section 1-M, RG 94, NA.

[21]Memo, AC/S G-1 for AG, March 7, 1934. AG 324.5 CCC (3-25-33) Section 1-M, RG 94, NA.

regulations of the CCC:

In delegating his authority to pass on appeals to Corps Area Commanders, the Director, Emergency Conservation Work, has gone a long way in meeting the wishes of the Army in a very irritating matter.[22]

The Army believed that its regulations were fair and consistent with the civilian nature of the CCC program and at the same time provided ample authority for the Army to maintain discipline. It was this provision of a semi-military discipline that led critics of the Army to suspect it of seeking to instill "militarism" on the CCC. This was indeed a sensitive issue, and after Mr. Robert Fechner had returned from his swing through the CCC camps in the South, he discussed with his Army advisor the entire problem of the Army's administration of the CCC camps, including discipline. The Army believed that with the return of the regular officers to their normal duties discipline would have to be tightened in order for the inexperienced reserve officers to meet with the success of the regulars in administering the camps. Fechner's concern over the situation in the camps was based on his reluctance to see the regulars return to their normal duties.

The Army used his concern over the administration of the camps as a wedge in which to gain his approval for strengthening the disciplinary training of the CCC enrollees. Colonel Major,

---

[22]Memo, AC/S G-3 for the AC/S G-1, March 15, 1934. AG 324.5 CCC (3-25-33) Section 1-M, RG 94, NA.

the War Department Representative on the CCC Advisory Council, informed the Director that the Army was anxious to "raise standards of excellence" in the CCC, and believed that by stressing discipline it was also an "opportunity to teach respect for authority and to make better citizens of the enrollees." In order to overcome the suspicions of Fechner, an old labor union official, Colonel Major stressed:

> We require many things in the Army, such as saying 'sir', knocking at a door before entering, that were in fact not military, but what might be expected of any well-bred civilian ... and the War Department felt that the opportunity should not be lost to stress these subjects more than had been done
>
> . . . .
>
> My impression is that Mr. Fechner would approve War Department action tending to improve the general tone of the CCC camps in the matter of uniformity in personal neatness and cleanliness of enrollees, better policing of kitchens, messhalls, etc.... The stressing of gentlemanly bearing of enrollees with their superiors as well as among themselves. I am of the opinion that the War Department might with propriety send out to Corps Area Commanders a memo embodying the above, and Mr. Fechner's approval would strengthen it and eliminate any charge of militarism.[23]

General Hugh A. Drum, the Deputy Chief of Staff approved of the idea of tightening up on disciplinary measures in the CCC, but hesitant about getting involved too deeply in the CCC, advised against any action pending determination of the future of the CCC.[24]

When it was decided that the Army would continue its

---

[23]Memo, Colonel Major to General MacArthur, January 15, 1934. AG 324.5 CCC (3-25-33) Section 1-K, Part I, January 1934, RG 94, NA.

[24]*Ibid.* Pencilled note by the Deputy Chief of Staff to the above memorandum.

participation with the CCC for at least another year, the War Department asked and received Fechner's approval to initiate disciplinary training. On January 29, 1934, Fechner signed a G-3 memo sent to all Corps Area Commanders which stressed that the

> Army's great mission is the rehabilitation of these young men mentally, morally, and physically so that they may return to their homes at the completion of their service better American citizens and with better chance to meet the various problems of life which the future has in store for them.[25]

With this in mind, the memorandum instructed the Corps Area Commanders to "exert every effort to bring about a more uniform standard of excellence" in all camps under their command, with attention being given to neatness, cleanliness, arrangement of equipment and the policing of the general camp area. As an aid to this goal, Corps Commanders were instructed to inaugurate physical exercises, and the stressing of "orderly movements of groups from one point to another." In addition, enrollees would be taught "respect for authority and other usual courtesies." Finally the Corps Commanders were instructed as a further aid to inculcating discipline that a

> formation will be held daily, except Sunday, Saturdays, and holidays, at reveille and retreat.... Inspection of camp and personnel

---

[25]Memo, AC/S G-3 for the AG, approved by Mr. Robert Fechner, January 27, 1934. AG 324.5 CCC (3-25-33) Section 1-K, Part I, January, 1934, RG 94, NA.

is to be held each Saturday morning except when work is scheduled for that day.[26]

This policy, approved by Fechner upon the initiative and under the influence of the Army, was certain to justify the suspicions of the anti-militarist critics of the Army. The War Department, having made itself vulnerable to charges of attempting to hoist "militarism" on the CCC, was reluctant to advocate any further semi-military training within the CCC. In February of 1934, the National Rifle Association urged Fechner to approve rifle shooting as a "sport" in the CCC, with equipment furnished by the Association. The Army had considered this idea and naturally was favorable to it but believed "we would subject ourselves to criticism" and therefore did not think it was "an advisable practice to institute."[27]

MacArthur envisioned the CCC as a potential enlisted reserve corps which could be used to supplement the Regular Army and the National Guard upon mobilization. He publicized his proposals along these lines when he testified before the House Military Affairs Committee in early 1935, at the same time that he presented his $405,000,000 program for modernizing the Army. In his testimony he alluded to the practicability of using the discharged

---

[26]Ibid.

[27]Minutes, CCC Advisory Council, February 28, 1934. RG 35, Records of CCC, NA.

CCC enrollee in a voluntary reserve corps and was requested by the committee to prepare a bill incorporating his reserve corps plan for submission to Congress. MacArthur, with the confidence and backing of the Military Affairs Committee, forwarded his legislative proposals to the committee on February 8, 1935. His bill provided that young men who had completed their six months enrollment in the CCC could volunteer for two months military training, and all those who underwent such training might enlist in an Auxiliary Reserve Corps. The bill provided that at the expiration of the enrollee's CCC service and military training he might be accepted at the

discretion of the Secretary of War in an organization known as the Auxiliary Enlisted Reserve. Subject to such regulations as the Secretary may prescribe for their proper identification, location, and physical condition, members of the Auxiliary Enlisted Reserve are to be paid in quarterly installments at the rate of $24.00 per year.[28]

MacArthur's bill and a bill similar to it were introduced into the House on February 12, 1935, and were referred to the Military Affairs Committee. Surprisingly enough the War Department was asked for its views on both bills which provided voluntary military training at the end of the CCC enrollment period. A draft letter prepared by G-3 for the signature of the Secretary of War, but which was not submitted to him, was unenthusiastic about

---

[28]Ltr, MacArthur to McSwain, February 8, 1935. AG 324.5 CCC (3-25-33) Section 1, February 1935, RG 94, NA.

military training for the enrollees while they were still legally enrolled in the CCC. Particular concern was expressed over the fact that "necessary funds for their pay and other expenses during this period would naturally come from funds allotted to the CCC." G-3 was also concerned over the implication such training would have on the legal position of the director of the CCC; as legal head of the CCC the director, a civilian, would ultimately be in charge of all training. Because of the vague ramifications of such proposed legislation, G-3 advised withholding any recommendations pending consultation with Mr. Fechner.[29]

Evidently the Chief of Staff was not as concerned as G-3 over the nebulous position of the Director of the CCC and was unwilling to leave the decision of military training up to Fechner. In a revised letter prepared for the signature of the Secretary of War for the Military Affairs Committee of the House, there was no mention made of the fact that military training would be part of the CCC and Congress was advised that the War Department was in "hearty accord" with the proposed legislation which would build up and maintain an enlisted reserve corps for the Army.[30]

MacArthur's proposals for initiating voluntary military

---

[29]Ltr, draft prepared by G-3 for the Secretary of War, March 13, 1935. AG 324.5 CCC (3-25-33) Section 1, February 1935, RG 94, NA.

[30]Ltr, Acting Secretary of War Harry W. Woodring for J. J. McSwain, Chm Mil Aff Com House, March 19, 1935, Section 1, March, 1935.

training into the CCC program after the expiration of the regular work enrollment period brought swift and vigorous reaction. Edwin C. Johnson, Secretary of the well-known anti-militarist group, The Committee on Militarism in Education, in writing to Secretary Dern, summarized the general opposition of liberal groups toward such a scheme. He noted that the Army's participation in the CCC should be terminated, and that it would be a "distinctly civilian enterprise ... and entirely free from every taint or suggestion of military contact or administration."[31]

The Chief of Staff's activities in writing the legislation for the House Military Affairs Committee were well known and there are indications that this did not set well with the President and Secretary Dern. MacArthur had been warned by Dern a year before against laying the War Department open to the charges of militarism in connection with the CCC. Dern told the Chief of Staff on March 8, 1934, that regardless of the great care taken by the Army to keep the CCC free from any suggestion of militarism

> there is an element in our society seeking to distort the policies of the President and the Department. Misrepresentations are made to the effect that the CCC is a military organization in disguise. ... I know that all of you are cognizant of the President's policy and are keenly alive to every opportunity to prevent distortion.... I believe that it would be advisable to guard against

---

[31]Ltr, Edwin C. Johnson to Secretary Dern, March 12, 1935. AG 324.5 CCC (3-25-33) Section 1, March 1935, RG 94, NA.

any statement which would in any way identify the CCC movement with National Defense.[32]

Knowing Secretary Dern's position on this matter, it appears that MacArthur took the issue to Assistant Secretary Harry Woodring, who was known to favor increased military activity in relation to the CCC.[33]

MacArthur's efforts early in 1935 to initiate some sort of voluntary military training into the CCC were a unique exception rather than the rule. The Army in general, chiefly because of the criticism that it would have engendered by publicizing the military role in the CCC, was extremely wary and cautious in advertising the military aspects of the CCC. The Army was on continual guard to avoid any overt manifestation or development in the conduct of the CCC which would react on public opinion to the detriment of the Army. This was in keeping with the avowed policy of the administration that there was to be no official connection between military training and the CCC.

Behind the War Department's efforts to avoid antagonizing its severest critics was the desire to make a conspicuously

---

[32]Ltr, Dern to MacArthur, March 8, 1934. AG 324.5 CCC, RG 94 NA.

[33]Woodring had drawn the ire from liberal anti-militarist and pacifist groups in the country for his article in Liberty, January 6, 1934, in which he indicated his approval of semi-military training for the CCC. One liberal periodical called him the "first dictatorial man on horseback in the America of the future." World Tomorrow (Vol 17, January 18, 1934) p. 29.

efficient record in handling the CCC. Undoubtedly, the Army did benefit from the popularization it received as an efficient branch of the government, and the popularizing of the Army officer in the public's eye. Subtly, without fanfare, the Army went about its efforts to gain the maximum publicity without gimmicks or ostentatious and elaborate programs.[34]

If the Army laid itself open to the charges of "militarism" in seeking to tighten discipline and in MacArthur's proposal for voluntary military training at the completion of the enrollment period, it was without challenge in respect to the expenditure of money and charges of waste and extravagance. Perhaps the most money-conscious agency of the government because of its past experience, the Army was well-equipped to insure that the CCC was conducted with the maximum economy. Early in the CCC, the General Staff admonished the Army Corps Commanders that any criticism of the War Department in connection with the "administration of the CCC activities is more likely to be for extravagance than attempting

---

[34]The Air Corps in an attempt undoubtedly to gain publicity early in the organization of the CCC, proposed that "wherever practicable," regular and frequent aerial flights be used to maintain communications between national headquarters and the corps and district headquarters. Memo, Chief of the Air Corps for the Deputy Chief of Staff, June 3, 1933, AG 324.5 CCC (3-25-33) Section 1-C, June 1933, Part I, RG 94, NA.

In reply, the General Staff informed the Air Corps that this proposal was at variance with the War Department policy of decentralization and would "create a confused situation which would have only serious results." Memo, AC/S G-1 for the AG, June 7, 1933. AG 324.5 CCC (3-25-33) Section 1-C, June 1933, Part I, RG 94, NA.

to economize."[35]

Because of its efforts to insure the success of the CCC mobilization in the spring of 1933, the War Department gave little concern to the long range plans and future status of the CCC. The Army felt that this was the responsibility and jurisdiction of the civilian leaders of the administration and that the Army should concentrate on the tasks of mobilization and the problems of efficient camp administration. It was evident early in the CCC program that no one in the administration, including President Roosevelt, had a clear idea concerning the long range plans of the CCC once the first enrollment period was completed in the fall of 1933. According to Roosevelt's Secretary of Labor, the President "conceived the project, boldly ushered it through, and happily left it to others to worry about the details."[36]

This indefiniteness of the President combined with the haphazard manner in which decisions and plans were made by the civilian authorities in respect to the CCC, were important factors which led the Army to seek withdrawal at an early date of all Regular Army officers serving with the CCC. War Department proposals for the administration and supply of the Corps were based on the principle that in such a program as the CCC, efficiency and economy were the touchstones and bedrock of a sound organization.

---

[35]Memo, AC/S G-4 for AG, June 19, 1933. AG 324.5 CCC (3-25-33) Section 1-C, Part I, June 1933, RG 94, NA.

[36]Frances Perkins, <u>The Roosevelt I Knew</u> (New York: Viking Press, 1946), p. 177.

This viewpoint conflicted with the basic outlook of Roosevelt's advisors who believed that the main purpose and effort of the CCC should be the relief of unemployment and were opposed to making a fetish of efficiency and economy. These people favored shorter periods of enrollment with a larger turnover of personnel in order to spread to a greater number of citizens the relief benefits of the CCC. The sacrifice of efficiency and economy in order to provide social and economic benefits for the unemployed was anathema to Army tradition and training.

Basic to the entire problem of Army supply and administrative planning for the CCC was the question of what the President had in mind for the future of the Corps. Was the CCC to be a strictly temporary organization serving as a work relief vehicle and aimed at providing unemployment relief, or was the Corps to be formed into a permanent type organization to provide a national work force for reforestation, reclamation, and other federal work projects? Both plans had their proponents, but in general the Army originally visualized the first type of organization and was cool toward participation in a permanent CCC.

During the fall of 1935, there was some mention made of the possibility of making the CCC a permanent government agency. In this regard, emphasis was placed on the non-relief aspects of the organization: vocational training for youth, reforestation, and the conservation of natural resources. According to Robert Fechner, the President first broached this subject in the spring of 1934, when he decided on the extension of the CCC for another year, from April 1934 to the spring of 1935. At that time Roosevelt did not discuss his own ideas on a permanent CCC, but instead voiced the opinion that it was up to Congress to make any decision in this regard. At a White House meeting in the fall of 1934 Fechner noted that the future of the entire relief program, including the CCC, was discussed but nothing definite decided. Fechner believed that "it is almost a certainty that the CCC is going on in some form.... If we can get unanimity of thought by all departments we can get Congress to agree to almost anything."[37]

As Fechner intimated, the bitterly opposed and widely divided government departments could not agree on a permanent type of organization for the CCC. In the Army, the suggestions and proposals for a permanent CCC were received with little enthusiasm, particularly if the future CCC contemplated more control being exercised by the civilian departments of the government. The _Army Navy Journal_ reported on October 13, 1934, that there was considerable speculation as to the status of the Army should the CCC be made a permanent organization. In any case, the Journal commented: "It is no secret that the War Department is not anxious to continue the administration of the camps." The Journal added that although

---

[37]Minutes, Meeting of CCC Advisory Council, October 4, 1934. RG 35, Records of the CCC, NA.

reservists were being extensively used in the CCC by the fall of 1934, there were still some 400 regulars with the CCC at various headquarters and that the Army felt that these officers should be relieved and returned to their normal duties.[38]

A year later, in the fall of 1935, the issue of a permanent CCC again came to the fore, and at a meeting of the CCC Advisory Council on November 14, 1935, Fechner suggested to his advisors that their departments give "serious thought" to submitting plans for such an organization for it was quite possible that Roosevelt would call for them. Fechner noted to the Advisory Council:

> The President is in doubt about asking for legislation in the coming Congress. When I talked to him last September (1935) he made the positive statement that he was going to recommend to the next session of Congress that this work be made permanent, but in talking to him on Tuesday, he said he did not intend definitely to make that statement. It is a very important matter and the next Congress is generally understood to be of short duration and will handle only important matters. It is election year and Congressmen do not want to have any controversial matters come up. While I do not think this is controversial there is no telling what Congress will run into.[39]

Fechner kept the Army informed on developments, both through the periodical meetings of the Advisory Council and through correspondence. Writing to the War Department on November 19, 1935, four days after he had told his Advisory Council of Roosevelt's reluctance to propose a permanent CCC to the coming session of

---

[38]Army Navy Journal, October 13, 1934, p. 146.

[39]Minutes, Meeting of CCC Advisory Council, November 14, 1935. RG 35, Records of the CCC, NA.

Congress, Fechner informed the Army that now it was Roosevelt's intention to recommend to Congress that the CCC be placed on a permanent basis, beginning July 1, 1936, with an authorized strength of 300,000.[40] The discrepancies in Fechner's advice concerning the thinking of the President on a permanent CCC can probably be explained by the fact that he was at this time thoroughly confused by the President's indirectness and ambiguity in respect to the CCC program. At this time Fechner was perturbed because he knew that a permanent corps of some 300,000 men would complicate planning, in view of the fact that the War Department had procured equipment and planned construction for 600,000 men and the result would be considerable waste and excess. In addition, it would be necessary to close around 950 camps by April 1936.[41] Fechner's letter to the War Department on November 19, 1935, informing it of Roosevelt's plans to set up a permanent CCC reflected a sympathy and understanding of the War Department's position and his frustration in being aware of the confusion pertaining to the CCC's future but being unable to do anything about the situation. On December 16, 1935, in another startling about-face, Fechner informed the Army that Roosevelt had again changed his mind and definitely would not ask Congress for a permanent CCC.[42]

---

[40]Ltr, Fechner to AG, November 19, 1935. AG 324.5 CCC (3-25-33) Section 1, Part III, November 1935, RG 94, NA.

[41]*Ibid.*

[42]Ltr, Fechner to AG, December 16, 1935. AG 324.5 CCC (3-25-33) Section 1, Part III, December 1935, RG 94, NA.

The General Staff in late 1935 had not as yet proposed that any policy study be undertaken concerning a permanent CCC and the role of the Army in such an organization.[43] This was probably due to the fact that the Army felt that there was no need for such a study as long as Roosevelt and his advisors viewed the CCC as a temporary expedient for the relief of unemployment. Only in the context of the CCC being transformed into a permanent conservation and vocational rehabilitation agency would such planning have validity.

---

[43]Note: A Colonel Ely of the Office of the Chief of Finance submitted to the Director a draft of a bill creating a permanent CCC. This was prepared and submitted at Fechner's request, and not submitted through the Chief of Staff for his approval prior to submission to Fechner because it was a "personal matter." The General Staff was nevertheless concerned that the draft might be taken and used by those "not understanding War Department organization as an expression of the views of the War Department." It was pointed out that only the Secretary of War and the Chief of Staff were qualified to make statements of such "far-reaching importance to the Army." G-3 recommended that the Director be requested to return Colonel Ely's draft together with the letter of transmittal. Memo, AC/S G-3 to the Chief of Staff, November 27, 1935. AG 324.5 CCC (3-25-33) Section 1, Part II, November 1935, RG 94, NA.

In a letter to Fechner on this issue, the War Department Representative on the CCC Advisory Council emphasized that the draft of the bill creating a permanent CCC was prepared without the knowledge and approval of the Secretary of War or the Chief of Staff. "Until that time no officer of the Army is authorized to express an official opinion on this subject without the prior approval of the Chief of Staff." Fechner was requested that if he had made known to any other government agency or department the draft of the bill made by Colonel Ely, a copy of the covering letter be furnished them, so that the "status of the War Department in this matter may be clearly understood. This letter has been written at the direction of the Chief of Staff and has his approval." Ltr, WD Rep on CCC Advisory Council to Fechner, December 2, 1935. AG 324.5 CCC (3-25-33) Section 1, Part II, November 1935, RG 94, NA.

In the fall of 1935 Colonel Duncan Major, who had been detailed from G-3 to serve as the War Department Representative on the CCC Advisory Council in the spring of 1933, and who had served in this capacity for over two years, made an extensive inspection of War Department activities and installations pertaining to the CCC in five corps areas. Colonel Major forwarded his startling observations and recommendations to the new Chief of Staff, General Malin Craig, on December 16, 1935.

He advised General Craig that there was no "diminishing of interests on the part of Corps Area Commanders and their subordinates of the Regular Army in the CCC." On the contrary, it was noted that all Corps Area Commanders visited believed that the Army should continue its present functions if the CCC was to be made permanent. Colonel Major claimed that the CCC was not interfering with the training of the Regular Army nor civilian components, rather it constituted an "excellent means of training for the Reserves." It was recommended to the Chief of Staff that every junior officer of the Regular Army, and not just the Officers Reserve Corps, be given a six months tour of duty with the CCC: "No better opportunity is presented in time of peace for practical leadership in command, administration, and supply, and the development of leadership and initiative."[44] It is difficult to analyze

---

[44]Ltr, WD Rep on CCC Advisory Council for Chief of Staff, December 14, 1935. AG 324.5 CCC (3-25-33) Section 1, Part III, November 1935, RG 94, NA. Note: General Malin Craig had succeeded MacArthur as Chief of Staff on November 14, 1935.

Colonel Major's thinking on this issue because he had long been one of the most sensitive of Army spokesmen who chafed under the prerogatives of the civilian Director of the CCC over the Army, and opposed any activity by Fechner, and other civilian officials, which in any manner impinged on military discipline and the autonomy of the Army. It may be that through his close attachment to the administration of the CCC, he developed a close affinity toward the organization, and his official position as Army spokesman on the CCC Advisory Board gave him a different perspective when it came to recommending future policy to the Chief of Staff.

Six months later Colonel Major again brought up the issue of the Army's role in the permanent CCC. This time, however, he was less enthusiastic. On June 30, 1936, he advised the Chief of Staff that after March of the succeeding year the CCC would expire and that new legislation would be needed; therefore, the Chief of Staff was advised that the General Staff prepare a "well-considered" plan in anticipation of future developments. With this in mind, the War Department Representative on the CCC Advisory Council recommended that if congressional proposals for a permanent CCC did not include the Army, no effort should be made at seeking inclusion; on the other hand, if the Army was included, it would be "unwise for the War Department to endeavor to have Army participation eliminated" and the best thing would be to try to guide the formation of legislation along the lines that would "best serve

Army interests."[45]

Colonel Major's lengthy memorandum went on to recommend that the present objective of the CCC, relief of unemployment, be changed and the main goal of a permanent organization be made the conservation of national resources and the "rehabilitation" of youth through vocational training. It was recommended that the War Department should "endeavor" to have military training included in legislation for a permanent CCC, and that under such legislation the Office of the Director of the CCC should be abolished and coordination among the various departments be obtained by creating a governing board to consist of the various department secretaries. If Congress retained the Office of Director, Major advised that the War Department should endeavor to have his functions delimited to coordination "so that he may be deterred from invading the functions of the Secretary of War as he has in the past." Furthermore, he recommended that in all matters of discipline the decisions of the Secretary of War should be final "and not subject to review by the Director." Concluding his long letter to General Craig, Colonel Major recommended that the term of enrollment for the CCC be extended to four years, one of which would be active CCC duty, and three years in a semi-military CCC reserve. The latter would be the result of a two-month period

---

[45]Memo, WD Rep on CCC Advisory Council to the Chief of Staff, June 30, 1936. AG 324.5 CCC (3-25-33) Section 1, June 1936, RG 94, NA.

during the active CCC duty year in which the enrollee would receive "extensive military training" and become a member of a special enlisted reserve corps.[46]

No immediate reaction was forthcoming from the Chief of Staff's office to Colonel Major's revolutionary proposals; undoubtedly Craig was not too enthusiastic toward them and realized that such radical recommendations stood little chance of acceptance by Congress and even less from the Roosevelt Administration, to which Congress would look for guidance on CCC policy. The failure of the War Department General Staff to give more serious consideration to the possibilities of enacting Colonel Major's recommendations reflected the fact that the General Staff realized that Roosevelt, although undecided on a permanent CCC, would be extremely cool toward any proposal that included military training and increased Army control of CCC activities. Army participation in the CCC was controversial, and any further efforts to increase this participation would exacerbate civil-military relations and bring forth the opprobrium of the White House.

Fechner advised the various participating departments on July 7, 1936, that Roosevelt wanted each of their departments to submit to the Director by September 1 of that year, a study on a permanent CCC. The War Department replied that it had given "much consideration" to the subject and had reached the conclusion that

---

[46] *Ibid.*

the Army should be excluded from any permanent CCC "in view of the entirely civilian nature of this activity."[47] Therefore, the War Department did not submit any plans for a permanent CCC. Roosevelt apparently hoped that by having each department submit its separate plans on a permanent organization, the final result would be a distillation of the best from each. Fechner ordered the Advisory Council to come up with a final plan which would be forwarded to the White House. However, because of the widely different proposals submitted by the various departments, the best that resulted was a memorandum for Roosevelt which incorporated in general the existing organization. The main point, as far as the Army was concerned, was the reference in the memorandum that it desired exclusion from any permanent CCC, but should the President direct the Army to continue its present duties, the War Department recommended that there be no change in the present organization and responsibilities.[48]

---

[47]Ltr, Colonel George B. Tyner to Fechner, August 7, 1936. AG 324.5 CCC (3-25-33) Section 1, Part II, August 1936. Note: Colonel Tyner replaced Colonel Major as War Department Representative on the CCC Advisory Council in July 1936. Major was promoted to Brigadier General and transferred to duty with G-3. This transfer may have been the result of his views toward "militarizing" the CCC.

[48]Memo, Advisory Council for Fechner, October 12, 1936. AG 324.5 CCC (3-25-33) Section 1, Part II, August 1936. Note: During the October 15 meeting of the CCC Advisory Council, the subject of the memo which had been submitted to Fechner three days before was thoroughly discussed. The memo dodged the entire issue of a permanent CCC organization and recommended that Congress by a resolution continue the present legislation to the end of fiscal 1938 (June 30, 1938), with the stipulation that a joint congressional

The Chief of Staff, General Malin Craig, wrote to Fechner on October 15 and explained in detail the War Department's position on a permanent CCC so that there would be no doubt in the mind of the Director when he discussed the matter with Roosevelt. Craig emphasized that should the CCC become a permanent organization

---

committee study the question of a permanent CCC and recommend legislation to the 2nd Session of the 75th Congress.

At the October 15 meeting Fechner noted his dissatisfaction with this recommendation and added that it was "not desirable to suggest to Congress to appoint a commission to study" a permanent CCC. "All they accomplish is to create more complications," Fechner remarked. What the Director clearly wanted was for those Departments having responsibilities for administering the CCC to plan a permanent organization that could be presented to Congress when it met in January 1937.

The Labor Department doubted if Congress could have time to come up with a permanent CCC in time before enabling legislation covering the existing program expired on March 31, 1937. Therefore, it was suggested that Congress be requested: (1) authorize a permanent CCC to be established at a future date; and (2) extend the present act for $1\frac{1}{2}$ years to provide for a proper transition period. Fechner disagreed with this proposal and pointed out that Congress was favorable to a permanent organization and would accept what was recommended by the participating organizations through the President.

The Agriculture Department noted that any recommendation from the Advisory Council would be the President's bill and that it was unlikely that he would want any congressional committee to study his bill.

The War Department, when asked for its comment at the Advisory Council meeting, pointed out that its representative was not permitted to discuss the matter as it would not be a part of the organization unless the President specifically desired.

Fechner resolved that he would go to Roosevelt and tell him that it was the opinion of the Advisory Council that present legislation should be continued for a sufficient length of time to let Congress study the situation and prepare its own bill. The Director of the CCC added that Roosevelt did not want to impose his thoughts on Congress concerning a permanent CCC and that the Chief Executive was not greatly concerned about "anything except to have it (CCC) continued as permanent." Minutes, Meeting CCC Advisory Council, October 15, 1933, RG 35, Records of the CCC, NA.

the Army should be excluded in view of the purely civilian nature of the CCC's mission and its personnel. However, Craig noted, the Army was willing to continue its present work with the CCC during a "transition period" and assist the new agency in preparing to take over the administration of the camps. Craig visualized this transition period as lasting approximately six months.[49]

The Chief of Staff's recommendations that the Army should be excluded from any permanent type of CCC organization was disregarded by Roosevelt, and in his annual message to Congress in January 1937,

---

[49]Ltr, Craig to Fechner, October 16, 1936. AG 324.5 CCC (3-25-33) Section 1, Part II, August 1936, RG 94, NA. Note: A recent study on the history of American civil-military relations implies that the Army became progressively enamored with the CCC as a vehicle for hoisting universal military training on the youth of the country. "In other respects the CCC was open to suspicion as a militarist device. Closely paralleling the work camps established in Europe it was like them a means of keeping the national manpower physically fit and partially trained for eventual military service. Army officers, backed up by the Secretary of War Woodring and American Legion spokesmen, favored a frank militarization of the CCC under Army control, but such proposals were objectionable to labor and peace opinion.... It is not surprising therefore that the Army eventually became enthusiastic over the CCC, accepting it as an admirable substitute for military training. But, despite mounting war tension in Europe and increasing pressure to turn the CCC over to the Army, Congress and the Roosevelt Administration refrained from including military training of CCC boys as a part of the expanded national defense program." Arthur A. Ekirch, _The Civilian and the Military_ (New York: Oxford University Press, 1956), p. 239. Ekirch's analysis is incorrect in maintaining that the Army became increasingly enthusiastic over the CCC potential as a military training program. Only in MacArthur's bold but imprudent proposals in the spring of 1935 did the Army openly seek some sort of military training for the CCC. This policy was vigorously repudiated by his successor in the fall of 1936 and later by Marshall. In this respect it should be noted that MacArthur's proposals included only voluntary training and the provision for a semi-reserve corps of former CCC personnel who would be willing to complement the Regular Army in an emergency mobilization.

the Chief Executive urged that the existing CCC organization be adopted as permanent. The President did not explicitly indicate what kind of a CCC organization he had in mind, but left that up to the discretion of Congress:

I intend shortly to submit a supplemental estimate of appropriations to carry the Corps from March 3, 1937, to the end of the current fiscal year; and I strongly recommend that Congress enact during its present session the necessary legislation to establish the Corps as a permanent agency of the Government.[50]

On April 5, 1937, in a letter to Congress Roosevelt again urged the adoption of the CCC as a permanent government agency:

Such continuance or establishment is desirable notwithstanding the great strides that have been made toward national recovery, as there is still need for providing useful and healthful employment for a large number of youthful citizens.[51]

The Senate voted to make the CCC a permanent institution, but the House voted that the CCC should be extended temporarily for two years. A conference compromise report bill, extending the CCC for three years, was passed by both houses on June 24, 1937, and was signed by Roosevelt on June 28.[52] The law specified that the

---

[50]"The Public Papers and Addresses of Franklin D. Roosevelt," Vol V, The People Approve, 1936 (New York: Random House, 1938), pp. 645-46.

[51]"The Public Papers and Addresses of Franklin D. Roosevelt," Vol VI, The Constitution Prevails, 1937 (New York: The Macmillan Company, 1941), p. 145.

[52]Congressional Record, 75th Cong., 1st Sess., Vol 81, Part 6, (Washington: GPO, 1937), pp. 6204, 6299.

President could order reserve officers to active duty with the CCC and provided that the Army would continue to carry out its various disbursing and supply responsibilities. The bill stipulated, much to the chagrin of the Army, that the Director of the CCC

> shall have complete and final authority in the functioning of the Corps, including the allotment of funds to cooperating Federal departments and agencies, subject to such rules and regulations as may be presented by the President in accordance with provisions of this act.[53]

The increasing military budgets after fiscal 1935, and in particular the rise in the enlisted strength of the Regular Army to the long-sought goal of 165,000, as provided for by appropriations for fiscal 1937, meant that the Army became less concerned over the CCC as a potential pool of military manpower and reserve personnel. Indicative of this position was the Army's reaction to various attempts in the late thirties to have military training instituted in the CCC. In a startling reversal from the position MacArthur had held in the spring of 1935, the Army in early 1939 vigorously refused to introduce any sort of military training into the CCC camps. The Army informed Congress that it was opposed to such a development on the following grounds: (1) really effective military training would cause a curtailment of work projects in the various camps; (2) to give instructions in weapons

---

[53]*Ibid.*, p. 6204.

was impracticable because of the location of certain of the camps; (3) to send an enrollee to any Army camp for military training prior to his assignment to a CCC work camp would be expensive and remove him from the basic mission of the CCC; (4) to enlist the CCC enrollee in a special reserve corps after enrollment would cause a considerable amount of administrative work and financial expense with no commensurate or proportional benefit to the national defense.[54]

---

[54]Ltr, Woodring to Senator Morris Shepard, Chairman of the Senate Military Affairs Committee, March 18, 1939. AG 324.5 CCC (3-25-33) Section 1, Part II, August 1936, RG 94, NA.

CHAPTER XIV

THE MILITARY BUDGETS OF THE EARLY ROOSEVELT ADMINISTRATION

The first military budget of the Roosevelt Administration, fiscal 1935, was drafted by Army planners in the spring of 1933 for submission to the Budget Bureau the following August. The Army's estimates for fiscal 1935 reflected to a considerable degree the curtailment of expenditures by the administration of appropriated military funds for fiscal 1934.

The Budget Advisory Committee of the War Department, in forwarding its study of Army estimates for fiscal 1935 to the Chief of Staff, stated that the maximum amount that was "practicable to even tentatively base the military estimate" was approximately $331,000,000. The Chief of Staff was advised that this figure was the minimum which would provide a "coordinated and well-balanced military program." The Committee further noted that full consideration had been given to the Chief of Staff's instructions that total estimates should not "exceed minimum requirements" in view of the "uncertainty as to the status of funds for fiscal 1934." MacArthur was informed that the original estimates of the War Department for military activities had reached a figure of $350,000,000. The Budget Advisory Committee had reduced this sum to around $331,000,000, including some $8,000,000 for mechanization.[1]

In September 1933 the Bureau of the Budget returned to the Army its estimate with the instruction that the Army was "authorized to proceed" with the preparation of the final military budget based on a limiting figure of approximately $247,000,000.[2] The final military estimate for military activities for fiscal 1935 that was forwarded to Congress by the Roosevelt Administration totalled approximately the above amount. In testifying before the House Subcommittee on Military Appropriations MacArthur noted that the estimate before Congress had been formulated "on the instructions" of Lewis Douglas, Roosevelt's controversial Budget director. According to MacArthur, the funds requested for military activities would provide for the "bare essentials" and that "little progress" could be expected in developing the effectiveness of the Military Establishment.[3]

MacArthur reviewed for Congress the situation that had been brought about by the action of the Roosevelt Administration in curtailing expenditure of funds approved for fiscal 1934. According to the Chief of Staff, the bill for 1934 which Congress passed had appropriated some $271,000,000 for military activities, and

---

[1] Memo, Budget Advisory Committee for the Budget Officer of the War Department, July 31, 1933. BOWD/111.

[2] Ltr, Acting Director of the Bureau of the Budget for the Secretary of War, September 1, 1933. BOWD/111.

[3] _Hearings_: War Department Appropriations Bill, 1935, pp. 19-21.

although this sum was considerably less than what the Army had received for the previous fiscal years it was deemed adequate to provide for the minimum needs of the Army for a single year on a "depression basis." MacArthur noted that plans of the Army for fiscal 1934 were "quickly disrupted" when the Director of the Budget, soon after taking office, proposed an additional cut of $90,000,000.

After reiterating for the benefit of Congress the serious inroads into the Military Establishment that would have resulted from Douglas' retrenchment schemes, MacArthur noted that "adjustment" of the basic requirements of the Army and the Administration's "retrenchment program" was the subject of "continuous and intensive study" by the War Department and "written and oral" presentations to Douglas. MacArthur noted that the Bureau of the Budget finally agreed to allow the Army some $224,000,000 for military activities, a reduction of some $47,000,000 below the appropriation figure made by Congress for fiscal 1934.[4]

In response to questions from the committee as to the effect that the "salient features" of the New Deal retrenchment had on the Army, MacArthur noted that practically all field training of the Regular Army had to be omitted, and that the civilian components had experienced similar debilitating effects. Whereas the procurement of new equipment, including a small mechanization

---

[4] Ibid., January 25, 1934, p. 12.

program, and R&D work had been provided for by the 1934 appropriations act, MacArthur claimed that curtailment of expenditures by the New Deal had forced the "abandonment" of practically all these projects, the most serious being the reduction of aircraft procurement.[5]

MacArthur then attempted to impress upon Congress the fact that the budget submitted by the Administration for fiscal 1935 in no manner met with the desired or necessary requirements of the General Staff. The Chief of Staff noted that the minimum needs of the War Department included a Regular Army of 165,000 men, a National Guard with a total strength of 210,000, and an Officers Reserve Corps numbering 120,000 with a summer training program for 30,000 reservists, and a ROTC and CMTC program maintained on the same basis as in fiscal 1932. Moving on to the materiel requirements of the Army, MacArthur said that the Army's goal was to assure that by the time troops were subjected to combat they would be supplied with weapons that were equal in efficiency to those of the enemy. In order to accomplish this goal, MacArthur claimed that constant research, the production of pilot models, and the accumulation of small quantities of new equipment, in order to develop applicable tactical methods, were the "outside limit of our efforts in peacetime rearmament."[6] Thus MacArthur was encouraging Congress to increase funds for manpower and training;

---

[5] Ibid., p. 13.

[6] Ibid., p. 16.

he was confident that a modest program for materiel was adequate in view of the economic situation of the nation and the fact that new weapons were expensive to produce in quantity and had a high rate of obsclescence.

The House Appropriations Committee reported its military budget out of committee on March 6, 1934. The total War Department figure came to around $280,000,000, some three million less than Roosevelt requested. Of this total $248,000,000 was scheduled for military activities and some $32,000,000 for non-military activities. Final House action increased the non-military part of the budget so that the figure that was forwarded to the Senate came to around $291,000,000.[7]

Dern, requested by Senator Copeland to comment on the House bill for the benefit of the Senate Appropriations Committee, noted that the estimate before the Senate would meet the essential needs of the Army in view of the overriding issue of economy in government spending. "With certain exceptions," Dern informed the Senator, "the estimates meet the most essential War Department needs in view of the existing economic situation." The Secretary of War added that at a cabinet meeting on the previous day the President, alarmed over the consequences of the Air Corps flying the mails, had requested that $10,000,000 be added to the budget

---

[7]New York Times, March 6, 1934, p. 11. March 8, 1934, p. 8.

for the Air Corps.[8] The Senate acquiesced in Roosevelt's request, but the final House-Senate conference report limited the sum for "improvement, development and augmentation of Army aviation materiel" to around $5,000,000.[9]

In late April 1934 the Army appropriations bill for fiscal 1935 was finally agreed upon by Senate-House conferees and the total budget figure that finally passed Congress came to around $316,000,000. The greater part of this increase over the original estimate submitted by the administration was in flood control work and other non-military activities, but the military items were increased slightly in order to provide increase funds for the Air Corps and to finance forty-eight drills for the National Guard.[10] Congress could be expected to do "everything possible to promote the efficiency of the National Guard," particularly in view of the fact that many congressmen were sympathetic to the idea that in times of "depression every drill with pay means a great deal to a very large number of National Guardsmen all over the country."[11]

---

[8] Ltr, Dern to Copeland, March 10, 1934. AG 111, RG 94, NA.

[9] Ibid., March 15, 1934, p. 12. Congressional Record, 73rd Cong., 2nd Sess., Vol. 78, Part 4, March 14, 1934, pp. 4505-07. US Statutes at Large, 73rd Cong., 1933-34, Vol. 48, Part 1, April 26, 1934, pp. 614-42.

[10] New York Times, April 22, 1934, II, p. 7.

[11] Congressional Record, 73rd Cong., 2nd Sess., Vol. 78, Part 7, p. 7103.

The effect of the reduction in the original War Department estimates for fiscal 1935 by the Bureau of the Budget, and congressional compliance with the budgetary leadership of the Executive, was to impress upon Army planners the probability of continued retrenchment in military appropriations. Commenting on Roosevelt's "economy wave" in a letter to all members of the General Staff, General Drum, the Deputy Chief of Staff, warned his colleagues not to plan on increased funds for future fiscal years. Drum's memorandum dated March 8, 1934, the same date that the House approved some $248,000,000 for military activities for fiscal 1935, stressed the fact that all military projects for fiscal 1936 should "contemplate adequate support of the essential military activities of the War Department, but the probable necessity for continued economy should be given full consideration." Alluding to the possibility that the New Deal might further decrease military spending, Drum instructed his colleagues that the former policy of using the level of appropriations of previous years as a standard for budget planning should be "used guardedly."[12]

While Congress was discussing the 1935 military budget the old scheme of expanding the Regular Army in order to alleviate unemployment was once again brought up for consideration. Introduced by Representative Clark Thompson of Texas, the new proposal sought to expand the Regular Army by providing 25,000 one-year

---

[12] Memo, Deputy Chief of Staff for AC/S G-1, G-2, G-3, G-4, WPD. March 8, 1934. OCS/20809-1, RG 319, NA.

enlistments annually for three years. Thompson also sought to increase the officer strength of the Regular Army by a total of 2,000 through annual increments over a five-year period. In addition Thompson wanted to give the Secretary of War authority to call reserve officers to active duty in order to provide the necessary officers needed for the increased enlisted personnel. Thompson's bill stipulated that the Secretary of War should call to active duty those reservists "whose personal financial condition most seriously requires employment."[13]

MacArthur hoped that possibly he could induce congressional support for the Army's goal of a standing army of 165,000 but he was unequivocally against any proposal which contemplated using the Army as an agent in unemployment relief. Testifying before the House Military Affairs Committee on the Thompson Bill, MacArthur urged an increase in the enlisted strength of the Regular Army, but did not endorse the proposal as a temporary measure to alleviate unemployment. According to the Chief of Staff, the Army would benefit more by enlisting 25,000 men for a three-year period than by taking in 25,000 men every year for three consecutive years and discharging each enlistee at the end of one year's service. Opposing any plan that contemplated enlistment in the

---

[13] Army Navy Journal, April 21, 1934, p. 683. The Thompson Bill was introduced into the House on April 16, 1934, as HR 9136. Congressional Record, 73rd Cong., 2nd Sess., Vol. 78, Part 6, April 16, 1934, p. 6689. Note: The hearings of the Military Affairs Committee on this bill were not published and the bill was never reported out of committee.

Regular Army as an ameliorant to unemployment, MacArthur countered with the comment that always could be relied upon to clinch any argument with Congress: "It is not economically practical to have a period of enlistment less than three years."[14]

Dern's remarks concerning the expansion of the Army from 118,750 to 165,000 enlisted men in the spring of 1934 were interesting for they reflect his reluctance to agree to any proposal which did not emanate from the White House and which did not have explicit White House approval, particularly when such a proposal contemplated expending additional funds. Writing to a member of the House Military Affairs Committee in late April, Dern noted that the Thompson Bill had his "personal endorsement." However, the Secretary of War, cognizant that increased military expenditure was not in harmony with administration policy, added that because the "measure had not been approved by the Bureau of the Budget and is not an administration measure" he could not give "official approval."[15] In his testimony before the House Military Affairs Committee in reference to the Thompson Bill, Dern reiterated his equivocal endorsement of the proposal to increase the enlisted strength of the Regular Army. The Secretary of War emphasized that an increase to 165,000 men was needed so that the Army could adequately carry out its three-fold mission of protecting

---

[14] New York <u>Times</u>, April 24, 1934, p. 5.

[15] <u>Army Navy Journal</u>, April 28, 1934, p. 697.

foreign possessions, training the civilian components, and serve as a ready force capable of meeting emergencies. Dern admitted that an increase in enlisted strength would call for additional funds and confessed that he had not taken the matter up with Roosevelt in view of the "President's ardent desire to balance the budget."[16]

Dern clearly implied that the Army could look for little or no support and encouragement from the Roosevelt Administration in its efforts to increase military expenditures in order to provide for increased manpower. If any augmentation of the strength of the Regular Army was to be forthcoming it would have to be at the initiative of congressional supporters of such a policy. However, Congress was hesitant about increasing military spending and reluctant to take unilateral action to increase the size of the Regular Army without the encouragement and approval of the Chief Executive. Congress deferred to the judgment of the President in

---

[16] New York <u>Times</u>, May 30, 1934, p. 4. <u>Army Navy Journal</u>, June 2, 1934, p. 809. Dern accepted the general idea that during a period of economic stringency the Army would have to curtail its activities. In his annual report for 1934 Dern noted that the force necessary to perform the various duties of the Regular Army had been the subject of frequent studies by the General Staff, and the conclusion had been reached that least force that could perform the mission was 14,000 officers and 165,000 enlisted men. With the "general intent" of these views, Dern said he was in "complete accord." However, the Secretary of War stressed the fact that the need for a "greater defense force" would have to be balanced against the "necessity for emergency expenditures in recovery programs.... In the interest of economy, and in view of the urgent calls on the Treasury for relief funds, it may be necessary to defer for the present any material increase in the strength of our military establishment." Report of the Secretary of War, 1934, p. 3.

matters pertaining to national defense, and as one congressional leader suggested, the President should "carry the ball" as far as national defense was concerned. According to this concept the President

> was the Commander-in-Chief of the Army and Navy and we would depend on him in time of war. If he wants another battleship, we should trust his judgment, because he is responsible in time of war.... He has all the information available from the Army and Navy as to their needs and from the State Department as to foreign relations and the strength of other armies and navies. What does a congressman know about these matters, except what he reads in the newspapers and that may be colored by the views of the newspaper.[17]

MacArthur well realized that Congress deferred to the judgment of a strong Chief Executive in matters of national defense, and sought to goad Congress into taking action regardless of the penurious policy of the administration. In his appearance before the Senate Appropriations Committee in testimony on the 1935 budget for the Army, MacArthur, with vigor and cogency, reminded the members of the upper chamber that they, along with the House of Representatives, had the ultimate constitutional responsibility for the maintenance of the Army. The Chief of Staff admonished the Senators that the Army over the years had received less funds than should be "consistently appropriated" in accordance with the National Defense Act, and that the responsibility for this insidious situation rested squarely with Congress and the Bureau of the Budget. Senator Townsend sought to rebut the Chief of Staff by

---

[17] _Army Navy Journal_, December 30, 1933, p. 357.

pointing out that Congress had only reduced appropriations some $7,000,000 over the past three years. The Chief of Staff replied that just because the Bureau of the Budget did not send to Capitol Hill the figures requested by the Army, Congress was not relieved from its responsibility of "raising and maintaining armies...." Concluding his peroration, MacArthur challenged Congress: "You are not bound by Budget figures. The Constitution places the final responsibility not upon the Budget, but upon one group alone, and that is the Congress of the United States." The Chief of Staff's forthright appeal for more money over the head of the President and the Bureau of the Budget caused Senator Copeland to admit with some chagrin that perhaps Congress had "hidden behind the petticoats of the Budget."[18]

Efforts by MacArthur to encourage congressional initiative in increasing military expenditures in disregard of the administration's position on the matter provoked a reaction by administration leaders. Late in 1934 Roosevelt instructed the War Department that all contemplated legislation requiring appropriations should be first submitted to the Bureau of the Budget for

---

18 Army Navy Journal, March 17, 1934, p. 588. MacArthur pointed out to the Senate Committee that because of the Budget Act of 1921, once the Bureau of the Budget submitted the War Department estimates to Congress the Army could not "initiate increases thereto." The Army could respond to suggestions from the Appropriations Committee or answer questions to whether more or less funds were necessary, but the Army could not initiate any increase to the various budget items. Hearings before Subcommittee on Military Appropriations Bill 1935 (Washington, 1934), March 12, 1934, pp. 25-26.

approval. In addition, the War Department was informed that any legislation not requiring appropriations by Congress would have to be first submitted to the National Emergency Council, whose chairman was Donald L. Richberg.[19] These instructions from the White House sought to curtail the independence of the Army in its relations with Congress, and undoubtedly were related to MacArthur's efforts to encourage Congress to increase the strength of the Regular Army, an issue that was likely to come up again during the forthcoming session of the new Congress.

The policy of channeling through Richberg all legislation pertaining to the Army raised the ire of military spokesmen. The influential Army Navy Journal claimed that this policy would hamper national defense and would hinder such needed reforms in the military establishment as the Secretary of War might desire to carry out. Richberg, the Journal pointed out, was "not responsible for the conditions in the Armed Forces ..." and his interposition between the Secretary of War and Congress would delay the decision-making process. The Army Navy Journal aimed its criticism not at Richberg, but against a policy which was clearly not in the "interest of good government."[20]

Not unexpectedly this provision did not preclude MacArthur from exercising what he considered was his responsibility as Chief of Staff to be military advisor to Congress. In February 1935 he

---

[19] Army Navy Journal, December 22, 1934, p. 355.

[20] Ibid., January 5, 1935, p. 386.

sent to Congress an outline bill for using the CCC as a source of a voluntary Enlisted Reserve Corps, clearly circumventing Roosevelt's directive. In addition MacArthur's letter to the Chairman of the House Military Affairs Committee in early February, incorporating the identical $405,000,000 arms modernization program that had been sent to the Bureau of the Budget and the President, was clearly meant as a recommendation for legislation. Furthermore, Congress was well aware of the position of the Chief of Staff on the issue of increasing the strength of the Army, and in various appearances before congressional committees the Chief of Staff was able to enunciate the policy of the General Staff.

At the same time the policy of referring all military legislation to the administration served as a convenient means to dispose of obnoxious proposals originating in Congress which did not meet with approval by the General Staff, or which were in opposition to War Department policy. By replying to congressional leaders that a given proposal initiated by them was not "consistent with the financial program" of the administration, the Army could tactfully refuse the importunities of Congress. An example of this occurred in the spring of 1935 when Senator Pat Harrison of Mississippi personally wrote to MacArthur requesting additional funds for the Air National Guard of his home state. This proposal was not in harmony with the policy of the General Staff, but desiring not to offend an influential Senator, MacArthur conveniently forwarded the proposal to the Bureau of the Budget so that the views of "higher authority" might be ascertained before taking action.[21] Thus the opprobrium for rebuffing Senator Harrison was placed on the Bureau of the Budget.

Roosevelt's ambivalence toward military spending --- a reluctance to approve substantial increases in the regular budget appropriations but at the same time an apparent favorable disposition to consider the use of relief funds for military purposes --- is evidenced again in the closing days of 1934.

It has been discussed in an earlier chapter that Roosevelt in the fall of 1933 had implied to Secretary of War Dern that he was disposed to use public works funds for the modernization of the Army, and although the Army request was not met in its entirety some $17,500,000 was allocated from relief funds for motorization of the Army and aircraft procurement.

In December 1934 Dern was directed by the White House to submit through the Bureau of the Budget for the consideration of the President information concerning the "urgent needs of the Military Establishment." This was a dear indication that Roosevelt was interested in this matter. In a letter sent to the Bureau of the Budget to be forwarded to the President, the Army stressed the fact that it had sought for some time to

obtain sufficient funds to effect a reasonable degree of motorization, modernization and mechanization of the Army, together with

---

[21] Ltr, MacArthur to D. W. Bell, Acting Director of the Bureau of the Budget, May 29, 1935. AG 111, RG 94, NA.

the completion of the program for the Air Corps provided for in the Act of July 2, 1926, and for completion of the necessary construction of housing for personnel and storage of supplies, and equipment, including ammunition.

Referring to the fact that some progress had been made through the use of public works funds, the War Department estimated that an additional sum totaling approximately $405,000,000 should be expended to meet the "urgent needs" of the War Department.[22]

No record is available in Army files to indicate what Roosevelt's reaction, much less that of the Bureau of the Budget, was to this rather expensive program. The fact that the identical estimate was forwarded to the hostile Public Works Board by the

---

[22] This total included the following items:

Ammunition	$44.9	Million
Antiaircraft	35.	"
Motorization	22.	"
of Field Artillery	37.	"
Mechanization (to include mechanized equipment for one brigade of cavalry, one regiment of medium tanks, one regiment of light tanks, one battalion of Field Artillery, seven separate armored car troops, and seven companies of light tanks)	15.	"
Aircraft	89.	"
Seacoast defense	21.	"
Modern Equipment (equipment needed for the active units of the Regular Army and National Guard in gas masks, mortars, fire control equipment and communication equipment)	8.	"
Army housing and technical construction	132.	"

Ltr, Deputy Chief of Staff to the Director of the Bureau of the Budget, December 12, 1934. AG 111 (1-23-34) Section 2-A, RG 94, NA. Note: As an enclosure to this letter the Army forwarded a map of the United States which indicated the principal areas of unemployment that could be aided by the disbursement of its $405,000,000 project.

War Department the following February[23] suggests that the Army had reason to believe that Roosevelt was at least not vigorously opposed to the use of public works funds for military projects. However, Roosevelt's deferment to the views of Ickes in the fall of 1933 on the issue of public works funds, and the demise of MacArthur's $405,000,000 program submitted to Roosevelt in December 1934, indicates that while the President may have favored spending public works funds on military activities the size of the Army estimates coupled with the antipathy of his New Deal advisors toward such a scheme precluded final approval.

Almost simultaneously with this curious incident Roosevelt again encouraged the War Department to think that the possibility of emergency funds for the Army might be forthcoming. In late 1934 Japan announced that after 1936 it would no longer abide by the Five Power Naval Treaty of 1923 pertaining to naval building. Roosevelt's reaction to this development was to request Secretary Dern to submit to him a statement of the effect produced on national defense from the "point of view of the responsibilities of the War Department, by Japan's denunciation of the Washington Treaty, and likewise my (Secretary of War) recommendations as to the action that should be taken in consequence."[24]

---

[23] Ltr, Dern to Federal Emergency Administrator of Public Works, February 21, 1935. AG 111 (1-23-34) Section 2-A, RG 94, NA.

[24] Ltr, Dern to Roosevelt, December 27, 1934. OCS/20827-2, Files of the Secretary of War, RG 107, NA.

Dern's reply to the President pointed out that the inherent strength of the American strategic triangle, Panama-Hawaii-Alaska, together with a "reasonable state of preparedness" would be a strong factor in obviating war with Japan. Dern was thus positing the deterent or insurance theory of defense: that by being reasonably strong the potential enemy would be deterred from instigating aggression. The problem in 1935, as today, in respect to the deterent theory was to obtain the maximum position of strength with the minimum expenditure of money. In advising the President, Dern noted that the Philippines, Guam, and the Aleutian Islands were extremely vulnerable and would have to be "considered as within the possibility of Japan to take." The Secretary of War then proposed the following three considerations for the President in order to meet the potential threat from Japan and increase American deterent posture in the Far East: (1) the Pacific Coast, the Panama Canal, and Hawaii should be made "reasonably secure" through the early completion of approved defense projects; (2) the strength of the Regular Army must be increased so that there would be adequate garrisons in the Hawaii-Panama-Alaska defensive perimeter, an immediate readiness force for use as an expeditionary force, and a nucleus of personnel to train the initial mobilization force; (3) the augmentation of War Reserve in equipment and ammunition so that shortages for the initial mobilization force could be met. Dern noted that the cost of increasing the Regular Army would be around $20,000,000 annually, and he stated that the cost of meeting equipment shortages came to approximately $360,000,000. This figure, Dern cautioned Roosevelt, constituted

> the irreducible minimum required to put the defensive means for which the War Department is responsible on adequate basis to meet the changed situation brought about by Japan's denunciation of the Washington Treaty. They are not only conservative but modest. They are not designed primarily with a view to give us adequate means to wage war but to obviate it.[25]

Dern's spectacular request for funds to improve the American deterent position vis-a-vis Japan in December 1934, went unheeded. The administration, if not the President, was cool to increased spending for military activities. This primarily reflected the fact that the "liberal reform" element of the New Deal was disenchanted with the insurance theory of defense and believed that increased military expenditures would lead to an arms race and this in turn would provoke and exacerbate rather than deter an international crisis, and ultimately lead to war.

Roosevelt, notwithstanding the opposition to increased military expenditures on the part of his New Deal advisors, definitely considered the idea of an emergency, or so-called "crash program" of military spending for aircraft in December 1934. The Army,

---

[25] Ibid. Written below Dern's signature is a note which indicates that the letter was personally presented to Roosevelt by the Secretary of War. OCS/20827-2. File #100 to #200, accession number #123, Classified Files of the Secretary of War, Series 300, Box 4, RG 107, NA. Note: Dern's request for $360,000,000 included the following: Ammunition - $67 million, antiaircraft - $36 million, modernization of Field Artillery - $38 million, mechanization - $22 million, aircraft - $133 million, Seacost defense - $23 million, and modern equipment for the field forces - $25 million.

advised of Roosevelt's position on this matter, estimated that the cost of 800 aircraft to be procured during the fiscal years 1936, 1937, 1938 would total around $150,000,000.[26] A month later the Army was informed that the President was definitely "contemplating allotting" from public works funds approximately $35,000,000 for the procurement of some 600 aircraft. The President wanted this sum to be utilized before the end of fiscal 1936, with the possible extension of spending to the end of fiscal 1937. This sum would be in addition to any amount which the regular budget would carry for procurement of aircraft.[27]

Although Congress prohibited the use of public works funds on military activities in March 1935, the Army never gave up the hope that it could persuade Roosevelt to initiate an emergency spending program on military activities. In June 1935, Dern appealed to Roosevelt again to approve spending $40,000,000 for aircraft procurement over a five year period.[28]

The Chief of Staff, undoubtedly realizing that his $405,000,000 program would be unacceptable to the Administration and the Public Works Board, appealed to Congress in an effort to

---

[26] Memo, AC/S G-4 for the Chief of Staff, December 11, 1934. AG 111 (1-23-34) Section 2-A, RG 94, NA. Eight hundred was given as the figure required to bring the Air Corps up to the strength of 2,320 aircraft as recommended by the Baker Board.

[27] Memo, AC/S G-4 for the AG, January 28, 1935. AG 580 I.R. (6-6-33) Section 1, RG 94, NA.

[28] Ltr, Dern to Roosevelt, August 2, 1935. AG 580 I.R. (6-6-33) Section 1, RG 94, NA.

obtain relief funds for the Army. In a letter to John J. McSwain, Chairman of the House Military Affairs Committee, on February 6, 1935, MacArthur outlined in detail the same program of spending $405,000,000 for the Army that he had forwarded to Roosevelt the previous December, and which he sent to the Public Works Board later in February. Hoping to rally congressional support for the passage of legislation incorporating his $405,000,000 program, MacArthur summarized the "materiel needs" that an "adequate" defense of the nation required. The importance of this bid for congressional support and the light it sheds on the material position of the Army in the early months of 1935 requires that it be discussed in some detail.

MacArthur pointed out that $89,000,000 was needed for aircraft procurement so that the Air Corps could be brought up to a strength of 2,320 machines as set by the Baker Board in 1934. In outlining his request for funds for mechanization, MacArthur stressed the fact that

> though we have developed a pilot model unquestionably the equal and probably the superior to any other in the world, our Army is equipped with tanks of World War manufacture, which are no longer of tactical value against modern forces. Comparatively few modern vehicles have been delivered, while only moderate numbers have been included in the 1935 and the 1936 bills. Because of the relatively short useful life of this kind of equipment and the expense involved in its acquisition and frequent replacement our program is so drawn as to derive maximum advantage from minimum quantities, and does not include armament for even the major portions of units of this type that will be promptly mobilized in an emergency.

MacArthur estimated that the cost for equipping the total number of mechanized units scheduled for initial mobilization would be approximately $90,000,000. Clearly such a large figure would preclude congressional approval and support. Instead MacArthur stressed the fact that the Army wanted only $15,000,000 so that it could provide "mechanized equipment for an adequate number of units."[29]

MacArthur went on to stress the need for spending around $35,000,000 for anti-aircraft weapons, noting that this equipment was "complicated in design, slow in manufacture and required highly-trained personnel for its most effective use." The Chief of Staff noted:

> At present, the six active regiments of anti-aircraft artillery in the Regular Army are at reduced strength and all are seriously lacking in essential items of modern equipment. The ten active regiments of the National Guard, except for two batteries, are entirely lacking in modern anti-aircraft equipment. These are first line troops and as a matter of first priority must be fully equipped and properly trained.

---

[29] MacArthur listed the following units that could be equipped with the expenditure of $15,000,000 in 1935: one mechanized cavalry brigade, one regiment of medium tanks, one regiment of light tanks, one battalion of Field Artillery, seven armored car troops, and seven light tank companies. This list of units is identical with the organization that the Army indicated could be equipped with the expenditure of $23,000,000 of public works funds in 1933. Slight progress seems to have been made between 1933 and 1935 in equipping a mechanized force in view of the fact that the 1935 request for equipment was some $7,000,000 less than in 1933. The total number of tanks that MacArthur estimated could be procured with the $15 million allotment were 285 light tanks, 162 medium tanks, 44 combat cars, 33 scout cars, and 76 half-track vehicles. Ltr, MacArthur to McSwain, February 6, 1935. AG 111 (1-23-34) Section 2-4, RG 94, NA.

In presenting the Military Affairs Committee with a request for $37,000,000 for field artillery weapons, MacArthur noted that this sum was needed to modernize the 75mm and 155mm howitzers with which the active units of the Regular Army and National Guard were equipped, and to procure new artillery weapons such as the 105mm howitzer, the 8" howitzer, and the 155mm gun. MacArthur urged that $8,000,000 be spent to procure new infantry weapons and equipment such as gas masks, 37mm guns, semi-automatic rifles, fire control equipment, 50 caliber machine guns, communication equipment, and bridge equipment. The Chief of Staff noted that the Springfield rifle, model 03, had been the basic infantry arm for a third of a century and should be replaced with the new Garand semi-automatic rifle. MacArthur added in this regard:

> In the 1935 appropriations 1,500 of these weapons were authorized and 1,870 are carried in the 1936 bill, making a total of only 3,370 now in sight. As rapidly as possible all Regular Army and National Guard units should be equipped with them, and the older rifles retired to reserve for emergency use.[30]

After reception of the Chief of Staff's letter McSwain called a "secret meeting" of the Military Affairs Committee, and invited MacArthur to appear before the group and present verbally his $405,000,000 program. Emphasizing to the Committee the urgent needs of the Army, MacArthur sought to have his entire program "woven into a bill designed to bring about a $405,000,000 army modernization

---

[30] *Ibid*.

plan."[31] MacArthur's efforts to persuade Congress to initiate a large scale army modernization program through the use of public works funds brought vigorous reaction from those members of Congress who were adverse to such expenditures. In late March 1935 Congress stipulated that none of the $4,800,000,000 public works bill, then pending in Congress, could be used for military or naval purposes. On March 12, 1935, Senator Borah introduced an amendment to the public works bill which would prohibit such use of public relief funds. The final amendment which passed Congress provided that

> no part of the appropriations made by the joint resolution shall be expended for munitions, warships, or military or naval materiel; but this provision shall not be construed to prevent the use of such appropriations for improvements in military or naval reservations, posts, camps...or for non-military or non-naval purposes in such places.[32]

It appears that one of the factors behind the enactment of this prohibitive amendment in the Senate was the fact that the House Military Affairs Committee, acting upon MacArthur's recommendation, had initiated a draft bill to authorize the use of public works appropriations for the $405,000,000 army modernization

---

[31] New York Times, February 9, 1935, p. 7.

[32] Army Navy Journal, March 16, 1935, p. 596. March 30, 1935, p. 645. Senate and House conferees on the $4.8 billion work relief bill accepted the Senate amendment barring use of the money for strictly military or naval purposes, but altered it so that funds could be used for construction as well as for improvements on military or naval reservations. Congressional Record, 74th Cong., 1st Sess., Vol. 79, part 4, March 13, 1935, pp. 3524-3530.

program that MacArthur had presented.[33] The Senate at that time was in the midst of its famous hearings on the munitions industry and the tempest over the "merchants of death" presented an emotional climate unfavorable for such a plan as MacArthur had visualized. Although the Borah Amendment had the support of the pacificist and anti-militarist circles in Congress, Borah himself denied that this was the motivation behind his legislative tactics. The famous legislator from Idaho was adamant that if the administration and the Army wanted to modernize the Army and increase military spending, such a program should be presented to Congress through the regular appropriations bill so that Congress could examine in detail how the money was to be spent. He did not approve of giving the Commander-in-Chief a carte blanche in respect to military appropriations. Borah claimed that he felt

> strongly that no discretion should be lodged in the Chief of the Army and Navy, as to how much should be expended in building up our Military Establishment. That should be determined by Congress.[34]

Although it is easy to dismiss Borah's remarks as a reflection of his basic "isolationist" sentiments there is some substance to

---

[33] New York Times, March 24, 1935, I, p. 28. The Times reported that Senator Borah initiated his amendment barring the use of public works funds for military activities when he was appraised of the fact that the House Military Affairs Committee had actually begun drafting a plan to authorize spending $405 million of the $4.8 billion public works bill for military activities.

[34] Congressional Record, 74th Cong., 1st Sess., Vol. 79, Part 4, March 13, 1935, p. 3524.

the fact that Congress was sincerely concerned over the constitutional issue involved in allotting a lump sum to be spent at the discretion of the Executive for military and naval purposes. After all it had been one of the hallmarks of Anglo-Saxon constitutional history that the legislative body zealously guarded its exercise of the power of the purse, and Borah felt that in allowing the Executive to spend a given amount as it saw fit on military activities, Congress was permitting the administration and the Army to usurp congressional prerogatives. In addition, it should be pointed out that concurrently with the Borah Amendment the Senate passed the military appropriations bill for 1936, which increased funds for military activities over the figure set by both the House of Representatives and the Bureau of the Budget.

Commenting on the action of Congress in denying the Army the only possibility that it had of obtaining any modicum of modernization in the mid-thirties, the Army Navy Journal showed unusual restraint. Without its usual strident comment in reference to congressional penuriousness, this influential weekly noted that funds for housing, technical construction, and repairs would be available; however, the Journal "regretted" the fact that the Army would "still be handicapped" by a lack of artillery, tanks, armored cars, and reserve ammunition.[35]

---

[35] Army Navy Journal, April 6, 1935, p. 656.

During the early months of 1935 Congress, while giving attention to the issue of using public works funds for military activities, concurrently undertook its annual perusal of the military budget for the coming fiscal year. The original estimate requested by the Army for military activities totalled around $341,000,000, the greater part of this increase over previous War Department budgets being to finance an increase in the strength of the Regular Army to 165,000 enlisted men and 14,000 officers. It was reported that Roosevelt would ask Congress for a modest increase in military appropriations over the appropriations for fiscal 1935, but at a figure well below Secretary Dern's original estimate. In particular, the Army's projected increase in strength had been received with "unsympathetic attention" by the Budget Bureau and President Roosevelt.[36] The final amount approved by the Bureau of the Budget and forwarded to Congress came to around $312,000,000. Provision for the increase in strength for the Regular Army, which would have cost around $20,000,000 for the first year, was eliminated by the Bureau of the Budget.[37]

On Thursday, February 1, 1935, Representative R. Ewing Thomason of Texas, disregarding the views of the administration concerning an increase in personnel for the Regular Army, announced

---

[36] New York Times, January 1, 1935, p. 11.

[37] Hearings: War Department Appropriations Bill, 1936, p. 11.

that the Military Affairs Committee of the House had approved his plan to increase the Regular Army by some 50,000 enlisted men and 2,000 officers.[38] On the same day that MacArthur testified before the House Military Affairs Committee in reference to his $405,000,000 equipment plan, the Committee recommended to the House that the Regular Army be increased to 165,000 enlisted men.[39]

In his annual appearance before the House Subcommittee on Military Appropriations in respect to the military budget for the coming fiscal year, the Chief of Staff reviewed with his usual cogency the situation in respect to the Military Establishment. According to MacArthur, the year 1932 had been the last year in which appropriations for the support of the Army had been "comparatively free from the disturbed economic situation...." The Chief of Staff then succinctly outlined the effect of this situation on the Army:

In distributing the successive reductions the War Department has endeavored determinedly to maintain the structural framework of trained personnel indispensable to orderly mobilization in an emergency. So far as possible every reduction has been absorbed by continuing in service obsolete and inefficient equipment, by limiting outlays for maintenance and for operation and training far below reasonable requirements and by slackening technical development. While grants from emergency appropriations have made good some of the resultant deficiencies, the adverse effect of the drastic retrenchment required are frequently cumulative and readily eradical.

The vital necessity for the acquisition of reasonable amounts

---

[38] New York Times, February 2, 1935, p. 28. Army Navy Journal, February 3, 1935, p. 459.

[39] New York Times, February 6, 1935, p. 19.

of modern equipment as promptly as possible is apparent.[40]

MacArthur then discussed the reductions in the military estimates that had been made by the Budget Bureau and specifically mentioned the fact that the latter had "disallowed" the proposal for an increase in personnel, reduced procurement of aircraft by some $8,000,000, curtailed mechanization and motorization projects by $3,000,000, and denied the Army procurement of the new 105mm howitzer and needed signal equipment. In presenting the cuts made by the Budget Bureau, MacArthur claimed that he was confining himself "to a bare recital of fact."[41] The Chief of Staff's testimony before the House in reference to the 1936 military budget is extremely important for it vividly reflects his efforts to lay before Congress the state of the Army and the need for moderate increases in military expenditure. MacArthur did not hesitate to indict the Bureau of the Budget and the administration for their parsimonious treatment of the Army, and he seemed contemptuous of the fact that he might be acting insubordinately toward the Chief Executive in his candid testimony.[42]

---

[40]Hearings: War Department Appropriations Bill, 1936 (January 14, 1935), p. 2.

[41]Ibid., pp. 11-12.

[42]Space forbids more than passing citation to some of the more interesting portions of the Chief of Staff's testimony. A few examples however will suffice:

Mr. Blanton. As Chief of Staff of the United States Army you, of course, bring to the attention of the President, through regular agencies, every urgent matter that you think is important

Realizing that there was little likelihood of getting the entire amount of the original War Department estimate reinstated by Congress, MacArthur brought his heaviest guns to bear on the issue of getting the personnel increase for the Regular Army reinstated into the budget appropriations bill:

Of the cuts, there is one that I think so fundamental and so basic that its application unbalances the bill from the standpoint of reasonable policy and may jeopardize the prospect of success in the case of major operations, I refer to the proposed increase in the enlisted strength of the Regular Army....The Bureau of the Budget indicated that we should have to confine outselves to 118,750 men. We estimate we should have 165,000.[43]

Influenced by MacArthur's emphasis and by the fact that the Military Affairs Committee had proposed a personnel increase, the Subcommittee on Military Appropriations integrated into its bill a provision for an increase in the enlisted strength of the Regular

---

regarding national defense and regarding new equipment?

General MacArthur. We have done so.

Mr. Blanton. And the President's Budget has cut you down in certain particulars?

General MacArthur. It has.

Mr. Blanton. Is it the purpose of you gentlemen to get us to enlarge those allowances?

General MacArthur. We are only going to present to the committee what has been approved by the Bureau of the Budget, unless the committee desires other enlightenment. I might say the differences between the estimates and the Budget we included in my statement merely because the chairman specifically requested in his letter of November 23, 1934. Hearings: War Department Appropriations Bill, 1936, p. 13.

Another interesting byplay ensued when the Chief of Staff stressed the role of the Bureau of the Budget in the preparation of the military estimates: Mr. MacMillan. For all practical purposes the Budget tells the War Department exactly what you can do and what you cannot do. General MacArthur. Precisely. Ibid., p. 22.

[43] Ibid., p. 21.

Army.

The appropriations bill that was adopted by the House gave the War Department some $378,000,000 for fiscal 1936, and of this amount some $318,700,000 was for strictly military activities. Cognizant of the fact that the Administration was opposed to an increase in personnel for the Regular Army, the House bill gave the President discretionary authority to increase the Regular Army from 118,750 enlisted men to 165,000 and the National Guard by some 5,000 men. In voting the largest military budget since the onset of the depression, the Chairman of the House Appropriations Committee noted that the House had been unable to provide for the $405,000,000 modernization program "demanded by the General Staff" and at the same time keep within the limitations of the budget laid down by the President.[44] The appropriation by the House of $318,000,000 for military activities represented an increase of around $38,000,000 from the previous fiscal year and of this increase a considerable amount was to be allotted to the "material betterment" of the Army.[45]

The provision in the appropriations bill to give Roosevelt discretionary authority to increase the enlisted strength of the

---

[44] New York *Times*, February 20, 1935, p. 13.

[45] *Ibid.*, February 22, 1935, p. 8. February 23, 1935, p. 8. February 23, 1935, pp. 1, 6. The increase in appropriations provided $24.5 million for aircraft including armament and communications equipment, $1.7 million for mechanization, $1 million for artillery equipment and modernization, and $1 million for motorization. *Congressional Record*, 74th Cong., 1st Sess., Vol. 79, Part 3, February 21, 1935, pp. 2412-29. February 22, 1935, pp. 2480-2500.

Regular Army was eliminated by the Senate Appropriations Committee. MacArthur viewed this provision as particularly obnoxious and an ingenious legislative device which would surely defeat his plans to increase the strength of the Regular Army. Testifying before the Senate Appropriations Committee the Chief of Staff emphasized that an increase in strength should be made mandatory and written explicitly into the final bill: "We believe a decision on strength of forces should be made clear-cut by Congress." MacArthur felt that granting Roosevelt "discretionary power" in this matter would add another burden to the already overworked Executive and impose upon him a duty always undertaken by Congress. According to MacArthur the House provision placed "a burden upon the Executive branch with regard to the strength of the Military Establishment which has never been placed upon it, either in war or peace." Questions relating to the strength of the armed forces, MacArthur told the Senate, "have always been decided by Congress."[46] It is rather ironic but MacArthur's main argument that Congress, rather than the Executive, had the responsibility to decide questions

---

[46] "War Department Appropriations Bill, 1936" Hearings before the Subcommittee on Appropriations, United States Senate on HR 5913, (Washington, 1935), February 27, 1935, pp. 4-6. Note: It would appear that the Senate Hearings on the Army bill for fiscal 1936 provided the first meeting between MacArthur and a freshman senator from Missouri, Harry S. Truman. Truman, apparently because of his previous interest in the National Guard and the CMTC program in Missouri, had been invited to appear at the hearings and bring up points bearing on the military appropriations bill. Truman's vigorous support of the General Staff's request for more funds for the CMTC undoubtedly made an excellent impression on the Chief of Staff. See also New York Times, March 2, 1935, p. 13.

relating to the strength of the armed forces was used by Senate leaders in defeating his bid for using public works funds for military activities.

The final bill as passed by the Senate provided for a mandatory increase in the enlisted strength of the Regular Army, and the bill that finally emerged from the House-Senate conference and which became law was indeed generous for the Army. Total appropriations approved for the Army for fiscal 1936 came to around $400,000,000, and funds for military activities were almost identical to the Army's original estimate that it had submitted to the Bureau of the Budget, $341,000,000. Besides authorizing $20,000,000 to provide for an increase in the enlisted strength of the Regular Army to 165,000, the bill also provided $500,000 for a strength increase in the National Guard.[47]

An analysis of appropriations for fiscal 1936 indicates that lower appropriations had been made by the House and higher ones by the Senate, and in general the compromise conference report tended to support the Senate figure. The action of Congress in appropriating funds for the military activities of the Army, well over the budget limit set by the Roosevelt Administration, was startling

---

[47] Congressional Record, 74th Cong., 1st Sess., Vol. 79, Part 5, March 29, 1935, pp. 4701-06. The Conference report agreed to a final bill that carried a total of $341,348,204 for military activities of the Army. This was approximately $23,000,000 more than the original House figure. Note: MacArthur had set $340,000,000 as the "limiting figure" to be used in the preparation of the military budget for fiscal 1936. Memo, MacArthur for the BOWD, August 6, 1934. AG 111 (1-23-34) Section 2-A, RG 94, NA.

and indicates that Congress was not as insouciant toward the American military posture of deterence, and indeed not as "isolationist" as is commonly presumed. The New York *Times* commented:

> The large increase and the disregard by both chambers of the limits set on budget appropriations in the budget estimates are viewed as being a result, at least in part, of the prevalent war talk.[48]

Congress felt that the essential requirements that had long been urged by the General Staff and MacArthur had been met:

> We have given the General Staff of our Army and our War Department everything that they have assured us they need in order adequately to protect and safeguard this Government.[49]

Army spokesmen were generally elated over the fact that Congress had seen fit to override the views of the administration and provide rather generously for the Army. Particularly congressional approval to increase the size of the Regular Army to 165,000 men, the long-sought goal of the General Staff, was received with exultant gratitude and satisfaction by the Army. Military leaders, although not unaware of the fact that from a materiel standpoint the Army was still in dire need of increased appropriations, proclaimed that for the first time in many years "adequate" defense could be obtained. This reflected the fact that military leaders were wedded to the belief that personnel and manpower were the prime prerequisites for the military

---

[48] New York *Times*, March 30, 1935, p. 9.

[49] *Congressional Record*, 74th Cong., 1st Sess., Vol. 79, Part 5, March 29, 1935, p. 4702.

preparedness of the nation, and that the materiel needs could be met through a modest R&D program in which "pilot" models could be produced which would serve as the prototypes to be turned out by American industry in time of emergency. This concept was questioned by the General Staff increasingly during 1935 and was repudiated after MacArthur left the Chief of Staff's office.

MacArthur, who retired as Chief of Staff in December of 1935 and left for the Philippines not to return to the country until 1951, commented that for the first time since 1922 the Army entered a new fiscal year (1936) with a "reasonable prospect" of developing a defensive establishment "commensurate in size and efficiency with the country's minimum needs." Referring to the fact that Congress had approved increasing the Regular Army to 165,000 men, MacArthur noted that "obstacles which had inhibited progress have been either swept aside by Congress or reduced in importance."[50] General Malin Craig, MacArthur's successor, likewise was of the opinion that the increase for fiscal 1936 was of immense significance for the Army:

> In general, it may be said that the increase in military appropriations for 1936 over those of preceding years marks an epoch in the period that has elapsed since the end of the World War.[51]

The Roosevelt Administration was opposed to the congressional action which provided a personnel increase for the Regular Army in disregard of the expressed position of the Budget Bureau on this

---

[50] _Report of the Secretary of War, 1935_, p. 41.

[51] New York _Times_, November 9, 1936, p. 10.

matter. In late June 1935, the Acting Director of the Bureau of the Budget, informed the Army that it was the "President's desire" that instead of receiving a total of $20,000,000 to finance the expansion of the Regular Army, only $11,000,000 would be authorized for expenditure.[52] It was explained that expenditure of the remaining $9,000,000 was deferred until January 1936, when a conference of the Bureau of the Budget and the War Department would be held and a decision made concerning expenditure of the remaining funds.[53] Apparently this move was a gambit on the part of the Bureau of the Budget to circumvent the mandate of Congress to increase the strength of the Regular Army. In its efforts to curtail increasing expenditures the Bureau of the Budget wanted to defer spending the required amount and postpone final action until the next session of Congress. At that time, if it appeared that Congress would continue appropriations for a 165,000 man Army for the next fiscal year, the administration could move to allot the remaining $9,000,000 to finance the expansion to 165,000 men. Understandably this tactic did not receive favorable reaction from the Army.

The General Staff was alarmed over the fact that the Budget Bureau not only withheld the total amount appropriated by Congress but directed that enlistments should be made in twelve equal

---

[52] Memo, AC/S G-1 for the Chief of Staff, August 17, 1935. G-4/30379-8, NG 319, NA.

[53] _Hearings_ before Subcommittee on WD Appropriations, U.S. Senate, 74th Cong., 2nd Sess. (Washington, 1936), p. 6.

increments spread out over the entire fiscal year. This meant that those individuals who enlisted early in the fiscal year would be a continuing obligation for pay, subsistence, and clothing allowances, and therefore would incure a "unduly high charge" against the total funds set aside for enlistment. The Chief of Staff was warned in August that if the rate of enlistment continued, by the end of August some 59 percent of the available funds would be obligated though only 32 percent of the approved increase in strength would have been procured. MacArthur was advised that "unless enlistments are curtailed funds will soon be obligated thus necessitating cessation of all enlistments."[54]

According to General Malin Craig, MacArthur's successor as Chief of Staff, the Army "found that we had run beyond our quota, so we had to stop. I think recruiting stopped just about the time I came in, about in October. We had then run up to about 139,000."[55] In December 1935 the Chief of Staff was advised the enlistment situation by the petulant G-3:

> The full amount of funds necessary for financing the increase to 165,000 has not been made available...and the reduction leaves us at a strength which the War Department considers to be below a figure consistent with absolute demands.[56]

---

[54] Memo, AC/S G-1 for the Chief of Staff, August 17, 1935. G-4/30379-8, RG 319, NA.

[55] Hearings: WD Appropriations, 1937, Senate, p. 8.

[56] Memo, AC/S G-3 for the Chief of Staff, December 4, 1935. AG 320.2 (12-4-35) Section 1, RG 94, NA.

In January 1936 the new Chief of Staff obtained the concurrence of the Bureau of the Budget to the use of the remaining funds to bring the increase of the Army to 165,000 men.[57] According to the Chief of Staff the Bureau of the Budget approved this allotment only if Congress saw fit to maintain the Regular Army at 165,000 enlisted men for the coming fiscal year, 1937. As Craig explained there would be no practical or economic sense for enlisting additional men to reach 165,000 and then discharging them again before July 1, 1936.

Further evidence that the Administration was attempting to hold down military expenditures was provided by events in the fall of 1935. At that time the President's supplemental budget message indicated that he would attempt to stabilize military spending for the current fiscal at around $300,000,000.[58] Roosevelt's efforts in this regard produced a sobering effect on the Army. G-4 was concerned that Army planners, taking liberty with the generosity of Congress in the spring of 1935, would over-step the bounds of prudence and plan projects based on unobtainable budget estimates. So that the pending retrenchment would have the least possible effect on the Army, G-4 urged that a study be prepared of savings and economics that the Army could initiate "in order to prevent serious embarrassment if efforts are made to continue all existing

---

[57] Memo, Chief of Staff for AC/S G-1, G-2, G-3, G-4, WPD, January 6, 1935. OCS/20822-29, RG 319, NA.

[58] New York Times, October 1, 1935, p. 9.

functions in their present proportions."[59]

The Administration throughout the fall and winter of 1935 indicated that it would be adverse to an expansion of the military budget so that all the requirements and needs of the Army would be met. The Army estimate for fiscal 1937, prepared for presentation to the Budget Bureau in August 1935, carried some $108,000,000 for procurement of aircraft, but the limiting figure received by the Army from the Budget drastically curtailed this program so that it was claimed that the number of aircraft that could be procured for fiscal 1937 would "barely replace losses" and would permit "no alleviation of the critical condition now existing as to shortages." Dern emphasized these points to Roosevelt and pleaded for the reinstatement of the War Department's original figure.[60] The President turned aside Dern's request for more money by stressing the fact that the amount approved by the Budget Bureau would improve the aircraft situation "though at a slower rate than that proposed by the Army." In addition, Roosevelt, cognizant that 1936 was election year, cautioned the Army in lucid and unambiguous terms that military expenditures must be stabilized, if not reduced:

. . . the amount of increased appropriations for the Army and Navy

[59]Memo, AC/S G-4 for the Chief of Staff, September 17, 1935. G-4/30529, RG 319, NA.

[60]Ltr, Dern to Roosevelt, January 13, 1936, Folder #200 - #300, ltr number 221, Secretary of War Classified File, Box 4, RG 107, NA.

have mounted each year during the past three years to such an extent that it is unwise, from the point of view of national finances, and incidentally from the point of view of public opinion, for me to recommend additional increases over those contained in the budget.[61]

---

61 Ltr, Roosevelt to Dern, January 15, 1936. Folder #200 - #300, ltr number 223, Secretary of War Classified File, Box 4, RG 107, NA. Note: this letter appears to have been personally typed by Roosevelt and was initialed in ink by him above his typed initials.

CHAPTER XV

LIMITED BUDGETS AND THE PROBLEMS OF MOBILIZATION PLANNING AND RESEARCH AND DEVELOPMENT

In September 1932 Secretary Hurley, concerned over the need for maintaining a viable Research and Development (R&D) program in the face of impending and active budget curtailment, inaugurated the Six-Year Program. In brief this program contemplated allowing around $4,000,000 a year for R&D for six consecutive years, beginning in fiscal 1935. In addition it was planned to make available corresponding amounts for procurement of new equipment and the augmentation and rehabilitation of the War Reserve of ammunition and equipment. Intrinsic to the program was the institution of a rigid system of priorities in both R&D and rearmament.

Soon after the initiation of the program serious objections were raised by many members of the General Staff concerning the scope and aim of the program. In particular objections were raised that the supply arms, such as Ordnance and Quartermaster, had too much authority in determination of the various procurement and development programs. It was felt that the problem should be restudied and that projects should be based more on the using arms and services and upon existing military units. The Assistant Chief of Staff G-4 recommended that the procurement of new equipment, the so-called "rearmament and reequipment" program, should include "standard items which have been approved for issue" by the using of combat arms.[1]

Underlying this request for a reappraisal of the Six-Year Program was an antagonism between the advocates of procurement and the protagonists of continued research and development. In general the using arms such as Infantry, Field Artillery, and Cavalry favored procurement and less emphasis on R&D, whereas Ordnance and Quartermaster supply experts favored expenditure on R&D at a continuing and relatively high level. At the same time the combat arms urged that procurement be closely related to the tables of equipment assigned to various units.

As War Department planning continued and as the "study of the needs of the Army progressed," particularly as a result of the preparation of estimates for the use of public works funds in the summer of 1933, certain elements within the General Staff thought that the Six-Year Program should be broader in scope and encompass more units, even if this entailed increased expenditures and costs. The Six-Year Program originally was designed to supply the active units of the Regular Army and the National Guard with those items of supply and equipment that were most urgently needed and which it was hoped could be supplied within the limits of the budgetary

---

[1]Memo, AC/S G-4 for the Chief of Staff, March 14, 1934. AG 111, RG 94, NA.

allowances imposed on the Army. G-4 urged that this limited goal be restudied and emphasized the opinion that "the requirements of the Army should not be limited to its present peace strength and to budgetary limitations." As a result there was drawn up after extensive work by G-4, in conference with the other General Staff Divisions, a statement of the supplies and equipment necessary to "more completely equip the first million men in the Initial Mobilization." G-4 claimed that National Defense would be imperiled if the War Department was content with only partially equipping the first million men scheduled for mobilization.[2]

The possibility that funds would be forthcoming from other sources than the annual appropriations by Congress in 1933 and 1934 gave an impetus to Army planners to contemplate the possibility of "personnel far in excess of current peace strength and appropriations overreaching current budgetary limitations." In setting its procurement sights higher than they had been the "staff established objectives whose attainment was far distant."[3] General Staff planners apparently believed that public works funds would be made available to the Army.

Disregarding the clear fact that additional funds would be unobtainable through the regular budget appropriations under the Roosevelt Administration, it was nevertheless felt that planning

---

[2]Memo, AC/S G-4 for the Deputy Chief of Staff, September 7, 1934. G-4/29552, RG 319, NA.

[3]Watson, Prewar Plans and Preparations, p. 39.

should be expanded on the possibility of obtaining funds earmarked for economic recovery and the alleviation of unemployment. G-1 proposed that all units scheduled for subsequent mobilization should be transferred to initial mobilization. Optimistic in regard to financing this expansion program, G-1 urged that the program should be placed before the proper Congressional committees and that efforts should be made "to secure the announced approval" of Congress to the "policy of providing in peacetime funds for rearming and re-equipping all units carried in the initial mobilization." According to G-1 such a plan would "enable Congress to visualize an ultimate completion even though it was spread over a long period of years, of the rearmament and reequipment program."[4]

G-3 counseled a more prudent and realistic approach to the problem and was not enthusiastic about revising the Six-Year Program to encompass more units. To the G-3 Division it was apparent that additional funds were unobtainable:

> While it was considered that the program was too restrained in not providing for enough units ... it is quite apparent that in other items it is too liberal and that to provide complete new materiel and equipment for those units would be impossible of fulfillment with the funds which it may be hoped that Congress may appropriate. ... To increase this objective would increase the number of tanks to be purchased in time of peace to 2213, with a consequent increase of cost to about $85,000,000.[5]

Although the Secretary of War approved the policy that the Six-Year

---

[4]Memo, AC/S G-1 for the AC/S G-4, October 23, 1934. G-4/29552, RG 319, NA.

[5]Memo, AC/S G-3 for the AC/S G-4, September 23, 1934. G-4/29552, RG 319, NA.

Program should plan to "arm, rearm, or reequip" all units in the Initial Mobilization Plan,[6] the Army never requested funds for this purpose from the administration. The Army, in its request for public works funds throughout 1933 and in December 1934, requested only enough money to equip a partial number of units scheduled for initial mobilization. Planning may have been ambitious, but in reality the Army understood that sufficient funds to equip even a partial number of units would be difficult, if not impossible, to come by. The ambitious and unrealistic Mobilization Plan of 1933 remained War Department policy throughout 1935 and most of 1936. At that time the Secretary of War, Harry W. Woodring, who succeeded to the office upon the death of George B. Dern, initiated a reappraisal of mobilization plans and corresponding budget estimates.

Concurrent with War Department plans to enlarge the scope of rearmament and procurement of equipment as outlined in the Six-Year Program, dissatisfaction was evidenced over the progress and accomplishment that had been made in Research and Development. As mentioned earlier, the Six-Year Program provided that over $4,000,000 was to be spent annually on R&D for the entire Army. During the summer of 1934, G-4 recommended that the Army draft a bill for presentation to Congress which would legally fix the minimum annual amounts to be spent for R&D for all arms and services.

---

[6]Memo, AC/S G-4 for the AG, December 31, 1934. AG 111, RG 94, NA.

This proposal was vetoed by General Drum, the Deputy Chief of Staff, who believed that such a plan was not necessary as

> ample authority now exists for a continuing research and development program for the Army, and the proposal would be no more effective in obtaining continuing appropriations than the requirement in the present Air Corps Act that 1800 airplanes be maintained.

At the same time General Drum directed that funds for R&D should be increased and that R&D estimates should be based on two limiting figures: a $7,000,000 program and a $9,000,000 program.[7] General Drum's memorandum, outlining plans to increase R&D funds for the Army, clearly indicates that central to the entire issue was the ever-present problem of the Air Corps and the need of providing this arm with an increase in R&D funds. According to General Drum, the Air Corps would receive approximately $5,000,000 for R&D under the $7,000,000 limiting figure, and in planning projects under the $9,000,000 ceiling the Air Corps estimates and those of other branches would be considered upon their "comparative merits."[8]

Drum's decision to increase funds for R&D, particularly the policy to raise the amount for the Air Corps, was the outcome of the recommendation of the Baker Board in July 1934 that more "definite and continuing appropriations should be available for

---

[7]Memo, Deputy Chief of Staff for the AC/S G-4, September 28, 1934. G-4/29552, RG 319, NA.

[8]*Ibid.*

research and development programs."[9] The effect of the Baker Board report was to increase War Department estimates for R&D above the

---

[9]Final Report of War Department Special Committee on Army Air Corps (Washington, 1934), p. 73. Section XVIII of the report covers the conclusions and recommendations, and paragraph 11 of this section includes the following recommendation in regard to finance. This section because of its pertinence to the topic of this entire study is quoted in full:

A considerable part of the present unsatisfactory situation in the Air Corps is due to lack of appropriations. The responsibility for this is divided between the Bureau of the Budget and Congress, with the ultimate responsibility in the Congress.

The general procedure of preparing estimates and processing the Budget from the War Department through the Bureau of the Budget to Congress is sound and tends to economy. Throughout the process, the estimating agencies, including the Air Corps, are given full opportunity to present their requirements and defend their estimates. Coordination in the process of preparing the final estimate for all military activities is and should be placed in the Office of the Secretary of War. Any restriction on him as to the use of his advisers on the General Staff, or of any other of his offices or agencies he chooses is basically unsound from every point of view.

Failure to complete the 5-year aircraft program was largely due to the failure of the Bureau of the Budget and the Congress to approve a financial program and coordinate it with the program for procurement of personnel and materiel prescribed by the law.

A balanced program covering all expenditures for military activities should be prepared and coordinated in the War Department. A separate budget uncoordinated by the War Department with other expenditures for military activities should not be provided for the Air Corps.

There should be submitted by the War Department a definite plan for the improvement of the whole Army, including the Army Air Corps. The plan for the Army Air Corps should be along the lines recommended by the latest War Department study. This plan should be accompanied by the War Department's estimate of the financial program necessary to carry it out; and this combined plan should be reviewed by the proper authority and if not approved the War Department should be given a directive as to basic changes to be made. The revised plan, including an approved financial program, thus coordinated, should then be presented to the Congress. Final Rpt of WD Special Committee on Air Corps, pp. 73-74.

average of $4,500,000 annually for the decade between 1923 and 1933.[10]

The recommendation by the Baker Board that the aircraft strength of the Air Corps be increased to 2,320 machines, presented the Army with an additional problem of obtaining the required increase in funds. The General Staff had to formulate an expenditure plan which would adequately provide for the recommendations of the Baker Board and at the same time meet the fiscal limitations of the administration. The General Staff was presented with two alternative plans: procure some 800 aircraft annually over a three-year period, or 500 aircraft annually over a five-year period. G-4 advised that regardless of which plan was adopted the annual budget estimate must be "reasonable" in order to obtain approval from both the administration and Congress.[11] It was decided by the Chief of Staff that planning would be based on the procurement of 800 aircraft per year for three years.[12]

The Chief of Staff was advised in September 1934 that in order to obtain the needed appropriations to finance the ambitious aircraft procurement plan it would be necessary to obtain the "approval and support" of the President. In addition G-4 believed

---

[10]Watson, Prewar Plans and Preparations, pp. 41-42.

[11]Memo, Deputy Chief of Staff for the AC/S G-4, August 16, 1934. OCS/20800-94, RG 319, NA. Memo, AC/S G-4 for the Assistant Secretary of War, September 1, 1934. G-4/29909, RG 319, NA.

[12]Memo, Deputy Chief of Staff for the AC/S G-4, September 7, 1934. G-4/29909, RG 319, NA.

that the initiation of aircraft augmentation, as envisaged in the Baker Board Report, should be delayed to fiscal 1937 rather than implemented in the forthcoming fiscal year of 1936. G-4 was not very optimistic over the results to be anticipated from such an ambitious program because of the fact that it was predicated upon such "problematic eventualities" as support from Congress and Presidential approval.[13] In order to obviate these financial problems MacArthur was urged to take the entire matter up with Roosevelt and get his unequivocal endorsement before presentation of the estimates to the Bureau of the Budget.

It is interesting to note that although the Baker Board report was completed in July 1934, G-4 did not recommend incorporating the contemplated augmentation into the War Department estimates for fiscal 1936, and instead advised procuring the first increment in fiscal 1937. Of course this was not welcomed by the Army aviators, who, although disappointed with the basic recommendations and conclusions of the Baker Board, welcomed the plan to increase expenditures for aircraft procurement. Naturally they could be expected to disapprove postponing procurement until fiscal 1937. G-4 remained skeptical of the ability of the Army to obtain the needed funds even for fiscal 1937, and in February 1935 MacArthur was advised that the augmentation of the Air Corps was of such vital importance and interest as to demand a "special communication

---

[13]Memo, AC/S G-4 for the Chief of Staff, September 25, 1934. G-4/29909, RG 319, NA.

to the President from the Secretary of War."[14] G-4 firmly believed that it was unwise to contemplate an expansion of the Air Corps unless Roosevelt unequivocally gave his support to the expenditure of the required funds.

MacArthur was cool toward this suggestion, and in particular was reluctant to adopt any tactic which would suggest that the Army sought an "emergency" expenditure program to build up the Air Corps. MacArthur informed his colleagues on the General Staff that it was "undesirable to bring this matter to the attention of the President at this time and that the War Department should renew its efforts to reach 2,320 aircraft through the annual estimates beginning in fiscal 1937." The Chief of Staff added however that an effort would be made to "secure Presidential approval" to the Air Corps augmentation program in the summer of 1935, "before the estimates go to the Bureau of Budget."[15]

MacArthur's position in this matter can probably be explained by the fact that he realized that the President was not very sympathetic to his continuing importunities and he did not care to receive another rebuke. MacArthur and Dern had presented the President in December 1934 with a comprehensive overall program that reflected the basic and "urgent needs" of the Army, and

---

[14] Memo, AC/S G-4 for the Chief of Staff, February 19, 1935. G-4/29909, RG 319, NA.

[15] Memo, Deputy Chief of Staff for the AC/S G-4, March 15, 1935. OCS/20800-124, RG 319, NA.

included $89,000,000 for aircraft in order to carry out the recommendations of the Baker Board. In addition the Chief of Staff's reluctance to undertake or plead an emergency or "crash" program for the Air Corps reflected his concern that any augmentation of the materiel needs of the Army must be on a "balanced" basis and should not favor any one branch or arm. Consequently the Air Corps was advised that it should prepare its estimates for a three-year procurement program for fiscal 1937, 1938, and 1939. It was the intention of the General Staff to handle this augmentation through the regular appropriations bill and to obtain Presidential approval of this program before the estimates were sent to the Bureau of the Budget.[16] The failure of the Army to press for more money in fiscal 1936 in order to begin augmentation of the Air Corps is explained by the fact the Army firmly believed that the administration would never approve the request being made of Congress. G-4 admitted in May 1935 that although it was desirable to build up the Air Corps as soon as possible to 2,320 aircraft, it was "not considered a propitious time to ask for further appropriations for fiscal 1936."[17]

In an interesting memorandum from the Chief of the Budget and Legislative Planning Branch of the General Staff for the Chief of Staff dated June 7, 1935, the problem of why the Army

---

[16]Memo, AC/S G-4 for the AG, March 18, 1935. G-4/29909, RG 319, NA.

[17]Memo, AC/S G-4 for the AG, May 7, 1935. G-4/29909, RG 319, NA.

did not request more money for fiscal 1936 to carry out the recommendation of the Baker Board was discussed in some detail. The memorandum advised the Chief of Staff that "it would have been useless to attempt more" than was requested in the way of funds for fiscal 1936. Attention of the Chief of Staff was invited to the fact that the Director of the Budget had informed the Army in the summer of 1934, concurrently with the final report of the Baker Board, that "every possible effort" should be made in preparing the military estimates for fiscal 1936 so that they would be "substantially below the amount of the corresponding appropriations for fiscal year 1935," and that estimates for military activities for fiscal 1936 would be established at the "lowest possible figure" consistent with basic needs and requirements. The memorandum declared:

> As it was we asked for $75,000,000 more than in 1935 including an increase in enlisted strength, Air Corps, Mechanization, training ammunition ... and miscellaneous items including the civilian components. The futility of asking for more is clearly shown by the Action of the Bureau of the Budget in entirely eliminating or materially reducing all of the items.[18]

The Army was of the opinion that augmentation of the Air Corps through increased appropriations would not have received favorable consideration by the administration and that the estimates for fiscal 1936 were the maximum that could prudently be requested. The Army was well aware of the fact that although the

---

[18]Memo, Chief, B&LP Branch GS for the Chief of Staff, June 7, 1935. OCS/17840-65, RG 319, NA.

Commander in Chief had given his "general approval" to Army plans to reach the 2,320 aircraft strength as recommended by the Baker Board, he had equivocated, as was his want, when it came to the actual expenditure of funds. Roosevelt had written to Secretary of War Dern that while the War Department plans in respect to the Baker Board's recommendations appeared sound, he was unable to estimate whether the necessary funds would be available to carry out then, but "as soon as funds became available the program should be made effective."[19]

War Department requests for funds to procure 800 aircraft during fiscal 1937, in keeping with the augmentation plan as recommended by the Baker Board, was disallowed by the Bureau of the Budget. When Secretary Dern pleaded with the President to reinstate the needed money into the budget, Roosevelt curtly reminded the War Department that it was necessary to reduce military expenditures and that he would not recommend additional increases over the budget figure for fiscal 1937 that was presented to Congress.[20]

In late 1935, coincident with a growing cognizance that the Army was making slow progress toward equipping its initial mobilization force because of the lack of appropriations, there developed a disinclination toward the continuance of expending

---

[19]Ltr, Roosevelt to Dern, August 31, 1934. G-4/29909, RG 319, NA.

[20]See Chapter XIII, <u>supra</u>., p. 391.

relatively large sums for R&D. This of course was in contradiction with MacArthur's previous policy that he had discussed frequently and at length with Congressional committees, and of which he had written cogently in his annual reports. At the danger of being redundant it should be reiterated that MacArthur believed that in a period of forced economy the Army should sacrifice the procurement of new equipment. However, he favored the development and procurement of advanced models in such amounts as to permit the "development of appropriate organizations and tactics and to supply the covering forces required in the early stages of an emergency." MacArthur had emphasized that

> The War Department plan comprehends no attempt to maintain the vast quantities of supplies that would be needed in active operations. Instead the plan looks for the barest requirements of peace-time preparation and depends for war supply upon the production of material after the beginning of an emergency.[21]

With MacArthur's departure as Chief of Staff, intimation of dissatisfaction over his policy on procurement developed and a change in policy was not long in coming. The new Chief of Staff, General Malin Craig, touched off the reappraisal of procurement versus R&D with a memorandum to his Deputy Chief of Staff. In the memorandum Craig noted that he viewed with alarm the "lack of standardization" of weapons for the Army. In Craig's opinion this lack of standardization was a

---

[21]Report of the Secretary of War, 1935, pp. 51-52.

distinct detriment to procurement as well as performance, and that standardization is essential, not only for efficiency but to counteract mounting costs of production. It is my idea that we can standardize, taking what we are actually using and what we have ... changing our standards annually when such change is indicated by the article in question.[22]

In addition to the pressure of budgetary limitations which prevented any large scale procurement of modern equipment, there was another current of opinion within the Army which prevented procurement and "standardization" of new equipment. This was the "philosophy of perfection held by many members of the General Staff, the using arms, and the Ordnance Department itself."[23] This philosophy implied that before a weapon was adopted for procurement it had to be as nearly perfect as possible, and its tactical capability had to be approved by the using arms. Thus before a weapon was adopted for service development projects extending over a long period of time were required.[24] Furthermore, the danger of obsolescence was another factor that militated against procurement. A piece of equipment that had finally been perfected and declared suitable for standardization could be rendered obsolescent by new and rapid technological advances

---

[22]Memo, Chief of Staff for the Deputy Chief of Staff, November 20, 1935. G-4/30562, RG 319, NA.

[23]Green, Thompson, and Roots, The Ordnance Department: Planning Munitions for War, p. 177.

[24]Ibid., pp. 175-76. The authors cite as an example the experience of the semi-automatic rifle. The development of this weapon took thirty-five years from the time the project was initiated until the time it was standardized as the rifle, semi-automatic, M1, on January 9, 1936.

before series production had begun. But the General Staff in 1936, eager to reequip the Army with available weapons, was forced to disregard this danger. One student of the Army during this period notes that Craig's emphasis on standardization and the discouragement of R&D work was not occasioned by hostility as such to R&D, but the

> dominant purpose was to get the existing Army re-equipped without further delay with the best equipment currently available. Appropriations for new weapons were still small, and the Staff was desirous of using the maximum of dollars for immediate acquisition of equipment rather than spending time exclusively in development work.[25]

In discussing the problem of standardization of weapons and equipment, the General Staff noted that before actual procurement of equipment the various War Department agencies made many changes in order "to procure the most modern and advanced types and models of equipment." Although this was a "praiseworthy effort," the General Staff believed it had caused "delay, budgetary and procurement difficulties, and increased costs in the items as finally procured in comparison with the costs used in the original preparation of estimates." The General Staff concluded that it was possible to hold down the cost of equipment by minimizing total

---

[25]Watson, Prewar Plans and Preparations, p. 42. Watson notes that the "halt" in R&D came late in 1936. This is true in the respect that the General Staff officially curtailed R&D estimates at this date for fiscal 1938. However it would appear that Craig initiated the change from emphasizing R&D to procurement soon after succeeding MacArthur as Chief of Staff in November 1935 with his memorandum on standardization.

changes in development and by procuring the types and models of equipment included in the original estimates. The Army was informed:

> The Secretary of War directs that all types and models of equipment included in the military program for fiscal 1937 and for each fiscal year thereafter will remain unchanged, for budgetary purposes, from the beginning of the preparation of estimates to the consummation of procurement. Exceptions to this rule will be made for cogent reasons only and then on the approved recommendations of the estimating agencies concerned.
>
> It is not desired that this directive be construed in such a manner as to impede or to discourage progress in developing new and improved types of equipment in accordance with approved programs for research and development.[26]

The widespread concern over the failure of the Army to obtain a modicum of equipment, except for an occasional "pilot model" of some item that was being constantly changed and altered in effort to perfect its performance, was the basis of the change in policy by General Craig. MacArthur had admitted that there were on the drawing boards weapons equal or superior to foreign models but that cost had precluded anything except token procurement. The General Staff, in late 1935 and early 1936, became acutely anxious over the fact that with the outbreak of hostilities in Africa and in China the American military establishment was poorly equipped with anything resembling modern weapons. Thus there was developed the tendency within the Army to place less emphasis and less money into R&D work and to spend more for the procurement of equipment then available. Knowledge that budgetary allowances would never

---

[26]Memo, AC/S G-4 for the Chief of Staff, November 23, 1935. A copy of this memo was sent to the AG for distribution to the Army on November 25, 1935. G-4/30562, RG 319, NA.

be adequate to maintain R&D at its previous relatively high level and at the same time provide for the procurement of new equipment led to the sacrifice of R&D work. As one spokesman of the General Staff explained:

> I would rather see R & D money held in reserve than money allotted for equipment. This is a general statement. If it were not for keeping trained personnel available I would take all R & D money for two years and get equipment with what we now have developed. . . . If it were a question of releasing R & D and taking it (funds) from somewhere else I would say no.[27]

Research and development, in the oversimplified view of the combat arms of using arms, entailed the expenditure of hard-to-come by funds for "non-essential" equipment. Understandably the equipment-starved combat arms questioned the expenditure of funds for such R&D projects as research on synthetic materials for the purpose of obtaining substitutes for critical raw materials. The developing arms on the other hand were cognizant of the fact that R&D demanded "heavy outlays" of funds, if there was to be any return at all, and at the same time they could not be certain of rewarding every investment. Thus the conflict between R&D and procurement was sharpened by the "skintight" military budget, and R&D took place without the sympathy of the Army as a whole who wanted present and existing needs satisfied.[28]

---

[27]Undated and handwritten memo for the AC/S G-4, initialed by EWA. G-4/31376-9, RG 319, NA.

[28]Terrett, <u>Signal Corps</u>, pp. 34-35.

In the fall of 1936 the movement toward standardization and the pressure for procurement of new equipment resulted in the War Department reducing funds allotted to R&D. The estimates for fiscal 1939, prepared in October 1936, planned to decrease expenditures for R&D from General Drum's previous ceiling of $7,000,000 to $9,000,000 to a limiting figure of between $5,000,000 and $7,000,000. In laying down the "new policy for Research and Development" the General Staff emphasized that the purpose was to manage the limited military appropriations in such a manner that the maximum results "may be obtained for every dollar expended." The General Staff decreed that new requirements for R&D were to be established only when a "real and insistent demand exists for new or improved items." In addition all funds were to be concentrated on development projects that were of the "highest priority to the War Department."[29]

According to G-4 there was too much frivolity and peripheral activity and needless expense in the R&D program and that the

> magnitude of research and development conducted by the Ordnance Department and the demands for further development made by the using arms and services only emphasizes the necessity for obtaining approval of all new projects prior to proceeding with their development in order that available funds and facilities will be expended only on those projects for which there exists a definite War Department requirement.[30]

---

[29]Memo, AC/S G-4 for the Chief, B&LP Branch General Staff, October 8, 1936. G-4/29552, RG 319, NA.

[30]Memo AC/S G-4 for the AG, October 20, 1936. G-4/29552, RG 319, NA.

The General Directive which outlined the new R&D policy included the following main points:

> The maximum amount of funds previously allotted to the War Department Research and Development Program is approximately $7,000,000. This amount not only should not be exceeded but should be reduced materially. As the major portion of development funds are expended on the salaries of technical personnel, this reduction should be gradual and extended over a reasonable period of time. The Army needs large quantities of excellent equipment that has already been developed. The amount of funds allocated to R&D in former years is in excess of the proper proportion for that item in consideration of the Rearmament Program. In the Rearmament and Reequipment Program for FY 1938 estimates, exclusive of the Air Corps, there was less than $7,000,000 allotted to the Arms and Services.
>
> Essential development projects should not be curtailed but all available funds and energy should be directed to complete the development of projects of highest priority to the War Department and to get the maximum amount of modern equipment in the hands of the troops.
>
> From a study of the projects under development there appears to be a definite tendency toward the development of unessential items at the suggestion of the arms and services. This procedure not only increases the demands for development funds but in addition dissipates the facilities and efforts of the developing services.
>
> . . . .
>
> To provide for the contingency of a reduction in all War Department programs and in order that essential development be not curtailed, careful study must be given in the preparation of the minimum program to the end that only the projects of the highest priority to the arms and services are included.[31]

The final War Department estimate for R&D that was set in the Directive for the Military Program for fiscal 1939 was limited to a total of some $6,500,000. The amounts made available to the separate

---

[31]Memo, AC/S G-4 for the Chief of Staff, October 30, 1936. Noted by the Chief of Staff on November 10, 1936, and signed by General Stanley D. Embick, Deputy C/S on the same day. Letters containing the G-4 memorandum were sent to all arms and services on November 11, 1936. G-4/29552, RG 319, NA.

developing agencies within the total figure, according to General Staff policy, was to be flexible and based strictly on priorities. The old practice of comparing each separate allotment with the amount set up in previous years was abandoned because it was felt that this had a tendency to "stabilize" the amounts at an unduly high level and made it difficult of the General Staff to "apply pressure and accelerate the effort on items of the highest priority to the War Department."[32] The $6,500,000 for R&D during fiscal 1939 was indeed a considerable reduction compared with the $9,000,000 figure that the War Department approved in February 1935 for the estimate for fiscal 1937.[33]

During the mid-thirties the Army, cognizant that its mobilization plans were unrealistic because of the tremendous financial expense required to equip the planned mobilization force, attempted to make its plans correspond more with the existing fiscal situation. In particular, equipment needed to supply the one million man

---

[32]Memo, AC/S G-4 for the Chief of Staff, March 10, 1937. The following R&D priorities were set by the General Staff: detection of approach of hostile aircraft, development of fire control instruments for antiaircraft artillery, rapid methods of mapping aerial photos, development of antitank weapons, development of aircraft cannon, development of aircraft and aircraft power plants, and improvement in navigation equipment for aircraft. G-4/29552, RG 319, NA.

[33]Memo, AC/S G-4 for the AG, February 18, 1935. Of this total the Air Corps was scheduled to receive over $5,000,000 and the Ordnance Department over $2,000,000. The remaining $2,000,000 was distributed to the other services who had research and development responsibilities: Chemical Warfare Service, Coast Artillery Corps, Corps of Engineers, Medical Corps, Quartermaster Corps, and the Signal Corps. G-4/29552, RG 319, NA.

initial mobilization force could not be procured during peacetime when the emphasis was on budgetary restrictions. It was generally felt that mobilization plans which did not reflect this economic fact were invalid and faulty.

The Secretary of War, Harry W. Woodring, appears to have initiated the revision of mobilization plans in late 1936, although the General Staff throughout the years since 1933 had voiced concern over the fact that mobilization plans were unrealistic because of budgetary limitations. However, contrary to this opinion the General Staff had sought in 1934 to broaden mobilization planning and visualized the equipping of a one million man force that would cover the initial mobilization. This development was based on the overly optimistic hope that public works funds would be made availble to the Army. By 1936 these hopes had been shattered: Congress had voted in 1935 to prohibit the use of relief funds for military or naval purposes, and the Roosevelt Administration gave no evidence that it would consider allocating to the Army sizeable funds required to meet the needs of the one million men scheduled for initial mobilization.

Woodring informed General Craig in December 1936 that as a result of his study of the 1933 Mobilization Plan it appeared that in the first several months of an emergency the supplies required by the mobilized manpower could not be produced by American industry in sufficient quantities. Consequently Woodring suggested that the General Staff consider the advisability and need of two mobilization plans. According to Woodring one plan should be a "paper plan" which would incorporate the total General Staff manpower mobilization, and a second plan, based on what Woodring called a "defensive policy," should be prepared to cover the speedy mobilization of a much smaller force for which materiel could be procured during peacetime. Woodring visualized that in the latter plan manpower and resources would be balanced.[34]

Craig readily followed up Woodring's suggestion and directed that the 1933 Mobilization Plan be called the War Department Mobilization Survey, and that it should be replaced as soon as possible by a Protective Mobilization Plan. The latter, based on a smaller number of troops, would provide for "the mobilization of a moderate but balanced force for the protection of the Continental United States, including Hawaii and Panama." The Chief of Staff emphasized that the smaller size and defensive character of this force would "permit its being speedily and properly equipped and armed."[35] According to the new plan the mobilization force would be capable of deployment to a "position of readiness" in a situation of actual or threatened war.[36]

It is interesting to note that because of its limited size

---

[34]Memo, Secretary of War for the Chief of Staff, December 6, 1936, OCS/13984-262, RG 319, NA.

[35]Memo, Secretary of the General Staff, Lt. Col. R. L. Eichelberger for the AC/S G-3, December 16, 1936. OCS/13984-263, RG 319, NA.

[36]Memo, Deputy Chief of Staff for the AC/S G-3, February 2, 1937. OCS/13984-263, RG 319, NA.

the new mobilization force did not directly encompass the concept of an expeditionary force or participation in offensive warfare. The availability of funds and the limitation imposed on procuring supplies and equipment forced Army planners to base mobilization plans on a force which would be capable of only defense and initial protection. As Secretary Woodring explained, it would be a force based on a "defensive policy."

General Craig noted that the revision of the mobilization plans should in turn modify the program for the "immediate rearmament and reequipment" of the Army. Craig directed the General Staff to pay close attention to the fact that new mobilization plans called for a much smaller force and expreseed the hope that this would be "reflected in our equipment planning and fiscal programs as early as practicable."[37] Craig was eager to have the reduction in mobilization requirements reflected in smaller procurement and rearmament estimates, thus aiding the Army to obtain funds from the Executive and Congress to reach the more moderate manpower goal. The Chief of Staff apparently felt that he could obtain support for a more limited program from both Roosevelt and Congress.

Sympathy and support for the revision of the 1933 Mobilization Plan was generally widespread through the Army. Knowledge of the fact that the Army was unable to supply even its minuscule standing force with modern weapons because of budgetary limitations

---

[37]Memo, Chief of Staff for the AC/S G-4, January 6, 1937. OCS/13984-285, RG 319, NA.

gave impetus to the revision of mobilization plans. It was the general opinion that mobilization plans should be based on mobilizing a force which would be supplied with its war reserve equipment during peacetime. The general feeling in the War Department was that it was unrealistic to plan for a M-day force larger than existing personnel and materiel would permit. Budgetary limitations imposed upon military expenditures as a result of the depression, and the need for economy in budget appropriations, indicated that it was hazardous to engage in unrealistic mobilization plans. As one General Staff officer succinctly described the situation: "There is no indication that an additional program can be secured, more elaborate or effective than at present."[38]

Another member of the General Staff envisaged a mobilization plan which would be relatively simple and include only the Regular Army and the active National Guard units. This plan would take the Regular Army, after overseas garrisons, GHQ Air Corps, and sundry overhead had been subtracted, and form it into "four real Regular Army divisions" ready for immediate concentration and available for any war plan. It was further recommended that "two real" National Guard divisions in each Army area be organized, with left over troops, including the Officers Reserve Corps, forming headquarters and Corps troops which could begin the subsequent mobilization. It was felt that by concentrating mobilization plans

---

[38]Memo, Unsigned for Col. Terry, G-4 Division, initialed by J.R.N.W., December 23, 1935. G-4/29729-1, RG 319, NA.

on a few well-trained and highly modernized units procurement planning would be assisted and such a moderate plan would be of help in "defending appropriations" as well as providing greater security for the nation.[39] Implicit in this recommendation to concentrate mobilization plans on a small, well-equipped Regular Army was the implication that it might be necessary, if a viable and effective mobilization plan was to be formulated, to curtail the participation of the Regular Army in training and supporting the civilian components.

The report of G-4 on the supply implications of the 1933 Mobilization Plan, and the comment on its revision, was presented to the Chief of Staff in great detail early in 1937. G-4 agreed with the study of the Assistant Secretary of War that the procurement of supplies for the 1933 Mobilization Plan was impossible of attainment. G-4 noted that the plan for the mobilization of 1,300,000 men by M-Day+30 and 3,600,000 by M-Day+180 was unrealistic because war reserves to supply this force through peacetime procurement would cost around $1,400,000,000, a figure which was "impracticable and impossible" of being fulfilled. G-4 noted that such a "staggering sum" would never be "made available in peacetime" and that mobilization rates should be "materially reduced." G-4 agreed that revision of mobilization plans was timely

---

[39]Memo, Lt. Col. Charles H. Corlett, G-4 Representative on Mobilization Board for the AC/S G-4, December 15, 1936. G-4/20052-102. Note: During World War II Corlett was a successful Division and Corps Commander in both the Pacific and European theaters.

and thought that it would result in providing a "moderate but balanced force which could be armed and equipped." The Chief of Staff was advised that although it would seem better to have manpower needs dictate mobilization planning, rather than the availability of supplies, in 1936-37 the opposite was true, although manpower limits should not be rigidly determined by supply. G-4 admonished the Chief of Staff:

> The ideal organization in order to be obtainable must take into consideration the probable annual budgetary limitations for national defense, and the necessity for a balanced maintenance program for the Army while attempting an augmentation or alteration program. Any fiscal planning which fails to give consideration to the above factors is unsound.

Warning against devising any mobilization plan that did not take cognizance of budgetary pressures for economy and limitation of spending, G-4 concluded its peroration:

> . . . based on basic defense policy and on budgetary limitations what is the desired size and organization of the moderate but balanced force to be speedily armed and equipped? Upon receipt of such decision the supply division and arms can go to work upon calculation of supply and procurement requirements and upon a fiscal program for augmentation of supplies and equipment to reach the goal.[40]

The Supply Division of the General Staff was well aware of the fact that planning was unrealistic and even dangerous unless it recognized the fact that mobilization plans were dependent upon

---

[40]Memo, AC/S G-4 for the Chief of Staff, January 13, 1937. G-4/20052-101, RG 319, NA.

the budget allocated by the Roosevelt Administration and passed by Congress. The Chief of Staff was cautioned that planning for a "moderate and balanced" force was in the last analysis determined by budgetary appropriations.

If the Supply Division of the General Staff was apprehensive over the fact that budget limitations precluded the satisfactory procurement of War Reserve equipment for the initial mobilization force, G-1 Division had its doubts about the feasibility of manpower procurement. MacArthur had premised the expansion of the mobilization force to one million men on the ability of the Army to obtain voluntary enlistments. The Chief of Staff believed that this was a valid assumption in view of the widespread unemployment that was rampant throughout the country.

By 1936 G-1 doubted the feasibility of MacArthur's concept on manpower procurement. The Chief of Staff was advised in unequivocal terms that MacArthur's plans were unrealistic:

> It is believed that the attempt to put an efficient fighting force in the theater of operations and increase the Army of the United States to over 1,200,000 men in 30 days, in a non-military country such as this, is entirely impracticable.

G-1 recommended that for planning purposes 300,000 men should be fixed as the M-Day+30 objective, with around 500,000 as the objective for M-Day+60, and 600,000 men for the M-Day+90 objective. Presumably after this date G-1 believed that Congress would enact selective service.[41]

One year before the official revision of the 1933 Mobilization Plan, G-1 had expressed serious doubts over the ability of the Army to obtain through voluntary enlistments the initial mobilization force. Among the various factors listed by G-1 as militating against voluntary enlistment in time of an emergency, one is of particular import for it reflects the manner in which social developments growing out of the economic depression affected the Army and its plans. According to G-1 the "subversive influences" throughout the country cast "grave doubts on the practicability of mobilizing the stipulated manpower," and it was believed that there would be strong reaction against the attempt by the Army to procure through voluntary enlistment the one million man initial mobilization force. G-1 claimed that the popularity of military training in the CMTC and ROTC, the presence of Reserve officers in many communities, the activities of the National Guard, and the widespread distribution of Regular Army officers assigned to the civilian components had made the people "conscious of our armed forces," and this factor might favorably affect recruiting during an emergency. On the other hand G-1 warned that opposition to "anything military" could be expected from

pacificist and radical groups such as the Civil Liberties Union, Communist League, National Council for the Prevention of War, or

[41]Memo, AC/S G-1 for the AC/S G-3, March 5, 1936. G-1/14116-4, RG 319, NA.

the various ramifications of the Federal Council of Churches of Christ in America, who will seek to make the war an unpopular one and discourage voluntary enlistments.

The Chief of Staff was advised that it was impossible to estimate with certainty the number of people throughout the country who had been "influenced" by the "specious arguments" of the above groups, but that their activities could very well thwart enlistments. Concerned over the inability of the Army to obtain through voluntary enlistment the manpower required for the initial mobilization, G-1 recommended that the 1933 Mobilization Plan be withdrawn.[42]

By April 1937 the new mobilization plans, called the Protective Mobilization Plan, was ready. This plan provided for an Initial Protection Force that would be capable by M+30 of a holding or protective action. It consisted of approximately 400,000 men organized into four Regular Army Divisions and fifteen National Guard Divisions, with corresponding Corps and Army troops.[43] Further sections of the mobilization plan called for augmentation of this force, but it was hoped that the 400,000 figure represented a moderate sized force that could be equipped through available and

---

[42]Memo, AC/S G-1 for the Chief of Staff, January 13, 1936. G-1/14137, RG 319, NA.

[43]Memo, AC/S G-3 for the Chief of Staff, April 10, 1937. AG 381 (4-10-37) Section 1, RG 94, NA. This memo was distributed to the Army as the basis of the new mobilization plan. See also: Kreidberg, Military Mobilization in the United States Army 1775-1945, pp. 468-78.

potential budgetary allotments.

Thus the Army in the mid-thirties found that its mobilization plans because of budgetary limitations were unrealistic and impracticable; it was forced to plan for a much smaller force and one that could possibly be equipped through continuing and adequate budget appropriations. At the same time the curious halt in R&D was brought about through the need to curtail "non-essential" activities and the opinion that use of corresponding funds should be spent on procurement of much needed new equipment for the Initial Protective Force.

CONCLUSION

The War Department appropriation bill for fiscal 1937 that Congress approved in May 1936, allotted to the Army well over $380,000,000 for military activities. This figure, as in the previous fiscal year, was a considerable increase over the amount requested by the Administration. Included in this budget figure were funds to provide for the increase of the Regular Army to 165,000 enlisted men; this provision for two consecutive years had not been recommended by the Budget Bureau. The appropriation bill for fiscal 1937 marks a convenient line of demarcation for the Army in the period between the two world wars. In particular, the provision to increase the strength of the Regular Army to 165,000 enlisted men, was considered by the General Staff as the fruition of its efforts to obtain the minimum establishment upon which an adequate and sound defense posture could be planned.

Despite the large scale relief spending of the Roosevelt Administration the military budgets in the years preceding fiscal 1938 (July 1, 1937 - June 30, 1938) reflected the policy of limiting and curtailing military expenditures. After fiscal 1938 the military expenditure program reflected to an increasing degree the deteriorating international situation and the efforts to prepare the military establishment for threatening developments. However, these succeeding budgets were the heritage of the depression years in the respect that they were never adequate to finance the complete rearmament and reequipment of the Protective Mobilization Force that was planned in early 1937. During the depression years equipment shortages and obsolescent materiel were the consequence of financial and budgetary restrictions. These factors, cumulative in effect over the years, were of such magnitude that the rearmament of even a moderate-sized "defensive" force (Regular Army divisions and active National Guard divisions) in the later 1930's was difficult to accomplish because of the enormous cost involved.

During the depression years the Army accepted the Administration's claim that it was necessary to reduce expenditures in order to balance the federal budget. To the General Staff, however, there were certain activities that could not be curtailed beyond a certain irreducible minimum. These activities pertained to the training of the civilian components and the maintenance of a trained military potential that could expand upon mobilization as the nucleus of a mass "citizen" army. The General Staff was inflexible, doctrinare, and adamant on this point; all else, including equipment and materiel in general, would be willingly reduced, sacrificed, or eliminated. Nothing could deter the General Staff from maintaining its policy that the skeletonized trained basis of a mass army must be kept intact at the expense of all other activities and projects. This meant that the highest priority was put on the maintenance of the Regular Army officer corps, Army schools, ROTC, Officers Reserve Corps, and the National Guard, with lower priority assigned to Ordnance equipment, mechanized warfare, and air power. This reflected the basic military doctrine of the American General Staff that in war it is man, and not weapons or technological advancements, that determines victory in battle.

The result of all this was to breed a conservative attitude in the General Staff toward military organization, doctrine, and training. From time to time various officers and others proposed the adoption of a radical reorganization of the defense establishment in order to achieve a more rational military program and more national defense for the money spent. The General Staff refused to reassess its doctrine, believing that any change would be costly as well as unsound. Furthermore, the War Department was jealous of the meager funds allotted to it and was reluctant to undertake any reappraisal; constant budgetary pressure instilled a habit of thought resistant to change and to new and possibly expensive ideas. The keynote of General Staff policy was preservation before progress. This was the direct result of the need throughout the early 1930's to maintain the military establishment at the irreducible minimum.

The shortage of funds during the prolonged economy period developed the reaction among Army planners that in preparing budget estimates for projects and programs, they should base their estimates on what funds to expect rather than on what was needed. Thus the availability of money dictated policy. Estimates were based on what the Bureau of the Budget had approved and what

Congress had appropriated the year before, and for efficiency in budget preparation it became the goal to "stabilize" military spending. The result was that as the economy righted itself in the late thirties the Army continued to plan on a budget which would provide for items of the highest priority and was reluctant to clamor for larger appropriations. However, it should be pointed out that during the years that the depression had its greatest effect on the military budget, 1931-1936, the Army appears to have exerted the maximum effort to obtain adequate appropriations. It must be emphasized that the Army took seriously the provision that it was the executor and not the formulator of American military policy. If it was national policy to reduce spending then the Army would cooperate and seek to curtail its activities. No better example of the acceptance by the General Staff and Army officers of the traditions of the American Republic, and the compatibility of the Army to these traditions, can be cited than the cooperation and support given by the Army during the depression to the national policy of the elected civilian authorities.

Another consequence of the limited military budgets during the depression years was to exacerbate inter-branch rivalry and jealousy within the Army. The annual scramble by each branch, arm, and service for meager funds and support, for what each considered "essential to national defense," served to sharpen the suspicion and animosity between the various units of the War Department. In particular, the annual "battle of the budget" served to increase the antagonism between the traditional ground combat arms, such as Infantry, Cavalry, and Field Artillery, and the young and aggressive Air Corps. Air Corps enthusiasts were unsympathetic to the doctrine of the General Staff that man was the final arbiter of the battlefield, and believed that they had found, in the strategic long-range bomber, an economical and radically new weapon which had made the General Staff's doctrine obsolete. The reluctance of the General Staff to consider the strategic bomber for the highest priority in budget allocation infuriated the army aviators.

The depression, with its concomitant social unrest and the incubation of ideologies opposed to the traditional order, increased the suspicion and distrust of various pacifist and "reform liberal" groups toward the Army. Perhaps because it was the symbol of the established social and political order, and thus shared in the responsibility for the social and economic cataclysm of the depression, the Army was under constant attack as a threat to American liberties and as the epitome of reaction. Castigated for its attempts to fasten on the nation a form of "militarism" and rebuked for carrying out what it considered was its role in maintaining national defense, the Army tended to withdraw more and more into purely military affairs and planning; sensitive to the attacks of its critics, it became cautious and circumspect in civil-military relations. Criticism of its role in the American domestic scene and of its machinations in the shaping of foreign policy tended to increase the Army's traditional clanishness and more sharply demarcate civil and military relations. This in turn precluded the Army from actively seeking additional funds for military activities. For public relations reasons the Army was reluctant to publicize the case for increased military spending; on the contrary it sought to demonstrate the fact that economy was synonymous with the military establishment.

Realization that allocations from federal relief funds, much less from the annual appropriations, would never be adequate to provide a modicum of equipment for units scheduled for mobilization led to a reappraisal of mobilization plans in 1936. Why did the Army wait until this late date to revise its plans and bring them into consonance with realistic fiscal resources? MacArthur, who was Chief of Staff until late 1935, premised his mobilization plans on personnel; therefore he believed that a force of over one million men, mobilized within two months, could be supplied with "essential equipment," presumably rifles and clothing, that was on hand in the war reserve. By the time this force was capable of taking the field, MacArthur believed that supplementary equipment could be produced by American industry from pilot models that had previously been developed through limited funds. The Chief of Staff believed that this was a sound plan given the economic situation of the country and the international situation during the depression years. MacArthur also believed that this was the maximum that could be accomplished under existing budgetary limitations.

In late 1936 the General Staff reversed this policy, and believing that it was exigent to equip a moderate-sized force with all its equipment during peace-time, sought to use available funds to equip a force to carry out a "defensive policy." This was the genesis of the Protective Mobilization Force of 1937, which included as a ready force some four Regular Army divisions and some fifteen National Guard divisions. The General Staff hoped that the size of this "defensive" force would be compatible with budgetary allocations. Thus the general trend that runs throughout this study and which continued on during the years immediately prior to World War II, and in the post- World War II years, as a heritage of the depression years: military requirements and needs must conform to the national fiscal policy of the administration. Military planning is not performed in a vacuum without consideration to various domestic political and economic factors, but is subordinate to the overall national policy of the Executive. If the activities of the Army, and the performance of its mission of national defense in the years 1929-1936, reflected the drastic financial curtailment imposed by both the Hoover and Roosevelt Administrations, this in turn was vivid evidence of the fact that United States military policy is clearly one aspect of the national policy and as such is subordinate to the political and economic programs of the Executive.

APPENDIX I

MILITARY ESTIMATES REQUESTED BY WAR DEPARTMENT, AMOUNTS ALLOWED BY BUREAU OF THE BUDGET, AND AMOUNTS APPROPRIATED BY CONGRESS, FISCAL YEARS 1929-1937. <u>Cater Files</u>, "1941 Folder," OCMH.

Fiscal Year	Requested by War Department	Allowed by Budget Bureau	Appropriated by Congress*
1929	$334,368,880	$317,115,318	$319,179,551
1930	349,986,426	328,727,164	332,114,899
1931	362,382,069	347,299,185	346,979,179
1932	351,304,294	343,170,810	339,767,644
1933	331,243,723	316,195,110	304,961,492
1934	320,900,513	277,746,841	277,066,381
1935	305,271,321	285,960,155	280,862,094
1936	361,351,154	331,799,277	355,538,204
1937	467,022,915	383,065,510	388,244,859

*Includes annual and supplementary appropriations.

APPENDIX II

SUMMARY OF MILITARY EXPENDITURES, 1925 - 1940

Exerpts from letter by Harry W. Woodring, Secretary of War, to House Military Appropriations Subcommittee, and to House and Senate Committees on Military Affairs, May 28, 1940. Cater Files "1941 Folder," OCMH.

During the 16-year period, 1925 to 1940 the amounts appropriated for the military activities of the Army totalled $6,169,300,000 including $371,300,000 from federal emergency funds. That total includes not only allotments for the Regular Army, but for the National Guard, the Organized Reserves, the Reserve Officers' Training Corps, the Citizens Military Training Camps and other military activities.

Of that total of $6,169,300,000 it should be noted that 86.1% -- that is, $5,314,744,000--were allotted for what are termed recurring charges and improvement of plant. Those items include pay, rations, clothing, repairs, research and development, planning, construction, training, operations, maneuvers, schools, and similar activities. Left for expenditure by the War Department, after those charges, were a bare $854,556,000 for augmentation, modernization, and replacement of arms and equipment, including new aircraft, spare engines, spare parts, bombs, new tanks, antiaircraft and anti-tank guns, semi-automatic rifles, trucks, tractors, field guns, machine guns, ammunition, and similar materiel.

It should be noted that of this $854,556,000, $509,900,000 went to the Army's Air Corps, a comparatively new, but nonetheless vital, branch of the land forces. In other words, of the total of somewhat over six billions appropriated for the military activities of the War Department over a period of 16 years, only $344,656,000 -- a bare 5.6% -- were available for the augmentation, modernization and replacement of arms and equipment for the ground elements of the Army of the United States. In view of these facts it is rather remarkable to me that we have been able to maintain any mobile ground army at all, especially when it is considered that the useful life of much military equipment, such as tanks and heavy motor vehicles, barely exceeds 5 years.

You will note from the breakdown that an average of only $21,000,000 per year has been allotted for the modernization, motorization, mechanization, and equipment of the Army's ground forces.

APPENDIX III

THE ARMY AND THE NEUTRALITY ACT OF 1935

The knowledge that budget limitations precluded the procurement of equipment and the placing of large-scale orders with private manufacturers for arms and other munitions, influenced the Army to favor in general the policy of encouraging various American arms firms to engage in the export of munitions. They favored this policy on the grounds that it would be an indirect method of subsidization for American arms makers, and thereby serve to maintain the war potential and industrial capacity of American industry. In case of an emergency these firms would be readily available and capable of meeting the requirements of the mobilization force.

Throughout the twenties the Army favored this policy, much to the chagrin of the State Department which in general sought to curtail this type of international trade. In 1930 the issue came up again when the Amtorg Corporation, the official Soviet Union trading company in New York, asked to purchase light tanks from the Cunningham Corporation in Rochester, New York. The latter firm referred the request to the War Department. In the face of the objections of the State Department, President Hoover concurred in the Army's approval of this transaction.[1]

---

[1]Ltr, Hoover to Hurley, February 3, 1930. AG 437.1 (1-20-30) (1) RG 94, NA.

The Army favored this kind of international commerce on the part of American firms because

> . . . the manufacture of tanks in general by a private firm in this country is to the advantage of the Government in building up an industry having this specialized knowledge and experience available for the production of such tanks as may be required by the War Department in time of a national emergency.[2]

During the Geneva Disarmament Conference in 1932 the War Department advised the Secretary of State that the nation should refrain from any agreement which would preclude international commerce in armaments and which would curtail the manufacture of munitions by private firms. MacArthur advised Secretary Stimson in 1932 that "any restriction of private manufacture that will limit its capacity for immediate war-time production will be detrimental to the national defense." Consequently, the Army advised the State Department to be more considerate of the problems of national defense in the deliberations at Geneva.[3] The Army made no secret of the fact that in its war plans private industry would have to produce the major portion of the required equipment and supplies. "Therefore the War Department has favored participation of American industry in munitions making and has encouraged the production of munitions for export."[4]

---

[2]Ltr, Chief of Ordnance to AG, January 27, 1930. AG 473.1 (1-2-30) (1) RG 94, NA.

[3]Ltr, MacArthur to Stimson, December 1, 1932. Ltr #12 in File #1-#100, Secretary of War Files, Box 4, RG 107, NA.

[4]Army Navy Journal, December 29, 1934, p. 359.

The threat to the general peace of Europe caused by the Italo-Ethiopian crisis precipitated the passage by Congress of the neutrality legislation of 1935. This legislation provided for the prohibition, in time of war between foreign states, or foreign civil war, of the export from the United States of arms, ammunition, or implements of war to any belligerent state, or neutral port for transshipment to, or for the use of a belligerent country. This much was mandatory on the President, though it was left to him to define the existence of war.[5]

When this legislation was first discussed in Congress in 1934, The State Department asked the War Plans Division of the General Staff for the views of the War Department on the proposed law. In a letter forwarded to the Chief of Staff the WPD commented that the enactment of the law would "tend to decrease the likelihood of the United States" being drawn into a war from an originally neutral position. It was also noted that if the nation was unavoidably drawn into a war the operation of the proposed law would not necessarily tend to decrease readiness for war. The Chief of Staff was advised that plans for economic mobilization by the Army had gone far to prepare American industry to make equipment for the war effort with a minimum of delay. According to the WPD, the war readiness of the country during neutrality could be insured by the addition to the neutrality legislation of a stipulation

---

[5]Samuel F. Bemis, A Diplomatic History of the United States (3d ed.; New York: Henry Holt and Company, 1951), p. 667.

authorizing the President to "bring the military and naval forces" of the country to the full strength authorized by law and to bring war reserves of equipment to the levels prescribed by Congress in time of peace. The letter noted that the "propriety and advisability of the legislation was outside the knowledge and responsibility of the War Department," but from the standpoint of national defense it was recommended that the enactment of the law was advisable and would prove to be of "profound advantage" for the nation.[6]

General Drum, the Deputy Chief of Staff, favored War Department endorsement of the legislation. According to General Drum this was an opportunity for the Army to take a stand on an issue which "will work for our benefit in the controversial matters now pending." This was a reference to the Nye Committee Hearings and the public charges against munitions makers and the "merchants of death." MacArthur was advised by his deputy that War Department support of the provision in the legislation which would permit the President to embargo any article designated by him as munitions of war would be an answer to the "publicity gained by the Nye Committee."[7]

MacArthur, however, took a much different view toward War Department policy on neutrality legislation and he advised the

---

[6]Draft of letter for Secretary of War, WPD to the Deputy Chief of Staff, December 10, 1934. WPD/3801, RG 319, NA.

[7]Memo, Deputy Chief of Staff for the Chief of Staff, December 11, 1934. WPD/3801, RG 319, NA.

Deputy Chief of Staff to return the draft letter to the WPD. According to the Chief of Staff there were "serious and vital" questions involved and the General Staff was unable to give its approval to such legislation unless all of the Great Powers concurred, and that the question should be considered internationally and not by the United States alone. MacArthur advised that no written document in reference to the War Department's position on the neutrality legislation should be sent to the State Department, but that during the next conference with State Department officials WPD should present orally the Chief of Staff's views on the matter.[8]

---

[8]Memo, Deputy Chief of Staff for the AC/S WPD, December 11, 1934. WPD/3801, RG 319, NA.

BIBLIOGRAPHICAL NOTE

In the preparation of this study main reliance for primary source material was placed on official Army correspondence, including letters, memorandums, and various other documents found in the National Archives in Washington, D. C. The official Army department charged with the responsibility of records management and records integration is the Adjutant General's Office (AGO). The AG copy of any document generally serves as the official permanent record copy for the AG files. These files, incorporating correspondence pertaining to the inter-war years, are located in the World War I Branch, War Records Division of the National Archives. This huge collection of source material is classified in a decimal system according to subject matter or content. The guide to this decimal system is described in a publication entitled: War Department Decimal File System (Washington: GPO, 1943). This is a listing of the decimal file classification and an alphabetical index for all War Department correspondence.

The decimal file numbers found most fruitful for the preparation of this paper were the following: AG 111 for material on budgets and appropriations, AG 320 for material on the organization of the Army, AG 470 for correspondence related to equipment, and AG 370 for data relating to the operation and employment of troops. In addition to these regular file categories there are a number of special files under the AG decimal system pertaining to the Economy Program, Industrial Recovery, CCC, and the Bonus Incident. These supplementary files were of particular value for they are related specifically to events that took place during the depression years. All material in the AG file in the National Archives is classified by Archives into Record Group (RG) 94.

Unfortunately for the student there are several disadvantages and handicaps that preclude a relatively simple and expeditious researching of Army documents in the AG files pertaining to the inter-war years. Primarily, the material has never adequately been catalogued and therefore the determination of what exactly is present in each box and folder depends on painstaking research by the student. There are a number of _Preliminary Inventories_ for War Department correspondence that hade been published by the National Archives, but for the period covered by this study they were found to be relatively useless. Included in this list is the _Preliminary Inventory of the Records of the Adjutant General's Office_ (Washington: National Archives, 1949). This inventory appears to be concentrated on an earlier period and is of little use to the researcher studying the late 1920's and early 30's. The professional archivists of the World War I Branch are experienced and exceedingly knowledgeable of records and correspondence pertaining to World War I but unfamiliar with the files for the later years. Thus researching for material in the National

Archives for the Army during the depression years was a slow tedious task of reviewing box after box for pertinent documents. It would appear that perusal of Army correspondence and records pertaining to these years, indeed, a study of the Army itself during the 1920's and 1930's, has been neglected. Researching in the AG files in the National Archives was a time-consuming task, and much material had to be reviewed before discovery of a document pertaining to the general theme of the study. In addition much of the material in the various decimal file classification was found to be incomplete and inconsistent; a document pertaining to training might very well be found in the file classification for equipment.

Besides the AG file located in the National Archives building at 8th and Constitution in Washington, much excellent source material was obtained at the World War II Branch, War Records Division of the National Archives. This archival depository is not located at the main Archives building, but is housed in a former torpedo factory adjacent to the Potomac River on King Street in Alexandria, Virginia. Although nominally the official repository for documents and other material pertaining to World War II, the Branch has some correspondence of the General Staff for the period of the 1930's and earlier. This correspondence is classified for filing purposes into the various General Staff Divisions, and each document has been abstracted by subject or content on a 5x8 card. Besides the short abstract, which reflects the content of the document, the date and file number are also indicated. A researcher is required to review a voluminous number of cards and cite the General Staff file number of promising abstracts. Researching of this material was found to be more fruitful and less time-consuming because of the fact that the information found in a document had been previously abstracted and catalogued before filing. This permitted the researcher to determine beforehand those documents and appropriate files which appeared to be related to the study. These documents are cited in the paper in the following manner: e.g. WPD/1338. This example indicates that the document is found in War Plans Division file number 1338. Usually these files are relatively small in size thus facilitating the problem of research.

The Library of Congress proved a relatively poor facility for research. The Manuscripts Division contained the following collections which were used for this study: the General Charles P. Summerall Papers, the George B. Dern Papers, and the General William Mitchell Papers. These collections were of little substantive value in the preparation of this study, in particular the George B. Dern Papers were disappointing.

For the military historian, the Washington, D. C. area has a plethora of libraries affiliated with the armed forces with courteous and efficient staffs quite capable and willing to advise and aid the student. The Army Library located in the Pentagon building, the Navy Department Library located in the Main Navy Building at 18th and Constitution Avenue, the National War College Library, and the Armed Forces Industrial College Library, the latter two located at Fort McNair in Southwest Washington, proved to be of inestimable value in providing military periodicals and congressional documents pertaining to military affairs during the period under study. The Industrial College Library has bound volumes of the _Lectures Delivered at the Army Industrial College._ The inefficiency and general confusion of the main reference section of the Library of Congress is in sharp contrast to the willing and helpful aid rendered by the various armed forces libraries.

Comment must be made to the superb facilities at the Office of the Chief of Military History (OCMH), Department of the Army. Charged with the mission of writing a multi-volume history of World War II and the Korean War, OCMH has integrated into its organization an excellent Reference Branch. This branch contains published works on military history, government publications pertaining to military affairs, a unique manuscript collection, and other unpublished and miscellaneous material. Included in this collection are the _Cater Files_ which were used extensively in this study, and Lawrence J. Legere's unpublished manuscript on the history of the unification problem entitled: _Unification of the Armed Forces_.

As most of the material for this study was derived from primary sources a selected and annotated bibliography of non-archival published material pertaining to the Army in the inter-war years will follow.

Civil-Military Relations: Bibliographic Notes on Administrative Problems of Civilian Mobilization. Chicago: University of Chicago Press, 1940.

An excellent reference for the study of mobilization problems during the 1930's and the relationship between mobilization plans and civilian society.

The Writing of American Military History, A Guide. Washington: GPO, 1956.

Prepared by the Department of the Army for distribution as an official publication this is a valuable and extensive guide to the general problem of writing on military affairs.

Van Riper, Paul P. "A Survey of Materials for the Study of Military Management," _American Political Science Review,_ XLIV, September 1955, pp. 828-850

A superb essay and introduction to writing on military affairs, including a description and guide to using various materials. Its value for the inter-war years is limited in that it focuses mainly on World War II and the post-1945 period.

GOVERNMENT PUBLICATIONS

Annual Report of the Secretary of War.

These published annual reports are basic documents required for a study of American Military policy. Besides a summary by the Secretary of War of the various activities and problems faced by the military establishment during the fiscal year; the reports include statements by the Chief of Staff and Assistant Secretary of War. The annual reports also include a useful detailed breakdown of the military budget.

Congressional Record.
Although not reflecting Army opinion, the debates in Congress reflect the political tenor of the legislative body in relationship to military policy and military expenditures.

Hearings on the War Department Appropriations Bill.
The annual published hearings are an invaluable source for an understanding of the problems faced by the Army during the depression years, and valuable for gaging the temper and thinking of the Army in the face of budgetary pressure. The relationship between finance and policy is vividly demonstrated in these publications.

In addition to these standard government publications mention should also be made of various special publications related to the Army during the depression years. The more important of these works are:

Department of National Defense. Hearings before Committee on Expenditures in Executive Department, 72nd Cong., 1st Sess. Washington: GPO, 1932.
These hearings sought to relate a unified defense establishment and an independent Air Corps with the economy program and the need to curtail military expenditures.

"General Johnson Hagood on National Defense and Reorganization of the Army," Hearings before Committee on Military Affairs, House of Representatives, 73rd Cong., 1st Sess., April 12, 1933. Washington: GPO, 1933.
A good summary of Hagood's plan to reorganize the military establishment and provide efficient defense at a lower cost.

Report of the Special Committee on the Army Air Corps. Washington: GPO, 1934.
This is the famous report of the Baker Board and must be considered as one of the landmarks in the bibliography of American Military History.

The National Defense Act, approved June 3, 1916 as amended to March 4, 1929. Washington: GPO, 1929.
A basic reference for the study of American military policy in the post-World War I years.

PERIODICALS AND NEWSPAPERS

Army and Navy Journal

Unexcelled as a reference for the study of American military policy. Besides reporting the day to day military and naval affairs of the nation, the editorial comments of the Army Navy Journal give an incisive and penetrating reflection of the reaction of the military establishment to the political and economic exigencies of the country. Exerpts from important congressional hearings and other official documents pertaining to the Army and Navy are to be found in this weekly periodical. In continual publication since 1863, this publication is of prime importance to the student of American military history.

The numerous service journals such as Infantry Journal, Field Artillery Journal, Cavalry Journal, and the Coast Artillery Journal must be mentioned as a good source for the student of the Army during the inter-war years. However, because of the availability of archival material and the overall coverage of military affairs given by the Army Navy Journal limited use was made of these publications for this study. They are cited because of their intrinsic value to the student of military affairs. The Army Ordnance, a bi-monthly periodical, was used somewhat in this study because of the problem of weapons and ordnance equipment in relation to budgetary limitations. To the student of military technology and weapons systems, this periodical is invaluable.

Little use was made of newspapers in the preparation of this paper because of the fact that the main emphasis was placed on primary archival material. However, limited use was made of the New York Times because of its convenient index for reference to various developments pertaining to the Army during the depression years.

SELECTED SECONDARY WORKS

Bernardo, C. Joseph, and Bacon, Eugene H. American Military Policy. Harrisburg, Pennsylvania: Military Service Publishing Company, 1955

A good cursory coverage of the history of American military policy. Little analysis of the problems during the depression years.

Craven, Wesley F., and Cate, James L. "Plans and Early Operations," Vol. I, The Army Air Forces in World War II. Chicago: University of Chicago Press, 1948.
Craven and Cate's account of the historical background of the inter-war years emphasizes the struggle of the valiant Army aviators against the reactionary General Staff. Stridently pro-air power.

Ekirch, Arthur A., Jr. The Civilian and the Military. New York: Oxford University Press, 1956.
A personification of the anti-militarist "liberal-reform" element in American political tradition. Critical and suspicious of the inroads of the military establishment against the liberties of the Republic.

Ganoe, William. The History of the United States Army. Revised edition. New York: D. Appleton-Century Company, 1942.
The coverage of the period between the World Wars is rather sketchy, the volume gives a good summary of the 1920 defense legislation.

Green, Constance, Thomson, Harry, and Roots, Peter. "The Technical Services, The Ordnance Department: Planning Munitions for War," The United States Army in World War II. Washington: GPO, 1955.
A detailed and excellent analysis of Ordnance development in the period between 1919-1943. Perhaps the best volume in the OCMH series pertaining to the problems of the Army during the prolonged economy period of the 1920's and 1930's.

Hagood, Johnson. We Can Defend America. Garden City, New York: Doubleday, Doran and Company, 1937.
A strong criticism of the General Staff and detailed proposals for reorganizing the military establishment. Hagood's basic premises are economy and efficiency.

Hoover, Herbert. The Memoirs of Herbert Hoover. Vols. II and III. New York: The Macmillan Company, 1952.
A basic source for Hoover's own account of the tumultuous years, 1929-1933.

Huntington, Samuel P. The Soldier and the State - The Theory and Politics of Civil-Military Relations. Cambridge, Massachusetts: The Belknap Press of Harvard University Press, 1957.
An excellent analysis of the history of civil-military relations in the United States. The account of the events in the post-World War I years is extremely valuable for an understanding of the effect of the depression on the Army.

Huzar, Elias. The Purse and the Sword: Control of the Army by Congress through Military Appropriations, 1933-1950. Ithaca, New York: Cornell University Press, 1950.

One of the best references for the study of the relationship between appropriations and military policy. A superb account of the relationship between appropriations and military policy. It must be considered as one of the major references in a bibliography of American military history.

Ickes, Harold L. "The Secret Diary of Harold L. Ickes," The First Thousand Days, 1933-1936. New York: Simon and Schuster, 1953.

The trenchant views of "Old Curmudgeon" toward the Army are indicative of the antipathy of the New Dealers toward the military establishment.

Kreidberg, Marvin, and Henry, Merton G. History of Military Mobilization in the United States Army, 1775-1945. Washington: GPO, 1955.

Published by OCMH, this work is an excellent account of the various mobilization plans devéloped in the 1930's and the Army's role in the mobilization of the CCC.

Lee, Edward B. Politics of National Defense. Washington: GPO, 1940.

A good analysis of the political controversy between the advocates of centralized and federally controlled forces and the proponents of a more decentralized defense structure.

Lyons, Gene, and Masland, John W. ROTC, Education and Military Leadership. Princeton, New Jersey: Princeton University Press, 1959.

The authors present a good historical account of the development of the ROTC. However, their claim that the Army failed to support the ROTC because it was disenchanted with the program's ability to supply an adequate number of officers in an emergency is in error. Under the General Staff's doctrine trained manpower had the highest priority and the Army always attempted to support the civilian components to the best of its ability.

Millis, Walter. Arms and Men, A Study of American Military History. New York: G. P. Putnam's Sons, 1956.

An absorbing historical account of American military affairs since that April day at Concord in 1775. However, in the few pages that are devoted to the inter-war years emphasis is placed on the fact that the Army had been reduced to its nadir of efficiency because of the lack of modern equipment. Millis fails to take cognizance of the policy of the General Staff that in a time of enforced economy emphasis should be placed on manpower rather than materiel.

________. Arms and the State, Civil-Military Elements in National Policy. New York: The Twentieth Century Fund, 1958.
The historical analysis of the civil-military relations in the period between 1930 and 1936 is disappointing. In the effort to emphasize the domination of the inter-war years by the idea of "isolationism" scant attention is given to the depression and its effect on national defense.

Myers, William Starr (ed.). The State Papers and Other Public Writings of Herbert Hoover. 2 vols. New York: Doubleday, Doran and Company, 1934.
A valuable reference for Hoover's speeches and statements on national defense.

Nelson, Otto L. National Security and the General Staff. Washington: Infantry Journal Press, 1946.
An analysis of the development of the General Staff. Surprisingly scanty treatment is given to the budgetary problems of the early 1930's. Valuable for organizational development.

Palmer, John McAuley. Statesmanship or War. Garden City, New York: Doubleday, Page and Company, 1927.
For the sake of economy and efficiency Palmer urges that the Swiss system of national defense, a strong militia force, be adopted by the United States.

Rich, Bennett M. The Presidents and Civil Disorders. Washington: The Brookings Institute, 1941.
A judicious presentation of the Bonus Incident of 1932.

Riker, William H. Soldiers of the States, The Role of the National Guard in American Democracy. Washington: Public Affairs Press, 1957.
A good political history of the National Guard.

Rosenman, Samuel (ed.). "The Public Papers and Addresses of Franklin D. Roosevelt," The Constitution Prevails, 1937. New York: The Macmillan Company, 1941.

________ "The Public Papers and Addresses of Franklin D. Roosevelt," The People Approve, 1936. New York: Random House, 1938.
A reference for Roosevelt's budget statement and remarks pertaining to National Defense and the CCC.

Helen-Jean Moore Library
Point Park College

Spalding, Oliver L. The United States Army in War and Peace. New York: G. P. Putnam's Sons, 1937.

A standard history of the Army from the Revolutionary War until the post-World War I years. Of little value for a comprehensive study of the period 1929-1936.

Terrett, Dulany "The Technical Services. The Signal Corps: The Emergency," The United States Army in World War II. Washington: GPO, 1956.

A good reference for the problems of research and development at a time when it was necessary to reduce expenditures.

Waters, Walter W. The BEF, The Whole Story of the Bonus Army. New York: The John Day Company, 1933.

An account from the point of view of the BEF of the entire bonus episode in the summer of 1932. Critical of Hoover's efforts to disperse the BEF after Congress adjourned.

Watson, Mark. "The Chief of Staff: Prewar Plans and Preparation," United States Army in World War II. Washington: GPO, 1950.

Although the major emphasis of this volume is concentrated on the period immediately preceding the outbreak of war in 1941, there is a good account of developments in the mid-thirties.

Index